Love's Creation

Marie Stopes in her laboratory, 1904.

Love's Creation

A Novel by Marie Stopes
Author of *Married Love:*
A New Contribution to the Solution of Sex Difficulties

With a Contextual Essay by **Deryn Rees-Jones**

sussex
ACADEMIC
PRESS
Brighton • Portland • Toronto

Introduction, annotation and organization of this volume,
copyright © Deryn Rees-Jones, 2012.
Love's Creation — A Novel by Marie Carmichael was originally published
in London by John Bale in 1928.

The right of Deryn Rees-Jones to be identified as Author of the Introduction
of this work has been asserted in accordance with the Copyright, Designs
and Patents Act 1988.

2 4 6 8 10 9 7 5 3 1

First published in this edition 2012 by
SUSSEX ACADEMIC PRESS
PO Box 139
Eastbourne BN24 9BP

and in the United States of America by
SUSSEX ACADEMIC PRESS
920 NE 58th Ave   Suite 300
Portland, Oregon 97213-3786

and in Canada by
SUSSEX ACADEMIC PRESS (CANADA)
8000 Bathurst Street, Unit 1, PO Box 30010, Vaughan, Ontario L4J 0C6

British Library Cataloguing in Publication Data
A CIP catalogue record for this book is available from the British Library.

Library of Congress Cataloging-in-Publication Data
Stopes, Marie Carmichael, 1880–1958.
Love's creation : a novel / by Marie Stopes ; with a contextual essay by
  Deryn Rees-Jones.
  p.cm.
ISBN 978-1-84519-419-2 (p/b : alk. paper)
  1. Women—Sexual behavior—Fiction. 2. Self-realization in women
—Fiction. I. Title.
PR6037.T68L68 2012
823'.912—dc23   2012005354

Typeset and designed by Sussex Academic Press, Brighton & Eastbourne.
Printed by TJ International, Padstow, Cornwall.
This book is printed on acid-free paper.

CONTENTS

CONTENTS

ACKNOWLEDGEMENTS

The Author and Publisher wish to thank the Galton Institute and the Royal Society of Literature for their assistance in determining the copyright status of Marie Stopes' novel *Love's Creation*.

Thanks to Betty Nixon, Maggie Fergusson and Harry Stopes Roe for their help at an early stage; to Tony Grahame for his patience and interest in the project. Thanks to John Lucas, Ralph Pite, Maurice Riordan, Alison Mark, and Jean Mills for helpful suggestions and comments on earlier drafts; to my friends and colleagues Jill Rudd, Alex Harris, Nandini Das and Dinah Birch for ongoing support, cheer and advice. As ever, thanks to Eira and Felix Murphy for their love and companionship, and to the late Michael Murphy whose enthusiasm about this project has buoyed it along, and whose creative spirit presides.

For Lesley Iwanejko,
who invited me into the lab.

INTRODUCTION

'At the heart of thought and creation', wrote C.P. Snow in his famous lecture of 1959, *The Two Cultures*, 'we are letting some of our best chances go by default. The clashing point of two subjects, two disciplines, two cultures — of two galaxies as far as that goes — ought to produce creative chances.'[1] Marie Stopes' *Love's Creation*, published under the pseudonym Marie Carmichael in 1928, offers just such one of those creative chances.[2] In a prefatory note to the novel, which acts as its drum-rolling entrance, Stopes, despite a guise of reticence, is keen to reveal the name of the author behind her pseudonym, explaining: 'As Lewis Carroll means to the public "Alice" and not mathematics; so Marie Carmichael means a novel . . . . Marie Carmichael is really another facet of Dr Marie Stopes.' In calling on the reputation of Charles Dodgson, who taught mathematics and logic at Christ Church College, Oxford, Stopes set herself up as the "scientist in disguise", who, like Dodgson, would manage to bridge an increasing divide between artistic and scientific thought. Stopes, who by the time *Love's Creation* was published was an internationally-renowned palaeobotanist and infamous author of the best-selling and controversial *Married Love: A Solution of the Sex Difficulties in Marriage* (1918), like many of her nineteenth-century predecessors, was no stranger to the arts, having by this point also written numerous plays, a novel and a collection of poems. Stopes' first attempt at a novel, *Love-Letters of a Japanese*, had in fact been published in 1910, a series of "real" letters "edited" by Stopes going under the pseudonym G.N. Mortlake. As June Rose has illustrated in her biography, the novel draws strongly on Stopes' failed relationship with the married Japanese scientist Kenjiro Fujii. Another novel, *A Man and His Mate*, still unpublished, is probably the one Stopes refers to working on in letters to friends as early as 1906, and which was also completed in 1910. By the mid 1920s it seems that Stopes was again turning to the novel as a vehicle through which to work through some of the events of her not uncomplicated life.[3]

Stopes had married Reginald Ruggles Gates in 1911, and, apparently unconsummated, the marriage was finally annulled in 1916. *Married Love* had been written as a response to the failure of that marriage. Stopes remarried in 1918, this time to Humphrey Verdon Roe. She gave birth to a stillborn child in 1919, and had her only child, a son, in 1924, at the relatively late age of forty-four. By 1925 Stopes had recorded her desire to move away from intellectual pursuits to "thinking about love", and, as such, *Love's Creation* represents for her an important turning point in her career. For while her periodical and scientific book publications are prolific until the mid 1920s, and sit with apparent ease alongside the publication of her plays and poetry, the novel — and perhaps mother-hood — marks Stopes' move away from "hard" science to an increasing commitment to literature and sexology.

Love's Creation centres on the lives of two orphaned sisters, Lilian and Rose Amber Rullford, who have fallen on hard times, and the two men with whom their lives become intertwined: Dr Kenneth Harvey and Sir Harry Granville. Early in the novel Lilian takes a position as a research scientist at the University of London, where she meets the scientist Kenneth Harvey.[4] Until he meets Lilian, Kenneth has been resolutely single. Kenneth's widowed mother, Mrs Harvey, longs for his marriage, and for grandchildren, and when Lilian and Kenneth fall in love and marry she is delighted by her new daughter-in-law. Meanwhile, Rose Amber, the more open-minded and liberal of the two sisters, who works as a secretary, appears to represent the artistic rather than the scientific point of view; she is described by her sister as a 'soul doctor' with a wish to become a professor 'of hearts' (*LC*, p. 53). Rose Amber develops a friendship with the older, wealthy and divorced Sir Harry, whom the sisters have known since childhood. The situation is complicated by the fact that Sir Harry has taken his terminally ill ex-wife Vera back into his home because she has been abandoned by her lover. Rose Amber, in her typically responsive way, befriends Vera. After the death of Vera, and of her sister Lilian in a freak bicycling incident, Rose Amber marries Sir Harry. At the same time she becomes a sympathetic ear to her brother-in-law Kenneth, who travels the world in a state of lassitude as he mourns his dead wife. Introduced into this mélange is the portrait painter Alistair O'Donnahaw (who bizarrely adopts an Irish accent but is in fact not Irish) and who also falls rather ruefully in love with Rose Amber; he is later deemed by Kenneth as being, like Sir Harry, a 'too dominant male' (*LC*, p. 179). In another convenient accident, Sir Harry, who at this point is becoming jealous of Kenneth's close relationship with his wife, falls off a cliff, leaving the way free for Kenneth and Rose Amber to marry, well provided for by Granville's fortune.

If the plot of *Love's Creation* is suffused with melodrama, and odd eccentric touches, it might also be said that it uses its fast pace and extrav-agant emotional tenor as a vehicle for less stereotypical and more tempered concerns: the desire for a union between women and men which fulfils bodily, intellectual and emotional needs, which *Married Love* had done much to explore; the importance of rethinking the division between arts and the sciences; and the impulse to offer a reinterpretation of Darwin's theories of evolution.

Love's Creation begins by situating itself 'in one of those innumerable interpenetrating worlds composing London', with a research scientist in his lab, clearing away 'half-dissected rabbits' (*LC*, p. 3).[5] Kenneth is pictured walking up and down the boards of his laboratory before putting on 'an old white linen coat', and beginning to 'examine a long series of brightly-stained microtome sections':

> His hands were streaked with crimson and violet splashes from the dyes which he had used to stain the tissues of the creatures he was studying so thoroughly that he knew the microscopic structure of their every cell. (*LC*, p. 4)

Kenneth Harvey is described as 'part-artist, part-creator: He had made the acquaintance only of the scientific side of himself as yet' (*LC*, p. 4). The description of Kenneth at work in the laboratory is written with calm and precise detail, and here (as the novel will again) seeks to flag up the shortcomings of Kenneth who, had he been an artist the novel suggests, would have seen his work differently:

> With a clean, bright knife he cut the strip into short segments of equal length. These he fixed on to the glass slides on which they were to be exhibited as objects for his microscopic exploration. . . .
> . . . The red-stained, delicate tracery of the tissue in the paraffin was repeated in each small section, forming a fantastic design. An artist, looking at his preparations, would have noticed the beautiful symmetry of the repeated curves of the coloured lines embedded in the white wax. Kenneth placed the sections in xylol, and the opaque films became translucent, evanescent and vanished. The sinking of the dissolving wax was only revealed by a rippling of the limpid fluid. He proceeded to mount permanently his series of sections in honey-coloured balsam. (*LC*, p. 5)

The contrast between these dichotomised positions of artist and scientist is countered by the figure of Rose Amber. Rose Amber's name, in contrast to her sister's, contains within in it some of the different strands which, in combination, the novel implicitly supports. Amber, of course, recalls geology, fossils, the captured past; and Rose suggests the natural world, a particular kind of femininity and transient beauty. The contrasts between softness and hardness, and the very duality of the name also points to the importance of the merger of dichotomies, and a willingness to "evolve" in terms of rethinking the feminine as well as the arts/science divide. Roses, in fact, and rocks, figure as opposing tropes throughout the novel: Mrs Harvey arranges pink and white roses at news of the engagement of Kenneth and Lilian, 'simple . . . but sweetly old fashioned. . . . symbolic of the purity and joy she brings. Sanctified as a wedding day . . . even more sweet' (*LC*, p. 44). Lilian, although a scientist, has only the flower-like quality of her name and describes her marriage as 'not like the usual frail barque of ignorant sentiment, swayed by gusts of instinctive feeling, to and fro along the waves of emotion! We're *rocks*!' (*LC*, p. 73). Nevertheless her union with Kenneth is refused by the narrative and what Stopes seems to be suggesting in her writing off of the Lilian/Kenneth union is that being a 'flower', or a couple who are simply 'rocks', does not represent progress in the modern world.[6]

As early as 1914, in the preface to her first volume of poetry, *Man, Other Poems*, Stopes had outlined the role of poetry as a form not of expression, but as a vehicle for knowledge and harbinger of truth which points up the inadequacies of science when she wrote:

> Only in poetry can humanity find expressions of the profounder truths which escape the stolid periods of prose. While scientific — i.e. *relative* — truth requires a prose exact, precise, even mathematical, such as prose can give, absolute truth is conveyed directly from heart to heart and, if it can be secured at all, must be enmeshed in words touched with magic.[7]

She continues:

> The chemist goes to his test-tubes, the geologist to the rocks, for his truths. Where is the poet to go? To the spaces shut apart from the commotion of matter, where his mind's receiver may synchronize with the everlasting verities. . . . (*Man*, p. ix)

Stopes defines Nature as that which is 'the life of this world unspoiled by man's urbanities' (*Man*, p. ix), suggesting that the poet becomes attuned to the currents of Nature's thought, 'cosmic feeling which can scarcely be described as thought':

> If poems vibrating through the ether are perceived even by me who am overwhelmed with other work, busy in lines of thought as remote and hard as natural science, it seems to me that it must be one of the fundamental facts of the universe — that the poet is not himself the creator, but is merely the tool in the hands of the poem. (*Man*, p. xv)

It is this return to the creating (mystical poetic) self which is central to *Love's Creation*'s attempt to find a new place from which science can interpret the world. For Stopes poetry and mysticism become elided and indeed love also becomes part of this synthesized triad of creation. Lilian and Kenneth, dedicated scientists, both come to poetry as something worthwhile as poetry in *Love's Creation* acts as the third way between a more general sense of the arts and sciences. As Kenneth puts it rather brusquely:

> Even that Tennyson fellow's stuff contains a lot of observation and ideas not badly put. There must be some psychological effect in the incompleteness of poets' thought and the rhythm into which they put it. (*LC*, p. 47)

Kenneth mourns the lack of a contemporary love poet who will write about modern marriage. When his mother makes the case for love's eternal nature Kenneth comes back, 'We go on calling it the same love because the poets have not redescribed it for us, but it is *not* the same thing, any more than Lilian and I are like our prehistoric ancestors' (*LC*, p. 47). Instead it is Rose Amber who comes to understand the complexity of human relations both outside and inside her marriage. She is the only person who can take on Kenneth's revisioning of evolutionary theory, and is thus set up as a figure who brings together the two cultures, just as she brings together, in her final union with Kenneth, the two genders in fruitful harmony.

Love and Marriage

Read in the context of women's fiction of the period it is tempting to see Stopes' apparently dogged idealisation of marriage as being unavoidably conservative, attaching her to models of masculinity and femininity that could only have been enmeshed in women's oppression in the still-recent Victorian past. Perhaps in answer to the more generally loitering sentiment proposed by Mona Caird in 1888 in her article 'Marriage' that marriage was a "vexatious failure", as the novel progresses Stopes is at pains to offer positive sexual experience as central to equality and happiness in a successful marriage.[8] Many of the most notable texts by women of the decade which focus on the problem of the single woman are also novels which refuse the demands of heterosexual romance. Radclyffe Hall's *The Unlit Lamp* (1924), for example, follows the life of its central character, Joan, whose desire it is to undergo medical training, but whose chances to settle with a lesbian companion, or to marry, are all denied her, compliant as she is to her mother's wishes. Sylvia Townsend

Warner's *Lolly Willows* (1926) addresses a single woman's attempt to avoid the obligation of family and patriarchal structures. Warner's heroine Lolly renames and reinvents herself by an embrace of spinsterhood, and a return to the country where she becomes a witch. Rosamund Lehmann's *Dusty Answer* (1927) painfully explores the differences between erotic and platonic ties, and the place in society of a single desiring woman. Sexual experiences outside marriage are also explored in Margaret Kennedy's *The Constant Nymph* (1924), a novel later made into a film in 1928, which was loosely based on the life of the artist Augustus John and his family. Most famously D.H. Lawrence's *Lady Chatterley's Lover* (1928), subject to an obscenity ban that was to last until 1960, despite its shortcomings in terms of gender equality, is notable for allowing its heroine sexual pleasures outside the framework of her marital relationship, without punishing her for them.[9] Same-sex love between women is explored in Radclyffe Hall's *The Well of Loneliness* (1928); also subject to an obscenity trial, the novel has at its centre a cross-dressing woman; while Virginia Woolf's *Orlando*, also published in 1928, with its gender-switching heroine, evokes the process of evolution through the transformation and interrogation of sex and gender over several centuries.

As Ross McKibbin has pointed out, Stopes was indebted to a swathe of contemporary thinkers on marriage and sexuality, including Edward Carpenter (1844–1929), Havelock Ellis (1859–1939), Ellen Key (1849–1926), Charlotte Perkins Gilman (1860–1935) and Auguste Forel (1848–1931).[10] That *Love's Creation* makes no sustained attempt to rethink female independence outside marriage does not, however, render it politically unthoughtful, although sometimes the ideology that underpins its assumptions is inconsistent. As a treatise on the need for equality within marriage which emphasized the importance of dispelling sexual ignorance, *Married Love*, a much more sexually explicit piece of writing, had narrowly escaped the censorship laws precisely because of its emphasis on sexual activity within marriage. There Stopes' famous invocation to marriage and motherhood is typically passionate in tone:

> Every heart desires a mate . . . neither man nor woman singly can know the joy of the performance of all the human functions; neither man nor woman singly can create another human being . . . and there is nothing for which the innermost spirit of one and all so yearns as for a sense of union with another soul, and the perfecting of oneself which such union brings.[11]

The fact that *Love's Creation*, unlike *Married Love*, is empty of any explicit descriptions of sexuality must, at least in part, reflect Stopes' previous experience of having novels rejected by Macmillan a decade earlier because of their sensuousness and "unwholesomeness". In fact *Love's Creation* deals with sexuality directly only once, and interestingly that experience is framed between women, through a conversation between Rose Amber and her mother-in-law. Rose Amber, unable to put her finger on her increasing sense of dissatisfaction in her marriage, confides:

> . . . my body, too, seems to mean so *terribly* much to him, and it is that which I feel I can hardly understand. I didn't realize quite *how* strong men's passions are. Do you know he hates my maid to undress me! Often he sends her away and undresses me himself, with a sort of reverent, passionate excitement. He even kisses my feet, and when he is beside me my body seems to stir him so that he quivers and pants and almost groans with the thrill of it, and I — I am frightened: I can't imagine *really* what he is feeling. It is terrible to stir anyone so much and not feel like that too, and not to understand. (*LC*, p. 122)

Stopes here is careful to make clear that it is not lack of affection on Rose Amber's behalf for her husband which leads to her problem. She is sexually unawakened, and it is never made entirely clear whether it is just that Rose Amber doesn't find Sir Harry sexually appealing, or whether it is something to do with his apparent excess of feeling which doesn't translate into something pleasurable for her in physical terms. While it is true that all sexual unions in the novel have marriage as their goal, and indeed the only woman to step outside marriage returns to it as a place of safety, appropriately punished for her adultery by a fatal illness, and the only man, Sir Harry, to indulge in sex outside marriage is also killed off, it is important to remember Stopes does not idealise marriage even though she offers it as a place where the ideal can be found. Although Rose Amber loves Sir Harry, the novel is quite clear that this union fails to offer her full sexual fulfilment:

> Harry's love, like a warm flame, surrounded her. But in spite of her eager willingness, it did not penetrate nor stir her uncontrollable pulses. She did not know the key which could unlock them, not the art or nature of their expression. The sweetness which she felt towards Harry was mental, spiritual, maternal. . . . Echoes within her consoled her with the old mis-statements that woman's part in love is and should be passive, that the rapture of the body known to man is not for her. These sophistries silenced the deeper instinct within her, and she consoled herself with them; for like so many modern women, she did not really know that they were mis-statements and threadbare. (*LC*, pp. 156–157)

Sir Harry's post-marital sexual dalliances with women before he married

Rose Amber come as a huge shock to her; the two miscarriages that Rose Amber later suffers are loaded with the metaphorical resonance of the failure of the relationship and Stopes makes a clear distinction between a marriage that might fulfil a man's sexual needs and a woman's emotional ones, and a marriage which becomes a spiritual and physical union of two people.

A key moment in the novel is the discussion between Lilian and Rose Amber about the need for a new way of understanding an inner life that moves away from heterosexual romance. Rose Amber points out to her sister that 'Our whole social life is built up of the idea of an old-fashioned novel, in which people fall in love, marry, and live happily ever after' (*LC*, p. 34), continuing:

> I can't put it into words exactly, but it seems to me what the world needs, at any rate what England needs, is someone to sympathize and understand the real *insides* of people's private troubles. We need some great person — big enough to be able to weld all the yearnings of all the people who are unhappy into something new, into some kind of new social conscience that will put things straight and bring happiness to everybody. (*LC*, p. 35)

Unlike many narratives of the fin-de-siècle — in the writings of the geneticist Galton and the novelist Sara Grand, for example, where passion in marriage was viewed as being at the lower part of the evolutionary scale — Stopes saw sexuality as 'the *creative* impulse . . . an expression of a high power of vitality'[12] which could be enjoyed by women if men were more attentive to women's sexual needs, and if women were similarly educated to explore their sexuality outside of a solely procreative model. Stopes' invocation to the new 'social conscience' to which we see Rose Amber aspire was of course already there in the unnamed figure of Freud. (Freud's *Collected Papers* were published in translation by the Hogarth Press in 1924–5.) But the insights that Freud might have offered Lilian and Rose Amber (and perhaps even Stopes herself) are an unexplored area of the novel. Instead it is a revisioning of Darwin that Stopes chooses to undertake and which underpins the thinking of the whole novel.

An Evolutionary Narrative?

Throughout her life the materialism that science offered her (Stopes' expertise was coal[13]) needed at all times to be countered with a more spiritual aspect, and the sections of the novel which address Darwinian thought are no exception. In fact Stopes steps directly into a debate with

Darwinism on two key occasions. The first of these occurs during an expedition Kenneth and Lilian make to the Natural History Museum. There, an attendant broaches the question of the relationship between the bible and evolution. The attendant is upset that he cannot reconcile his faith with the environment in which he works everyday and the evidence which is placed before him. Rose Amber returns to the museum to try to help the attendant harmonize his scientific knowledge with his religious belief. Lilian, and Kenneth's mother, are 'surprised at Rose Amber's vehemence on the subject of religion for the working-classes' (*LC*, p. 63); yet again we see Stopes, through the figure of Rose Amber, attempting to accommodate apparent opposites, this time bringing together science and religion.

Stopes' second, and more sustained engagement with Darwin, sits at the centre of the novel in a long chapter which purports to be Kenneth's ground-breaking re-reading of evolution. Given the close connection between eugenic thought and interpretations of Darwin that were so prominent in the period, and to which Stopes herself often, though in modulated ways, subscribed, it is hard not to be wary of the treatise that Kenneth lays out. Kenneth's theory draws on a range of post-Darwinian thinkers, Bergson, and almost certainly Nietzsche and Jung, in its offering of a theory of 'the Greater Unit' which proposes the interconnectedness of all things. Kenneth states that 'palaeontologists like Osbourne (sic) Smith Woodward' are questioning the fossil record, and indeed his description of the Greater Unit could be conceived as similar to Osborn's, described by Brian Regle as 'a quirky and nuanced conglomeration of Lamarckian adaptation, Darwinian selection, spiritual elevation, and the mental gymnastics of metaphysical free will'.[14] The most problematic of the passages in this section sees Kenneth discussing the poor:

". . . Look at the diseased city dwellers among us, down-trodden, stunted creatures filling the slums in every country in the world. How did they get there? Largely by the supposition that we are separate individuals, and that the 'fittest' must survive, that the weakest must go to the wall, that a strong, successful, rich man is good to carry on the human race, that the rich material success of the few is all that matters. It is *not* all that matters." He spoke fiercely. "Every one of these miserable, dwarfed specimens of humanity are diseased tissues, fleshy sores in the body of the Greater Unit. Do you think if people realized that such things are not isolated strains doomed to individual extinction, but are diseases in the greater, sublimer creature of which we form the tiny parts, they could allow it to go on? No! Consider your own body. If you have an ulcer in your tissues, can you do useful work? Is your consciousness able to deal with noble and beautiful things? Then how should this Greater Unit, with festering sores in its side, be able to do the greater, super-work that is its part in the universe?

"Yet it is *our* responsibility, ours! We make its tissues. Consider the analogy of our own bodies again. If you get a bit of dirt in your finger and it festers, what is happening? One set of the little unit cells that compose your body, the phagocytes, are perturbed; they come along in crowds to cleanse and sweeten and set the tissues right again. Though they have no realization of *us* they act as if they knew that if a part is diseased the whole unit suffers. So they destroy the diseased fragments — eat 'em up and give the sound tissues a chance. Are we, as thoughtful men and women, to be put to shame by the unconscious phagocytes of a man's body and fail to do our part for the life of the Super-conscious-ness? Oh, the effects of this new conception should reach from the geological laboratory to the farthest corner of our social system. . . . " (*LC*, p. 150)

The kind of language used here — the metaphor of the phagocyte, and Kenneth's use of the word 'cleanse' with its violent configuration of poverty as social disease — feels immediately repellent to contemporary sensibilities, not least to us now because of an acute awareness of the horrors of Fascism that were to come. Stopes was, without question, deeply involved in eugenicist thinking, as were many of her contempo-raries; despite her defence that the chapter bears no relation to the novel's plot, the ideas within it are, of course, unavoidably implicated in Stopes' thinking about love and procreation. In her favour it is also true that the passage expresses a legitimate anger at the suffering and degradations of the working classes, and even though they are portrayed in terms of disease and malformation, social inequality and injustice are also config-ured as unholy in their nature, with the sick and the poor not seen as "other" but as a part of a whole self which must be healed. Nevertheless, while there is a scepticism about Kenneth's capacity to understand other-ness elsewhere in the novel — when, for example, he is lost in Penang — and despite the scepticism of Sir Harry and the distinguished professor with whom he discusses his ideas — by this point the novel appears to support and glorify his views which reach their extreme in his descrip-tion of the devastation of war as being part of the natural reordering of the world (*LC*, p. 152).

H.G. Wells, a friend of Stopes, who had been taught by T.H. Huxley, also an acquaintance, wrote to Stopes chiding her for the inclusion of this long chapter with its bracketed apologia: 'This chapter does not carry the story and should only be read by those who think'. Wells' letter is telling in the way it conflates Stopes' aesthetic errors with her gender, and is worth quoting at length:

Congratulations on your birth (*Love's Creation*) as far as it has gone. But writing a novel is a business even more subtle and delicate than making love and it has to be learnt.

You are still but half-delivered from that pamphlet-writing woman, M.C. Stopes. The most difficult form of the novel is the novel of ideas and your little hands have still to master most of its technique. When you have, you will not put notices to tell people not to read particular chapter unless they *think*. Tut. Tut![15]

Although Wells doesn't seem to take issue with the ideological implications of the chapter, what's interesting is that in his tutting Wells conflates creativity with childbirth in a way in which he is perhaps hoping will chime with Stopes' own thinking about sexuality and procreation. He is also thus equating her failure as a novelist with her failure as a woman to reproduce, and her failure as a novelist becomes intimately connected with her gender. Wells equates novel writing not simply with Stopes' *treatise* on love-making but with love-making itself; similarly there is a slippage between delivery as a form, and self-delivery as a byword for transformation from ideas writing of the pamphlet tract and the more difficult form of the novel which attempts to hold ideas in a different way. Stopes' preoccupation with a perfect sexual and emotional union, however, in one important way saw her far removed from the social Darwinism that underpinned eugenicist thought. As Gillian Beer has pointed out, for Darwin the emphasis on *The Origin of Species* is 'always upon productivity rather than congress; on generation rather than sexual desire'.[16] This emphasis on the perfected sexual union as the key to creativity — and throughout her writings Stopes uses the word create a great deal — becomes yet again mirrored in the preoccupation with uniting the two worlds of the arts and the sciences, as much as it does two individuals. That procreation is the name of the game at the end of the novel validates Stopes' enterprise at the same time perhaps as letting down the novel's more radical potential. Woolf, like Stopes in *Love's Creation*, ends *Orlando* with marriage and childbirth, but for Woolf the creativity of the woman author is also figured through her desire to write. Marriage is sidestepped and displaced by the act of writing and the acknowledgment that desire can exist that transgresses marital ties:

She was married, true; but if one's husband was always sailing round Cape Horn, was it marriage? If one liked him, was it marriage? If one liked other people, was it marriage? And finally, if one still wished, more than anything in the whole world, to write poetry, was it marriage? She had her doubts.[17]

Unlike Woolf, Stopes' need to separate, as it were, form from philosophy, sees her at a distinct aesthetic disadvantage — one about which Wells might in some respect at least have been right. Like Woolf, however, Stopes seemed to be connecting a writing style with an understanding of evolutionary theory which ran in parallel to an unfolding evolution in women's writing, itself not an unproblematic enterprise. In *Love's Creation* there is nothing outside the union of marriage and the child that will spring forth from that union, as the novel ultimately sanctions a status quo whereby the male genius is supported by his understanding wife.

Mrs Stopes and Mrs Woolf

Had Virginia Woolf read *Love's Creation?* Or indeed any of Stopes' sexological works? Given Woolf's own ambivalence about her sexuality and motherhood which were also being worked through in her novels of this period, Stopes' writings, or even the idea of them second-hand, cannot fail to have had deep resonance. Woolf was forty-six when she published *A Room of One's Own* (1929), her complex and groundbreaking exploration of women's exclusion from the literary tradition, and had almost certainly come to terms with the fact that she was not going to (choose to) have children of her own. There is a constant return in *A Room of One's Own* to images of women with children, and of fertility, strong indicators that Woolf was thinking through the relationship between herself as a woman who makes the decision not to have children, and her own creativity, a constellation of thought for which Stopes becomes a touchstone.[18]

A Room of One's Own does in fact makes covert, but extensive reference to Stopes via Woolf's reference to Mary Carmichael, and her novel *Life's Adventure*. Several commentators have picked up on the connections between the two texts, not always accurately as Christina Alt has suggested.[19] Elizabeth Abel, who seems to have been the first person to discuss the connection between Stopes and Woolf, suggests that

> *Life's Adventure* is politically more adventurous than *Love's Creation*, but the echoes in title and setting, as well as in the author's names, affiliate women's literary production with a social discourse in which issues of reproduction have shifted from the margin to the center.[20]

Elsewhere, Donald Childs has argued that Woolf's remembering and misremembering of Stopes' novel is particularly pertinent 'because of the focus that the figure of Stopes could bring to Woolf's eugenical concerns about literary descent, sexual activity, and biological inheritance' and cites a letter in which Woolf expresses her awareness of Stopes, and her deep ambivalence about procreativity and unlicensed sexual activity. Woolf writes:

> I admire, but deplore, such an old maid, they make me feel. "And how do you manage not — not-not to have children?" I ask. "Oh, we read Mary Stopes of course" Figure to yourself . . . before taking their virginity, the young men of our time produce marked copies of Stopes! Astonishing![21]

The displacements that are going on in Woolf's reconfiguration of Stopes' novel are typically complex, elusive and telling. In using a variation on Stopes' pseudonym, a pseudonym which in fact sees Stopes drawing on her own mother's maiden name, Woolf creates her own "unmarried" author, the daughter too of an "unmarried" mother. The shift in title from "love" to "life" surely too makes a glancing playful reference to Woolf's novel of the previous year, *Orlando*, whose central character, based on Woolf's lover the poet Vita Sackville-West — also plays around with ideas of "vitality" and poetry. Perhaps even more significantly the shift from the idea of "creation" to "adventure" in Woolf's title sees her moving away from the generative model of life to a more open ended one. Thus the subtle shift in author and titles of the novels points to a narrative for Woolf which on the one hand favours a maternal line while on the other eschews the biologically maternal.

Although Woolf is at first rather sceptical about the imagined novel, which both is and is not Stopes' *Love's Creation*, it is Mary Carmichael who famously leads the way for Woolf in generating a new kind of women's fiction. Mary Carmichael's novel grows on Woolf; her desire for novels, in the famous Chloe and Olivia passage, to show more the relationships between women must in some part have been met by *Love's Creation* which is also very interested in women's relationships with other women: the relationship between the two sisters; Rose Amber's unconventional relationship with her soon to be husband's ex-wife, Vera; and her close friendship with her mother-in-law, Mrs Harvey, are perhaps the most affecting in the book.

Most of the fifth chapter of *A Room* is taken up with a circling round and a return to *Life's Adventure* which Woolf begins to read, pen in hand, disconcerted by the 'terseness' of the sentences, and its demands that she rethink her expectations of women's fiction by famously breaking the woman's sentence:

Something tore, something scratched; a single word here and there flashed its torch in my eyes. She was 'unhanding' herself as they say in the old plays. She is like a person striking a match that will not light, I thought. . . . For while Jane Austen breaks from melody to melody as Mozart from song to song, to read this writing was like being out at sea in an open boat. Up one went, down one sank. This terseness, this shortwindedness, might mean she was afraid of something; afraid of being called 'sentimental' perhaps; or she remembers that women's writing has been called flowery and so provides a superfluity of thorns; . . .

Mary Carmichael is playing a trick on us. For I feel as one feels on a switchback railway when the car, instead of sinking, as one has been led to expect, swerves up again. Mary is tampering with the expected sequence. First she broke the sentence; now she has broken the sequence. Very well, she has every right to do both of these things if she does them not for the sake of breaking, but for the sake of creating.[22]

Does this, with its use of the word creating, describe the style of Stopes' novel? As always with Woolf, irony upon irony are piled up one against the other as Woolf gestures towards Stopes through the figure of Mary: 'I cannot be sure whether she is being herself,' Woolf writes 'or someone else.'[23] While Stopes' style, or to be more accurate, the style which Stopes' writing evolves into in its transmission into Woolf's treatise, is meant to break the sentence, stylistically Stopes' novel is unremarkable; if anything, accusations laid against Stopes' prose style see her as over-effusive and Meredithian in the flow of her prose.[24] Discussing *Married Love*, however, Paul Peppis has pointed usefully to the way in which

Stopes was acutely aware of the gendering of scientific discourse, as well as male modernism's appropriation of impersonality, suggesting that not only was Stopes questioning the division between the sciences and liter- ature, but that her sexological works modernize sentimentalism by conjoining idioms of scientific rationality and impersonal detachment with vocabularies of lyric sentiment, thus affirming the continuing rele- vance of sentimentality to modernism's efforts to reform gender by rewriting sex.[25]

Similar comment could be made about the scientific observations in *Love's Creation* which step in as a bulwark against potential cliché or senti- mentality and constitute the most lively prose in the novel. *Life's Adventure*, however, Woolf complains, is 'heaping up too many facts':

She will not be able to use half of them in a book of this size. (It was about half the length of *Jane Eyre*.) However, by some means or other

she succeeded in getting us all — Roger, Chloe, Olivia, Tony, and Mr
Bigham — in a canoe up the river.[26]

For Roger, Chloe, Olivia, Tony and Mr Bigham do we read Kenneth,
Rose Amber, Lilian, Sir Harry, and O'Donnahaw, all crammed implau-
sibly into a narrative which cannot properly bear them?

In two separate passages which may well have appealed directly to
Woolf, Stopes addresses the relation between time and narrative in a
more radical way than the implausibility of *Love's Creation*'s plot might
suggest:

> I think the philosophic idea of discontinuity, which is so fruitful in ordi-
> nary life, has a lot to answer for in creating some of the worse muddles
> we scientists have got into. Now we cannot think of *time* without
> cutting it up into minutes and seconds, but most of us have the sense to
> realise that it is perpetually flowing — flowing on without a break. I'm
> beginning to wonder whether perhaps a life is really something like time
> — a perpetual stream. . . . (*LC*, p. 42)

And:

> [S]ometimes . . . there *is* no beginning — or it is all beginning and
> finished in a moment, and then a whole life is tangled up. I really know
> people whose stories are like that, and you can read of them often in
> the divorce court proceedings, let alone in novels and plays. (*LC*, p. 49)

These passages, spoken by Rose Amber, position Stopes much more
clearly as a modernist thinker, if not a modernist writer. One obvious
link between Stopes and Woolf here is Hardy, and that link becomes
more distinct if we remember that Stopes did herself live in a lighthouse,
where Hardy was a visitor, a fact which seems quite tantalizing in terms
of Woolf's own interest in lighthouses, especially given that Woolf might
well have known of the friendship between Stopes and Hardy.[27] Hardy's
description of humanity as 'one great network or tissue which quivers in
every part when one point is shaken, like a spider's web if touched'[28]
shows a similar preoccupation with such theories of interconnectedness
which can also be seen in Woolf and most likely originates in their
reading of Bergson's influential discussions of human consciousness, most
relevantly here his *Creative Evolution* (published in French 1907; translated by Arthur Mitchell, 1911). Woolf's descriptions of the emergence
of the woman writer in *A Room of One's Own* are similarly seen in evolutionary terms which also evoke Stopes, however implicitly, in their
paleontological references:

... This organism that has been under the shadow of the rock these million years — feels the light fall on it, and sees coming her way a piece of strange food — knowledge, adventure, art. And she reaches out for it ... and has to devise some entirely new combination of her resources, so highly developed for other purposes, so as to absorb the new into the old without disturbing the infinitely intricate and elaborate balance of the whole.[29]

This passage comes at the end of Woolf's famous Chloe and Olivia section that discusses the failure of novels to explore the complexities of relationships between women. Chloe and Olivia work together in a laboratory; one of them has children. In *Love's Creation* there is only one woman scientist, but, as she continues, Woolf returns again to Mary Carmichael and the woman scientist as the imaginative touchstone for what the women's novel might be, moving between speculation and warning: 'I am afraid', she writes,

that she will be tempted to become, what I think the less interesting branch of the species — the naturalist-novelist, and not the contemplative. There are so many new facts for her to observe. She will not need to limit herself any longer to the respectable houses of the upper middle classes. She will go without kindness or condescension, but in the spirit of fellowship, into those small, scented rooms where sit the courtesan, the harlot, the lady with the pug dog. There they will sit in the rough and ready-made clothes that the male writer has had perforce to clap upon their shoulders. But Mary Carmichael will have out her scissors and fit them close to every hollow and angle.[30]

In *Married Love* Stopes writes that 'the man and the woman are each organs, parts, of the other. And in the strictest scientific, as well as in a mystical, sense they together are a single unit'; love's creation is not simply an ability to reproduce biologically, but for the union of two people to create a new being through sex, a 'super-physical entity created by the perfect union in love'.[31] In *Women and Fiction*, one of the lectures which were eventually to become *A Room of One's Own*, Woolf writes in a manner that is strikingly similar in its creation of a third space in which creativity occurs. What is more curious in Woolf's thinking is that such a merger is framed metaphorically in terms of a wedding night. The creative synthesis occurs 'at the hush of midnight':

Not a light must burn; not a wheel grate on the cobbles. Draw the curtain, & let the marriage take place, & never presume for a moment to say, now I am a woman, now I am a man; they have to be allowed to do that job for themselves. So the only way to attain this oblivion is to exercise day after day, night after night, every faculty freely; so that when the marriage night comes you, the writer, can sink into oblivion . . .[32]

Woolf's passage here is excised from the pages of *A Room*, but the preoccupation with a fusion of male and female in her image of the Coleridgean androgynous mind figured by the man and woman who share a taxi cab in *A Room*, or her troubled and troubling image of 'the Fascist poem', which does not have a 'mother' *and* a 'father' but which has two separate heads — 'a horrid little abortion such as one sees in a glass jar in the museum of some county town' — remain.[33] It is in her vision of androgyny that Woolf might be seen most to take on Stopes' mystical ideals of a synthesis in marriage which creates another self. For Woolf — here at least— androgyny appears to be being equated with a liberatory oblivion that might elsewhere be described as orgasm.

Woolf's and Stopes' ideas concerning feminism and female identity are not always readily aligned and the differences between the two writers count as heavily as the connections which are established. For if Woolf aspires to an identity in which gender is irrelevant, for Stopes a self is incomplete without its ability to merge creatively with a biological other in order to transmute into a higher spiritual being. These connections, it is important to point out, too, must on Woolf's part, be read in terms of a continuous and provocative dialogue. Nevertheless, *Love's Creation* undoubtedly allows us to return to Woolf's writings with fresh eyes. Can a reading of Stopes' novel here see us relocating Stopes not as the "great" novelist, but in Woolf's terms, when she discusses Mary Carmichael, as an example of the woman writer who is paving the way for women writing in the next hundred years? Has Stopes in writing her novel 'forgotten she is a woman, so that her pages were full of that curious sexual equality which comes only when sex is unconscious of itself'?[34] Would such unconsciousness be desirable for Stopes? The answer to all these questions remains both yes and no. That, for example, Stopes' woman scientist is killed off and that her passion for science lives on only through her male protagonist represents one of the novel's many blindspots and incongruities, and is particularly ironic when set against Stopes' own pioneering life and work.

If *Love's Creation* gives us a fascinating insight into the pleasures Stopes felt looking back at her early career as a scientist, her simultaneous and various engagements with the arts — writing plays, children's stories, poems, novels — provides testimony to a certain intellectual restlessness, even a dissatisfaction, with the scientific work in hand. After the publication of *Love's Creation* Stopes continued to write plays and her final volume of poems was published in 1952. She did not, however, attempt to write a novel again. Although her ideas were to harden as she aged, Stopes' exploration of creativity and creation, in all their complexities, offers a fascinating insight into early twentieth-century debates about science, love, marriage, feminism and aesthetics. Surprisingly and pleasingly for us here, her novel also makes for a compelling and provocative read. Published in that landmark year when universal women's suffrage had become a reality, *Love's Creation* still demands our attention: with all its faults, and its not inconsiderable verve.

Notes to Introduction

1 *The Two Cultures*, with an introduction by Stefan Collini (Cambridge: Cambridge University Press, 1998), p. 16.
2 *Love's Creation* (London: Bale and Danielsson, 1928). Hereafter all page references to this new edition, *LC* in the text.
3 See *Marie Stopes and the Sexual Revolution* (London: Faber, 1992).
4 Stopes had herself studied for her B.Sc. at University College, receiving her Ph.D. from the University of Munich in 1904 and her D.Sc. from University College. She was subsequently a fellow and lecturer there before taking up a lectureship in Manchester and it is interesting seeing the way in which she transposes her own experiences as a woman scientist, reconfiguring and redistributing them between her characters. So, for example, Stopes' own travels to Japan in 1907 become transposed into Kenneth's travelling in the Far East. Stopes certainly seems to identify much more strongly in terms of her own biography with Kenneth as the science figure, rather than Lilian, and the novel could be said to be working through her own gendering of her scientific and artistic "sides".
5 In using the term 'interpenetrating worlds' Stopes perhaps takes up the discourse of theosophy (an interest of Dodgson's also). It is just as likely, though, that in the phrase we can also hear the influence of Coleridge and Shelley, and that such interpenetration looks forward in the novel to Kenneth's discussion of the interconnectedness of all things and his theory of 'the greater unit'. See Sally West, *Coleridge and Shelley, Textual Engagement* (Aldershot: Ashgate, 2007), p. 105. West cites Shelley's 'A Vision of the Sea': "Of living things each one/ And my spirit . . . / Interpenetrated lie".
6 In *Maisie's Marriage*, the film written by Stopes, originally called *Married Love*, the image of the rose is transformed into an image of a baby. For a fascinating discussion of the film, see Annette Kuhn, *Cinema Censorship, and Sexuality 1909–1925* (London: Routledge, 1988).
7 *Man, Other Poems* (London: Heinemann, 1914), p. viii. Hereafter *Man* in the body of the text.
8 Caird's article was first published in the *Westminster Review* (August 1888, pp. 186–201). Reproduced in *A New Woman Reader: Fiction, Articles, and*

Drama of the 1890s, edited by Carolyn Christenson Nelson (Ontario: Broadview, 2001), pp. 185–199; pp. 195–6.

9 Famously the novel was decried by Kate Millet and Germaine Greer in the 1970s, and the equality of orgasmic experience Stopes advocates is very different from Lawrence's demand for a male induced female orgasm.

10 See *Married Love*, edited, with an Introduction and Notes by Ross McKibbin (Oxford: Oxford University Press, 2004), pp. xxiii–xxxiii.

11 *Married Love*, p.17.

12 *Married Love*, p. 37.

13 For a detailed account of Stopes' scientific work, and that of her contemporaries, see H.E. Fraser and C.J. Cleal 'The Contribution of British Women to Carboniferous Palaeobotany During the First Half of the 20th Century' in *The Role of Women in the History of Geology*, edited by C.V. Burek and B. Higgs (London: The Geological Society, 2007), pp. 51–82.

14 See Osborn Henry Fairfield in the *Complete Dictionary of Scientific Biography*, 2008. Encyclopedia.com, 7 February 2011. www.encyclopdia.com.

15 Cited by June Rose, *Marie Stopes and the Sexual Revolution* (London: Faber, 1992), p. 189.

16 Gillian Beer, *Darwin's Plots: Evolutionary Narrative in Darwin, George Eliot and Nineteenth-Century Fiction* (third edition) (Cambridge: Cambridge University Press, 2009), p. 116.

17 *Orlando*, edited with an introduction by Rachel Bowlby (Oxford: World's Classics, 1992), p. 252.

18 Stopes in fact gave birth to a stillborn child in 1919, and had her only child, a son, at the surprisingly late age of 44.

19 *Virginia Woolf and the Study of Nature* (Cambridge: Cambridge University Press, 2010), pp. 115–16.

20 *Virginia Woolf and the Fictions of Psychoanalysis* (Chicago: University of Chicago Press, 1989), p. 88.

21 Cited by Donald Childs in *Modernism and Eugenics: Woolf, Eliot, Yeats and the Culture of Degeneration* (Cambridge, Cambridge University Press, 2001), p. 70.

22 *A Room of One's Own and Three Guineas,* edited, with an introduction and notes by Morag Shiach (Oxford: Oxford University Press, 1992), pp. 104–6.

23 *A Room of One's Own*, p. 105.

24 Stopes quotes Meredith's *Diana of the Crossways* (1885) at length in *Married Love*, and indeed Meredith's narrative, whereby an unsuitable husband is replaced by a better one after his death, must have had some bearing on her own plot, allowing a way out of a difficult marriage without the legal and moral complications of divorce.

25 "Rewriting Sex: Mina Loy, Marie Stopes, and Sexology" in *Modernism/Modernity* 9.4 (2002), pp. 561–79; p. 575.

26 *A Room of One's Own*, p. 105.

27 See Marie Stopes, 'Thomas Hardy Came to my Lighthouse'. I shall never forget series — 6, in *John O'London's Weekly*, Vol. XLIV, No. 1, 133, December 27, 1940, page 1. Cited in *Marie Stopes: A Preliminary Checklist*

Of Her Writings Together With Some Biographical Notes, compiled by Peter Eaton and Marilyn Warnick (London: Croom Helm, 1977).

28 See Beer's discussion of this passage in *Darwin's Plots*, p. 157.

29 *A Room of One's Own*, p. 110.

30 *A Room of One's Own*, p. 115.

31 *Married Love*, p. 103.

32 *Women and Fiction: The Manuscript Versions of* A Room of One's Own, transcribed and edited by S.P. Rosenbaum (Oxford: Blackwell and Cambridge: Harcourt, 1992), p. 145.

33 *A Room of One's Own*, p. 134.

The Novel

Publisher's Note

The public will be interested to learn that this first novel is by an author already world-famous for other works. She is taking a new pen name for her fiction so that readers may not be confused and find themselves in possession of a type of book different from that they expect. As "Lewis Carroll"[1] means to the public "Alice" and not mathematics; so "Marie Carmichael" means a novel and not sexology or palaeontology.

"Marie Carmichael" is really another facet of Dr. Marie Stopes.

CHAPTER

1

SOME LONDONERS

IN one of those innumerable interpenetrating worlds composing London, the clatter of departing students still echoed in the zoological laboratory. The attendant and his boy satellite cleared away the half-dissected rabbits pinned out on small wooden trays, which had nominally been occupying the minds of thirty young men during the afternoon.

"How that formalin² stinks!"

"We need some lady students with scent — like they 'ave downstairs, Sir."

"God forbid!"

"They'll come, and p'raps you learn more'n you'd think, Sir."

"Clear up."

"Right, Sir."

Dr. Kenneth Harvey had been demonstrating for three hours, and was now free to go about his own pleasure, but he walked up and down the bare, stained boards of the laboratory floor with his hands in his pockets musing on microscopic revelations.

The attendant's boy, his work finished, rattled a bunch of heavy keys at the door. "Will you be staying late, Sir?" A bullseye was in his cheek, but he was articulate.

"Yes, Tom. Give me the key." Harvey noticed that Tom had parted his hair in the middle and had oiled it. His mind asked itself — "Surely this is a new departure?" It irritated him slightly, for it was an indication that Tom was outgrowing his job, and consequently there would soon be a new cub of a boy to be broken into the precise and careful routine of the department. So Kenneth Harvey stared at him, and the growing lad, acutely self-conscious, slipped his hand up and smoothed the back of his too oily head.

"Good night, Sir."

Harvey's responsive good night was a purely reflex action; his mind was already projected into the research work which was going to entrance his evening.

3

He slammed the door of his own little research room off the laboratory, put on an old white linen coat, sat down and began to examine a long series of brightly-stained microtome sections.[3] He was tall and well-built, and his shoulders had not yet been hunched up over the microscope sufficiently often to give them the permanent roundness which would be their inevitable fate if his career followed its normal course. Tonight they were consciously hunched. The low lamp on the table illuminated one side of his face, outlining vividly the contour of his well-cut nose, and, shining through the bright brown hair, close cropped upon the forehead, created the illusion that it was golden. His hands were streaked with crimson and violet splashes from the dyes which he had used to stain the tissues of the creatures he was studying so thoroughly that he knew the microscopic structure of their every cell. His finger-nails were broken by the rough work entailed by the various manipulations of his technique, but that did not hide their oval shape, and their setting in his long, sensitive hands. Kenneth Harvey had never yet turned upon himself to examine himself impartially; he was still unconscious that he was part-artist, part-creator. He had made the acquaintance only of the scientific side of himself as yet; and if he was still ignorant of his own complexity at this stage in his career, Kenneth Harvey had still less discovered humanity and the world at large.

Dr. Nicholson, his co-lecturer and an old Oxford blue, knocked and entered smelling of rank smoke. Kenneth did not look up, but said, "Cut along, I'm too busy for you."

Dr. Nicholson was in a mood to chat: the students bored him. "Take a little leisure to consider humanity and all the social problems that are now so clamorous." He teased in a pompous voice.

"Rats."

"Be a pal."

"It takes the whole of a man's energy to master and keep abreast of one branch of science nowadays, when so many devotees have piled up mountains of loose data which one has to fuse before building one's own citadel."

"Shop, I don't want that."

"That's how I feel."

"But I want to talk."

"I don't."

"Tell me what you do in a train or 'bus without a volume or pamphlet in your pocket?"

"Ruminate on the details of my work."

"Then ruminate aloud now," pressed Nicholson.

"Wordy warfares are a waste of time."

"Doesn't the vast extent of the universe oppress you?"

4

"Too busy working on my own problem," he replied, with half-closed lips and eyes intent on his specimens.

As a mysterious whole, the universe did not trouble him greatly. The perceptions had not yet awakened which might join him to the company of those few rare souls to whom everything is transparent, and who go through life with a continual realization that they are on a globe which is whirling through infinite space.

Under a large glass box-lid a long strip of paraffin ribbon was laid out on a sheet of white porcelain. He rose and closed the door and window to prevent some errant gust of wind from blowing the light filaments across the room and destroying them. Then he took off the lid. With a clean, bright knife he cut the strip into short segments of equal length. These he fixed on to the glass slides on which they were to be exhibited as objects for his microscopic exploration.

"Jolly good series," he muttered to himself. "Quite complete."

Nicholson, nursing his knee on a bench, watched him with trained eyes and guessed what he saw.

"Progress, I perceive," he said.

Kenneth grunted.

"A six-plate quarto in the Transactions, eh?"[4]

"Seven plates at least."

The red-stained, delicate tracery of the tissue in the paraffin was repeated in each small section, forming a fantastic design. An artist, looking at his preparations, would have noticed the beautiful symmetry of the repeated curves of the coloured lines embedded in the white wax. Kenneth placed the sections in xylol,[5] and the opaque films became translucent, evanescent and vanished. The sinking of the dissolving wax was only revealed by a rippling of the limpid fluid. He proceeded to mount permanently his series of sections in honey-coloured balsam.

Ordinary folk, who look at the outside of things, do not realize how they would appear in a series of fine transverse plans. But to the two men the sections were like ground plans to an architect. From them they could picture and reconstruct mentally the complex interior of the once living object rigidly preserved for ever from ordinary decay. They could roam about inside the solid architecture of the microscopic creature.

"Clear out, old chap," said Kenneth.

"Unsociable brute." Nicholson rose to go. "Ta-ta and pure dreams."

Till half-past seven that evening the outer world did not exist for Kenneth Harvey. His mind was absorbed, projected down the funnel of the bright, brass microscope tube, through which the stimuli of potential sensations hurried up to him. A new set of patterns of the carmine tissues on the slide sent messages up the tube to his brain. He visualized the new arrangement of the minute cells composing the tissues and projected his mind among them so that it wandered there, at first as a tourist wanders through the halls of a great palace, only half understanding; but in an hour he had conquered the intricacies of the structures and his mind was master of a new conception.

But by seven-thirty the physiological rhythm of his own organism asserted itself.

"Jove, I'm hungry!"

He carefully covered up the slides again, put away his microscope, came down the stone steps where the vast shadows echoed his footsteps, and found his way out of the deserted quadrangle.

He was tired, so that when dinner was finished and he and his mother were together in the drawing room he relaxed for a few moments. His head sank to rest comfortably against the cushions of the couch. The gaze of his half-closed eyes wandered lazily. The soft blues and greys and mauves of his mother's room were reminiscent of the veil of opalescent peace cast by distance over sea-girt isles. His mother, observing him with fleeting, tender looks, thought how becoming was this languor to his manhood's strength. His head, half nestling in the cushions, tugged at the heart-strings of her memory, and impelled a caress. Her soft silks rustled as she rose and laid her hand on the bright brown hair.

"You work too hard, dear," she said, and her arms ached for him to be small enough to be entirely enclosed within them.

He looked up and kissed her soft, white fingers. "Isn't a man to be allowed to use his capacities?" he asked, teasing her.

"But not to tire himself *too* much."

"A man who uses himself, whether brain or muscle, always has a few moments of weariness afterwards. You don't know what work is till you have enjoyed the sensation of having done enough of it."

"I believe work represents to you the whole of life." Her breath was the echo of a sigh.

"Well," Kenneth laughed up at her. "Was that not what was prescribed for me when I was a boy? The last thing that you and father said to me before I went to the University."

"You do not regulate your life now by what I said about fairies and little pigs going to market, when you were in short frocks, do you?"

He mocked lovingly. "Do you mean to confess that you are repudiating all the foundations of my manhood? Do you mean to tell me that you do not think that work is the most important thing a man has to do in the world? Of course it is," he replied with a grim little smile. "I won't have you turn traitor to your own teaching."

She laid her hand upon his knee.

"My dear boy, do you remember how old you are?"

"Not often," he grunted.

She nodded at him. "Yes, it seems incredible, but you are thirty."

"Well," he maintained, in self-defence, "I have done a great deal in my time. I have published the results of two quite important researches and a lot of minor ones, and I've — "

She stopped him by laying her fingers on his lips.

"My dear boy, I was going on to remark that thirty is manhood, and then to add that you are my only son." She smiled into his eyes. "Don't you understand what I mean, dear?"

He looked at her in bewilderment, then put his arms round her and kissed her.

"My dear little mother, you mean that you are lonely! Now that father is not here, and you have no daughter, you're awfully lonely here by yourself when I'm away all day at my scientific work. Is that what you mean?"

She shook her head. "No, dear, I'm not lonely. You come home to dinner every night, and I have the day to think about you. I was really thinking about you. Are *you* not lonely?"

"I?" Amazement edged his voice. "Good Lord! No. My work absorbs me and there are a lot of fellows whom I know and like, and bless me, haven't I got you?"

She looked at him and laughed. "Are you Peter Pan, the boy who never grows up, I wonder?"

"Have I not just explained that it takes a man's whole time to do scientific work? Don't you want me to get on in the scientific world? If so, I must work hard, as I am doing!"

"Now, my dear son, we are talking about different universes."

"Well, what are you driving at, little mother? I really don't know."

"Don't you know," she said softly, "that I think you are beautiful and adorable and a most delightful person, the kind of person whom the world will always have need of?"

"Oh, I say! Come, little mother. This is too much. What's up?" His mother's tenderness, though loved and cherished in memory, made him shy in its moments of expression.

"For years in a general way, for months in a more acute — and really these last few weeks with a passionate longing I have been dreaming of a copy of you in the world, dear," she said, in a low, tense voice.

He started, and looked into her eyes. He recognized in their translucent clarity a tenderness unwontedly tense, unveiled.

"My dear little mother, what on earth do you want me to do?"

With a laugh and a sob together in her throat, she took his hand, "Marry, my dear."

"You want me to — what's that proverb, 'My son's a son till he gets him a wife'? I thought mothers always hated their sons marrying, particularly only sons."

She folded her hands and the light caught the diamonds on her finger. Kenneth suddenly wondered if the light came *through* the edge of her fingers, they were so transparent.

"Of course they do hate their sons marrying, but they hate it still more when they don't." She sailed unruffled on her sea of feeling, its waves subdued.

He appealed to Heaven. "Oh, Woman, thy name is incomprehensibility!"

She remembered suddenly how he had felt one day when he was a year old and she had bathed him. Such delight *must* return to the old earth. She said to him:

"I don't believe you ever made love to a girl." She thought with envy of the girl to come.

"Do you mean seriously?"

"Of course, dear, I mean seriously."

He muttered furiously, "No, then I jolly well haven't."

"But why not?"

The question was put with a soft wistfulness. It vibrated complex chords in its hearer.

"Good Lord! I never knew my mother was like this. Why on earth should I?"

He noticed the pattern of the lace on her grey silk gown, and it seemed rather like that made by the oft-repeated carmine sections he had studied that afternoon. He wondered if there is a limited number of patterns in the world.

"Does scientific work really absorb all a man's energy so that he has no longing for a human existence?"

He considered for a moment, and suddenly chuckled at the memory of a professor who was world-famous in his science and almost better known to the demi-monde. "Oh, well, not always. Of course not. Not always. When a man's older and has had more time to think and get his mind into a routine, I suppose subsequently he may fall in love and all that sort of thing — some time or another. Many of my colleagues are married."

"Then you — "

"Oh, I'm not that kind at all. I am one of the bachelor sort."

"What a dreary lot of bachelor sorts wither in the University. I am *so* sorry for their mothers. But among *them*, I am sure there are none so healthy and so beautifully straight as you."

"You absurd, impossible little person, making love to your own son like that." He stroked her fingers one by one.

"I wish I could infect you with love-making! My plan in life has been to try to make things make themselves. *You* are awfully proud when you make some discovery or write a scientific paper. But work like that comes to an end of itself; it just stops when you've made it. But I long to make things which go on making themselves, like Dame Nature in the Water Babies,[6] and somehow I thought, when father and Nature and I between us made *you*, that the pattern was there and that it would go on repeating itself."

"You modern women are quite beyond a man," he gasped.

She bridled with indignation. "Modern woman? I?"

"Oh, yes you are. You're all modern women nowadays. Though you are quite charming in the way you dress, you are a modern woman. Only a modern woman could think of things in the way you do."

She rose, leant over the back of the sofa, and put her two soft hands round his neck.

"I am only an old woman with a longing that her little boy should not miss the beautiful side of life by keeping his nose too close to the grindstone. I'm the oldest fashioned thing, an old woman with a longing to see her grandchildren."

Leaning over the top of his head, she kissed his forehead and slipped swiftly from the room.

He stared into the fire with a queer lump in his throat.

"Good Lord," he muttered. "What a state of affairs! Just when I've got that last consignment of things from the Antarctic. Dash it — I — ."

He thoughtfully lit his pipe and went into his study, where he opened a large quarto volume, and was soon immersed in a paper on the structure of the nuclei in a lowly family of animals which seemed to throw some light on one of the problems in his own work.

He forgot that his mother existed.

But when he went to bed he could not sleep. Pictures of his life presented themselves like dissolving cinematographs — the simple, easy circumstances of the unpretentious gentleman's household in which he grew up. At seventeen he had wished to become a university student, to study and devote his whole life to science; no serious objections had been raised. A university career was eminently suitable for the only son of his father.

He remembered how, unconscious of the leading strings, the lad Kenneth had been broken in for his university career at Cambridge by living in London with his parents and taking a preliminary course at London University.

When he was trusted with the freedom of Kings by the Cam, his mind was already harnessed to the idea of *work*. How little else he remembered of Cambridge! After taking his degree, he was guided through the inevitable piece of post-graduate "research work." Then he had decided to continue for life his explorations into the unknown, and meanwhile to supplement the tiny income left to him by an aunt, by lecturing in a university. In this way only did he see a prospect of keeping secure sufficient leisure for his research. How he hated routine, and how it cut into and destroyed his peace of mind!

Now, ten years after he had first enrolled as a student at the University of London, he was within its walls in a position of authority over a whole class of zoology[7] students. In the scientific world he was already well known for his researches on the morphology of a family of animals and its bearing on evolution.[8] The Royal Society[9] had published two of his papers.

"The real key to the problem of the evolution of life lies within my grasp," was his last drowsy thought. And as he slept he wandered clad in a magic cloak through realms unexplored and full of iridescent lobsters and amoebae.

CHAPTER

2

THE TURNING WHEEL

S IMULTANEOUSLY, in another of those innumerable worlds comprising London, a maliciously smiling Fate had given Lilian Rullford her heart's desire. She now possessed a university degree and was a post-graduate student. She, the one-time heiress of a wide and lovely estate, she whose parents had planned her for "Society," was now adrift in the whirl of the battle for existence in learned London. No longer petted and protected, she and her younger sister, Rose Amber, were "working girls."

That afternoon the back sitting-room of a house in Carlingford Road, Hampstead Heath, had the air of awaiting someone. Rose Amber had managed to give that attitude to the easy chairs and cushions by her deft touches. Whenever she went out, knowing that her sister would return before she did, she always left the room with this expression imprinted upon it so that it should welcome her sister with a tender breath of home. The room smiled, incompletely beautiful, but conscious of charm, and Lilian felt its charm. She sank into the sofa lazily, keeping her hat on, and dreamed. The dreary furniture of horsehair, with all its garnishings of crochet mats and covers which the walls had so long known, returned to her mind and gibbered at her. She saw how Rose Amber had banished it all before they settled into the house. She smiled and sighed to remember their early recklessness when they had bought the deep, springy Chesterfield and chairs in harmony with it.

Yet what a comfort it had been! Old and well-loved cushions and embroidered hangings retrieved as relics from the spoliation of their home were like mirrors with memories chasing across them. Bitter sweet memories. The stately home of her childhood, the crowd of friends, the devoted and gracious parents — all swept into other worlds. The black day when she and Rose Amber were told they had only a hundred and fifty pounds a year between them and the abyss of real struggle. Before they had fully realized the shadowy virtues of their landlady they had bound themselves to her by incurring the expense of a fresh, plain paper for their walls. The papering had made appear not too abrupt the removal of the enlarged photographs and the prints of sterling, virtuous Newfoundland dogs. The blue china cats, the photograph frame with the miniature thermometer on one side of it, and the ticking clock, once taken down from the mantelpiece, never seemed to have the vitality to enforce their own return. The polished wood "chiffonier" and the small tables, the sole original inhabitants of the room, thus severed from their more vulgar companions, took on a new air of gentility. The room was habitable — but — Lilian sighed. Rose Amber had brought in riotous armfuls of flowers and purchased the necessary glass vases to hold them. A cramped but smiling air of comfort spread over it, and became its habit.

The landlady was their cross. Lilian once again heard her flat voice from the back area below confiding to a crony. "You can see they're ladies," Mrs. Potter had remarked supporting herself against the bending grey laths of the dividing fence. "Not like the last lot — no pleasure to 'ave them in the house, jumped-up people they was, with no bottom to 'em. Now these, though, they is girls, 'ave got a real solid past."

Lilian shuddered and half rose to take off her hat. Her eye caught her reflection in the mirror. She gave it unwonted attention. "What am I now?" she thought. Her eyes were deep, serious and still. Her own sweet smile, a little elusive unless some special interest brought back to reality the thoughts that always seemed to be wandering into far horizons, was invisible to her. "My eyes shall see new truths,"[10] she whispered to herself. She felt dedicated; she exulted with an intensity akin to that of a mediaeval knight girding on his armour after a vigil of prayer in a dim chapel. She felt as one consecrated, setting out upon a glorious adventure. She was entering on the career she had longed for all her life.

Rose Amber came in with the cakes, and Lilian enquired of the landlady. She felt she must utter inanities or she would weep with joy.

"What has she been doing to-day?"

"Oh, the record has not been a bad one to-day," laughed Rose.

"You have forgotten the burnt porridge this morning."

"Of course! Then she broke the soap dish in my bedroom, brought my lunch half an hour late and swears we have finished the jam, otherwise she has been irreproachable."

"We're imprisoned by the cost of that wallpaper."

"I wish the weak and shiftless creature would allow me to go into the kitchen!" Lilian said that it was perhaps a blessing that they did not know what the kitchen was like, but Rose Amber had her mimic rages because she could not come down a few minutes before her sister and save the porridge from being regularly burnt.

"Tea." Rose Amber danced off to wheedle Mrs. Potter from the top of the kitchen stairs, down which she was not allowed to go. The light from the doorway showed the worn, oval patches in the ugly linoleum, made by Mrs. Potter's patient, shuffling feet on their innumerable journeys up and down the steep stairway.

Rose Amber, leaning against the frame of the doorway, waiting until her call was answered, wondered idly whether the holes would be half the size they were had Mrs. Potter come up and down the stairs half the number of times she had done; "and if they would be," she noticed she was saying to herself, "then Mrs. Potter's forgetfulness has increased the untidiness of her stairs by two, for she *never* makes one journey when two will do."

Rose Amber wished that it was not impossible to have a short and concise conversation with Mrs. Potter, for the air which came up from the stairway was moist and heavy with steam, each separate particle of which seemed laden with a greasy or stuffy smell. But she coaxed her into bringing up the tea almost punctually.

Meanwhile, Lilian went upstairs to wash off Gower Street grime, and on returning stopped in the narrow hall with a shock of disappointment, for mingled with her sister's voice were the lower tones of a man. Something in the deep, well-bred accents recalled the past, but she could not at once put a name to the personality they suggested. She did not care who it was, it was enough — it was too much — that a man should be there to-day. She opened the door a little impatiently, and found Sir Harry Granville with her sister.

Sir Harry rose, and exclaimed with delight, "I really am in luck's way to find you both in; this is far more than I deserve."

Lilian observed for the thousandth time the sympathetic brightness of her sister's face, and the strange, limpid clarity of her eyes. It was as though Rose Amber could see into hearts and drop into them just the soothing balm each one needed, without fully realizing or being able to analyse its pain. In the little room to-day Lilian was vaguely conscious that her coming seemed to have broken through some fine plane of sympathy. She was half aware of disturbed and elusive harmonies quivering in the air. It was as though she had gone for an evening walk in a garden whose paths she knew and had encountered the flying ends of a broken cobweb that bound her intangibly, and made her feel that she had been guilty of unconsciously disturbing a work of harmony and significance.

Yet there was nothing in the renewal of the old friendly gaiety between Rose Amber and Harry Granville which appeared to justify Lilian's unusual perceptions and she wondered if perhaps she were over-tired and fanciful.

Sir Harry Granville, with the scent of good cigars upon him, and the pleasantly comfortable air of being able to disregard time and money, acted as a stimulant. If it had ever been there the clouded sadness which Lilian had fancied she saw when she first came into the room vanished from Rose Amber's eyes like a mountain mist in the sun, and she sparkled.

"I have been from pillar to post seeking you," said Sir Harry. "Not one of your old set seemed to know where you were. You must not blame them; they said you positively would not give them your new address."

"But why should we?" Lilian enunciated with leisurely indifference. "We cannot keep up with that life any more, and we have work to do. If any of our old friends had come once or twice out of kindness they would have seen the contrast between our lives, and the friendship could not but have dwindled away, however kind they intended to be. A dwindling friendship is far worse than a dead one. Whereas by going completely away and not allowing anyone to know where we are so that they cannot visit us — well, we may appear again some day, like a plant cut down in Autumn which springs up with the turn of the season — supposing we ever have the luck to go back into that world again."

"Good," Sir Harry exclaimed. "I am glad at least to hear you say, 'if you have the luck to go back.' I have heard that you despise us completely. They say that you are a hopelessly confirmed blue stocking wasting your sweetness on skeletons and spectacled professors."

Lilian laughed. "There is some truth in that, perhaps," she said. "I am applying for a scholarship and am hoping to work on some very big problems, and that makes it rather difficult to enjoy the kind of life led by you and jolly people like you. A job like mine seems to take one's very life blood to do it. Why, there is no day on which I ever do more than half of what I am expecting to do each morning when I get up."

Sir Harry Granville assumed his old cloak of pretended gravity. "Do scientists never learn by experience?"

Rose seconded him gleefully. "No. They are celestial beings, quite inhuman. If I were not here to look after her, I don't believe that Lilian would ever think of her dinner, and only once a week or so would she go to bed."

"Ah! Rose Amber, we all come to you, we human beings, don't we? To be mothered and patched up and put on our feet again." The mockery was gone and the man spoke seriously. Lilian turned to examine his face. He did not seem to be quite so gay as she remembered him. Sorrow and experience rather than the few years since she had seen him last had cut new lines round his eyes. On his dark head were streaks of silver; but nevertheless his whole form seemed to radiate strength, a strength and mastery newly won. Lilian was now incredulous of her idea that she had surprised a childish, pathetic look in his eyes when they were turned on her sister as she entered. She put the thought away as being purely imaginary. She had little faith in her own power to read faces.

14

"As you have found us out, I suppose we shall *have* to see something of you," Lilian said lightly. "But unless you promise not to pass on our address you will force us to move again."

"And that would be my job," said Rose, "and I'm not having any. So take care."

Lilian asked politely, "How is your wife?" and was startled to see the shadow that passed over Granville's face. Rose acted as though she had not heard her sister's question, for she tapped her heels gaily and loudly on the floor and cried out, "You are going to stay with us all the evening, aren't you? It's so jolly to see you."

Simultaneously Sir Harry rose and explained that, though he would not care a straw about throwing the man over, he really had an engagement to dine at his club. Lilian encouraged him to keep his promises. He said he would break this one without a moment's hesitation, but he knew it was not really the right thing to do, so he took his leave, asking permission to come again. Lilian gave it in conventional words. Rose said, "Of course," and looked at him with something that seemed half compassion.

A few moments after he had gone Lilian got up and said, in an aggrieved voice, "Bother that man!"

"Why on earth?" asked Rose. "It was awfully decent of him to come. He's the first of the old set who has really troubled to find us out."

Harry Granville continued to visit them and began to take them about. Rose Amber pointed out to Lilian that he was even more friendly instead of less and that her fears of what would happen when their old friends realized that they were poor had all been unfounded.

"But that is different," said Lilian. "Harry was such an intimate friend. You'll see Vera doesn't come."

Rose Amber looked at her sister enquiringly. Then Rose Amber told her sister in a matter of fact, unemotional tone why Vera did not come. Vera had gone away; had gone, and then had begged Harry to divorce her and Harry had done so, chivalrously, as the only means of putting things approximately right. Rose Amber told her sister quickly what Harry had found so hard to tell her himself. Lilian could not explain wherein she felt outraged, so she received the news in a frozen silence.

Lilian felt again that strange cobwebby feeling in the air, as though there was something, to her intangible, that was real to them and affected other people, that they understood and could seize upon, but that just touched her elusively in the dark.

Lilian brooded for a while after Sir Harry Granville had left them. Should she or should she not tell Rose Amber about those papers she had found among the few undestroyed notes and letters left by her father? She pondered silent for so long that rose Amber wondered what was wrong.

"What is it, Lilian?"

Then Lilian pulled Rose Amber down on to the sofa beside her. "I am going to tell you now about a letter that dear old Professor Sir George Bailley wrote father. You remember that Professor of Philosophy at Oxridge University who used to visit us so often?"

"Yes," said Rose, enquiringly.

"Well, he wrote father a letter after that last garden party we had — a kind of story he had made out of what he noticed about you and all of us. Would you like to see the letter?"

"Yes," said Rose Amber, "but why have you never told me?"

"Oh, I don't know," said Lilian, "difficult in a way, I thought perhaps father would never have shown you, but — "

"Show me," said Rose Amber.

Lilian rose, and from a locked dispatch box at the bottom of a drawer took a letter. It was dated 1914, signed "Your devoted Bailley," and began:

Oxridge,
June, 1914.

"Dearest Rullford:

Those are lovely girls of yours! The second one especially. All her life have not her smiles, her laughter, her baby-kisses been begged for? Even distinguished men and greybeards like myself loved to feel the soft touch of her fingers as she tottered knee-high beside us; even the silken laps of beautiful ladies contended for her when she was a bundle of fine muslin and pink ribbons. Are not all your maids and men-servants proud of her? At present she does not know that these pre-ordained and fundamental circumstances make her herself. What will she be when her vivid personality has established itself?

At your delightful party yesterday I was ensconced in that secret clipped yew seat — caught there, as a matter of fact — and heard the most fascinating chapter of what might be a novel, but was real life, you know. I have written it out for you, for parents never know their own children, and I love you all so much I could not bear to make a copy of it for any eyes but yours. You will see why I want you to read it.

A philosopher is handicapped by his passion for probing into human character, but even I had some compunctions about my note-taking, and I was strolling along that glowing pergola of yours to the corner of your old grey house, skirted by banks of lavender, when I encountered the nymph again. The penetrating little hussy! What do you think she said? Looking right into my face, she asked me: 'Why are you looking *through* everything instead of at it?' I told her I was wondering if the brightness would be dimmed if the laughing, god-like figures on the lawn realized the drear outer places of the earth, where men and women toil in grim anguish, where young girls have not time even to dream of untasted happiness, and youths are stunted ere their muscles harden. I asked her, Is hideous pain the inevitable reverse of light and lovely joy? Is life like a lamp? A light that can burn brightly only at the top of the wick, and into whose burning must go the very fibre of the dull ones submerged in burning oil? Tears brimmed to her eyelashes, but all she said was one word, 'Cruel.'"

Rose Amber sighed. "I remember that day! So lovely and bright and remote. Another world!"

"For *you* especially. I'm sorry."

"Where is the manuscript with it?"

"I destroyed it," said Lilian. "It was a sort of story about you."

"Me?" said Rose Amber, wonderingly.

"The manuscript written in Sir George Bailley's writing, was headed 'YOUTH: of a pre-destined Heroine.' It was all about you and Harry Granville and Vera. I didn't think daddy would ever have shown it you. But he might have *told* you not to — to — mix yourself up in people's affairs as you did then."

"I was only 14. What a ridiculous kid he must have thought me," said Rose.

"Who?"

"Harry Granville."

"Oh! Well, don't forget that once a kid, always a kid to one's elders. He probably thinks you a ridiculous kid still."

"Perhaps I am."

"Don't be."

"I only wanted to *help*."

"Helping married people is always ridiculous," said Lilian.

CHAPTER
3
COMPLEXITY

A WEEK later Lilian returned hurriedly to Rose, waiting to hear whether her sister had won the longed-for scholarship.

"Got it," she jubilated briefly. Rose sprang up and kissed her.

"What were they like?"

"Splendid!"

"The professor is just what I have always dreamed a professor should be, and his chief lecturer — the man I shall have to work with most — is awfully keen on his subject. I could tell that at once."

Rose sat on the edge of the table, swinging her long, shapely legs. She raised her hands to heaven in gladness, and Lilian appreciated the gracious beauty of her sister as she sent her hat into the corner of the sofa.

"Tell me all about it," Rose asked eagerly.

"My dear baby, where am I to begin? The laboratory is very well equipped, it — "

"Begin with the men," interpolated Rose. "What did the professor say?"

"He started by congratulating me on getting the scholarship and said he quite approved of the research work I wish to do. He had had a letter of recommendation from the Committee, but said he specially wanted to know what *I* felt about my work. So I tried to let off a little steam about my ambitions in biological research, but it would not come out the way I wanted. And anyway, what's the good of enlarging on things like that to a man who knows all about them? I believe that I actually did say that I am frightfully keen on doing research. Baldly idiotic, wasn't it? Then he went into the details, mostly in words of five syllables — ."

"All right, cut that out. What did he say next?"

"Um — yes. Well, he wanted to know why I first went to a *ladies'* college if I felt the way I did about doing work with him, so I had to tell him, of course, that I was sent there by my parents, who would have been frightfully shocked at my mixing with a lot of men I didn't know. He smiled and nodded. 'And very right and natural of them,' he said. 'I am going to send my own youngest daughter to the same college.'"

"Golly!" ejaculated Rose, "how queer parents are! I should have thought he would have sooner kept her under his own eye. But perhaps he is a gentleman and only said that not to make you look foolish."

"*Of course* he is a gentleman. He is the chief man on this subject in the world."

"*Does* that make him a gentleman, in these days of board schools?"[11] queried Rose, maliciously.

Lilian ignored her. "Then he wanted to know why I was going to a mixed college now, and I explained that I was of age and that father and mother were both dead, and you and I could scrape along for another couple of years with the help of this scholarship, when I hope to get some sort of post in the University and be able to keep on my research work. He just nodded and tapped his fingers together; then he asked if I could talk French and German."

"Well, it's lucky you can," said Rose. "Is it going to be some use having had French and German governesses after all?" She slipped off the table. "I hope he will treat my distinguished sister nicely."

"Don't be a goose, Rose Amber," remonstrated Lilian. "Distinguished indeed! When one heads the List at a little hole like that women's college and gets a university scholarship and a degree — even with first-class honours — it only shows that one has learned the *alphabet* of a subject."

Rose looked at her critically. "I like your modesty; keep it, Lily-sweet. Now, my function in life being to mother you, I am going to discover the dinner. I am quite certain that our limp rag of a Mrs. Potter has forgotten it."

After dinner Lilian and Rose sat together sewing. Their talk flickered between long intervals of silence. The drawn curtains and the sphere of lamplight enclosed them within a magic circle of limitations. The restful limitations of a small room shut out the remembrance of an external universe too vast for comprehension. It ensnared a happiness profoundly real. Lilian breathed contentment and hope. "I like this little room," she said. "I think it is only the exceptional person, the seer, the prophet who can enjoy anything so unmanageably vast as dwelling in the infinite. Humanity is only happy when its horizon is limited."

"A craving for a ceiling is one of the most primitive instincts of man," said Rose.

"Inherited from his cave-dwelling ancestors."

"Something — whether it be a material object, a thought or an idea — which can be completely grasped, some job which can be perfectly accomplished is attuned to man's capacities."

"Like the Village Blacksmith,"[12] said Rose, "at the end of the day with something accomplished."

"There is more ponderable joy in the making of a successful pudding or a wood-shed than is ever harvested by the planner of an unfinished city."

Within the charmed circle of the lamplight Rose sighed contentedly. "It *is* extraordinary how we have enjoyed ourselves in these dull little rooms, isn't it, Lilian? I should never have believed it possible."

"Don't you yearn for parties?" Lilian could never be convinced that Rose was really so contented with the solitude as she was herself.

"I suppose I shall after a bit, but there has been so much to do, and it is so peaceful just to do it."

They did not notice a ring at the front door. A thunderous knock on their own panel barely warned them of the untidy head of their landlady suddenly thrust in with the announcement, "A gentleman to see you."

Before they could move, Sir Harry Granville came into the circle of light. "What luck! Caught you both! I have got a taxi outside in case you would like to go down to Covent Garden with me to the Opera."

Rose Amber looked up with sparkling eyes and flushing cheeks. She clapped her hands.

"You don't mean to say you are going to take us to the Opera?"

They were both too excited to offer him a seat. He sat with a deliberately excessive air of calm.

"Why not — when the taxi is waiting and my box at the Opera is standing empty and forlorn."

"How perfectly lovely!" Rose Amber glowed. "We have not been to the Opera for more than two years."

Lilian folded her work. "We shall have to dress like lightning. You have got the taxi ticking all this time?"

"Don't trouble to dress any more than you are," said Granville. "Why should you? You look perfectly charming now. Just put on cloaks."

Rose danced on tip-toe with excitement. "Do you think I am going to lose a chance of getting into my very best frock? Lilian won't let me wear it when we are by ourselves; she says it looks absurd, and the poor thing is quite huffed with being in a wardrobe so long."

At Covent Garden even Lilian felt the waves of excited anticipation throbbing round her and a delicate flush stole over her cheeks. She turned to Sir Harry with laughter in her eyes.

"I had almost forgotten how delightful it all is," she said.

Harry Granville suddenly felt very selfish. The box had been standing empty many nights. How the girls must have been cut off from everything to be so excited over this trifle of an outing! For a moment he was inclined to resent the fact that this little act of kindness should play him the mean trick of making him feel selfish. The music had not yet begun and he glanced over the house to see who he knew in it. Rose wanted to chatter. She turned to him with a provoking smile of mischief in her eyes, knowing that she would administer a shock.

"The last time we went to the theatre we were in the gallery," she announced.

"You don't mean it!" Sir Harry was horrified.

Lilian interposed. "Be quiet, rose, you are perfectly aggravating."

Lilian was dismayed. Why need Rose have so frankly revealed the humiliation of their poverty? Rose seemed determined to torment her.

"How shocked she is. Look at her?" She appealed to Sir Harry. "Isn't she characteristic of the past when everybody was genteel and pretended they never rode on 'buses or bought things at sales. I am very proud of having been in the gallery. What do you know of the audience of a theatre when you only go to the boxes and stalls? . . . when I marry a millionaire, and I do not see why I should not — "

"I am sure you will," Sir Harry sounded convinced.

"Well, when I marry my millionaire I shall make him have a box at Covent Garden and go up to the gallery every now and then and sit the performance through there."

The last lights were lowered, and as the first notes of the overture trembled into existence, both girls were absorbed by the world of the stage.

When the interval threw them back upon his hospitality, Sir Harry asked his guests what they would like to do.

Lilian hesitated, but Rose was prompt. "Sit here and watch the people without being recognized. I don't want to meet anybody, for we should only be uprooted from our peaceful life."

The opera was discussed, uncritically, but with emotion.

"I love it," said Rose, "but it makes me want to laugh in the most serious places."

"And that is why Society likes it so much," said Sir Harry. "The opera is more fashionable than any real theatre because no one *can* believe it."

The opening of the box door behind them made them both turn. Sir Harry stood up to see who it was and remained standing. A tense look set his features, and in the hand that was clutching the back of his chair the knotted veins seemed ready to burst.

The girls wondered who the strange lady in the marvellous black satin dress could be. She seemed vaguely familiar to them. Her face was pale, and seemed to be the mere echo of once sparkling eyes and a pouting mouth. Perhaps she was the sister of someone they knew and had forgotten? The girls turned away, politely pretending to be unconcerned,

21

but wondering who it was. This pale face with the violet-shadowed eyes was more than a memory, and subtly suggested sorrows they had not known.

The stranger stood hesitating within the door. "I am sorry," she whispered. "I did not know you had people here with you; but I must rest a moment." She sank into the chair Granville pushed forward, panting and exhausted.

Whose voice was it? Rose Amber wondered. It was like the faint travesty on a phonograph of a voice she had known and loved.

The voice continued hurriedly, catching at the breath that came in irregular gusts. "I had no idea you had someone here. When you asked me to come this evening and I refused, I felt then I could not come — I was too ill and tired and it was so long since I had been anywhere — but after you had started, I thought of the music and lights and I craved for them somehow, as one might for champagne. I thought perhaps they might do me good."

How ill she was! The girls pitied this strange lady who had had the first offer of the box. The first half-heard undertone in the voice suddenly reminded Rose Amber of the bright past, when its possessor was their friend. A flush slowly mounted into her cheeks and ran along her forehead.

She clasped her hands and leant towards her sister.

"Oh, Lilian, *it is Vera Granville!*"

The same thought had half formed itself in her sister's mind, but when she heard the words uttered by Rose this thing of terror and pity shocked her.

"What *shall* we do?" she appealed for guidance to her younger sister. The situation seemed to her too much fraught with drama to be real. But Rose did not listen to her; she stood up quickly, dropping her gloves and scattering programmes and opera-glasses in a cascade and went swiftly to Vera Granville's side and held out her hand eagerly.

"Have you forgotten me? You used to know us when we went about in short frocks and pink sashes, you know." She stretched out her hand and touched Vera's slender, blue-veined fingers clasping the back of the chair. Vera looked at her with eager affection in her eyes and half rose.

"I must be going now," she said. "The woman who knew you then is quite dead, and I am very nearly dead. I — I should not have come to-night — but I had no suspicion that you two, or anyone whom I could harm — would be here."

An incongruous pride compelled her to make her position clear. She stood with her head thrown back, braced and strengthened by the tenderness in Rose Amber's eyes, but too proud to take it under false pretences. Her voice did not falter.

"You know Harry has behaved like a brick. I am now living with him in his house and he is caring for me, but I am not his wife any more, you know. Everybody knows he was good enough to divorce me when I wanted it, and now, when I am deserted and a pauper he is taking care of me. People mustn't know. I would not have allowed him to do it, but it is for such a short time — the doctors only give me three months."

Sir Harry Granville spoke quickly, his hands opening and closing on the back of his chair.

"What nonsense, Vera; doctors be hanged. We are going to set you up finely."

Vera smiled a subtle, inward smile. She had grown accustomed to the cheering assurances all invalids learn to know so well. She saw through the well-intentioned kindness, divined in the secret depths of Harry's heart the wish that she had died on the way rather than bring her sordid and pitiful beggary within touch of the girls for whom he was responsible that evening.

He had adored her passionately, and when that was shattered he had forgiven her for the anger and pain with which she had seared his life. He was now doing far more for her than Society could allow was right; but she knew that he really shrank from her presence there, demanding by her very weakness his encouragement and protection.

Lilian did not turn; she looked steadily down at the people below her. She would have liked to be kind, but she did not know what to do, and it had filled her with horror to see her younger sister holding out her hand and speaking to the divorced wife of Sir Harry Granville, a divorced wife who was now living once more in her former husband's house. She wondered, miserably, whether fate had any more cruel coincidences in her lap; whether perhaps the owner of some keen pair of eyes downstairs might damage her younger sister's fame. Minutes passed as she sat in helpless inactivity.

"I'm going this moment," said Vera, rising. She stood against the door for its support, rubbing her fingers lightly up and down the woodwork of the frame.

"Dear Rose Amber," she whispered, "I shall never forget you. I wish I could look forward to seeing you again, but that must not be.

"Why not?" said Rose. "If you would like to see me, I should love to come and see you. Mayn't I?"

A bitter laugh rose in the midst of Vera's cough. "May you? No. My dear girl, you may not." She spoke with determination. "Let us hope that no one has seen me here. I expect they haven't. A black dress would not show up very much at the back of the box, and I am so changed. I wonder how you recognized me?"

"It was your voice," said Rose simply.

"Thank goodness no one but you has heard me speak, so perhaps you will be safe." She drew a film of black chiffon so low over her hair as almost to hide her face. No one could recognize her.

As Harry began to follow her out of the box, she pushed him back. "Don't come with me, Harry; I would rather you did not. *Much* rather. I won't have it. I won't. The car is waiting, as I knew I should only stay for one act."

He persisted.

"No," she repeated, almost with anger, "I will not have you come; go back to the girls at once."

And he sat down again beside his guests.

The lights were down and the music had begun, and closing his eyes in the dim refuge of obscurity, his head fell forward in his hands.

None of the three saw very much of that act.

At the end of the play he endeavoured to cover the intense pain of the experience with a superficial cloak of indifferent talk, and the girls helped him as best they could. The tenor's mannerisms were a gold-mine for chatter. But in the car going home Rose Amber quietly broke through the light veil of pretence and said to him quietly and directly, "If I had known that Vera would like to see me I should have gone to see her last week."

"Dear Rose Amber, how good you are," he replied. "And yet I acknowledge that I do not think you ought, and I hope you won't come."

The darkness of the taxi concealed Lilian's start of amazement and her helpless look of indignation.

"Good night," she said stiffly, with puzzled indecision and a helpless longing to add something kind. "It was very kind of you to take us, we have not had such an evening for a long time."

He couldn't make the conventional reply.

"Rose Amber," breathed Lilian icily, breaking the taut silence of the room in which they were undressing, "do you mean to tell me that you *knew* Vera was living with Harry again?"

"Yes," Rose Amber acknowledged simply, "he told me last week."

Lilian remembered that subtle, vague feeling of being outside some harmony of understanding between her sister and Harry Granville which had puzzled her so often when she came in and found them talking. She wondered miserably whether she was cut off by something in her nature from the full comprehension of human experience.

"Why didn't you tell me?" she asked.

"It was his secret and hers. Anyway, I thought you would be shocked. I could not bear to have you misjudging him, for when Harry Granville took her home again he did the most generous thing a man could do.

The man he divorced Vera for would not marry her and just left her when she was ill and nearly dying. She was too ill for anything and hadn't any money. She wrote to Harry asking for a little money; but instead of refusing it, or just sending a cheque, as most men would, he went to her and treated her like a brother, only far better than most brothers would."

"But he need not have her back in his house," persisted Lilian.

Rose Amber's grave eyes answered her. "But that is just the splendid thing about it, Lilian. Think how lonely she would be in a nursing home or somewhere like that."

"But if she has a spark of decent feeling left she must see that she is harrowing him." Lilian was tenacious of her indignation.

"I don't believe she does harrow him so much as you think," said Rose. "That is where he is so splendid. He has got over all that part of it now and he feels only an immense compassion for her. He told me he feels that the Vera he married died long ago, or never existed, and this is her sister's poor ghost whom he longs to help as much as possible through the valley of the shadow."

"And if they are divorced and have not married again they are living together — in sin!"

"Living together!" Rose flamed in anger. "I told you that he treats her just as though she was his sister."

"Yes, but — "

Rose cut her short with a wild gust of temper.

"Lilian, your conventional pig-headedness makes me wild!" she jumped into bed, turned over and would say no more.

An hour later Lilian stirred, and Rose, whom she thought was asleep, put out her hand, and, crossing the narrow abyss between the beds, touched her.

"Forgive me, Lilian, darling. But you know you live right away in a world that is a mixture of the heroic and the conventional. I know you only judge him because you have a higher and *simpler* standard for Society than most people. I find life too complex to judge so surely. *I* feel that Harry Granville has behaved in quite a *Christ-like* way over this."

Lilian confessed in the darkness. "I don't *only* judge, quite often I feel out of my depth with you when problems like this come up. It is as though there are great and terrible things in the world that I do not understand."

"I know," said Rose, with mother-comfort in her voice, "and I love you for it. You are a saint and most of the world are sinners."

CHAPTER

4

THE INVASION

THAT same evening, in another part of London, Kenneth Harvey lay back in his arm-chair watching his mother at work. He mused, considering why he did not understand the reason why it fascinated him to see her hands flying in and out of the butterfly-like fragments of linen on which she was occupied. It seemed absurd that such a dainty collaboration should ever produce anything of real use; and the absurdity of it always touched him. The light of the lamp shone on her silver-grey hair and the sheen of its radiance flooded the upper part of her dress, while round her feet the red glow of the firelight lent its gay geniality to her frosted loveliness.

Kenneth stretched back wearily in his chair. Like a half-slumbering volcano, between puffs of smoke, he emitted, "Here's a pretty kettle of fish!"

His mother looked up from her work, her smile a sympathetic question.

He continued grimly. "For all these years we have managed to escape the new plague — learned women. Yes, our department has had all the luck. Quite free from the creatures. And now, what do you think? We have gone and capitulated to the enemy without even a show of fight on the part of the professor. I really believe the old fool is flattered because a pretty girl wants to come and 'do research' with him. But, of course, he will go and shove most of the bother of it on to me in the way he generally does."

"Why?" exclaimed his mother, with veiled eagerness. "Is a lady going to do research with you?"

The young man grunted ungallantly.

"What is she like?" Her voice was alive with curiosity.

"How do I know? Have I ever been able to describe anyone's personal appearance to you in my life?"

His mother laughed and shook her head. "Well, is she anything like me?"

"Ye gods! No! If you really want to know her style, she is rather like

26

that, if you can imagine *her* pale and sanctified." He pointed to an engraving of the famous, lovely face of Lady Hamilton.[13]

Mrs. Harvey was startled. "Like that! A student?"

"Of course, she is not so — so — alluring — but she has got the same sort of enormous eyes in her head. If you can imagine a modern, intellectual Lady Hamilton you will get some idea of her appearance. She has those deep eyes that sort of go through you, but her hair is not so dark as that. It is the same make of hair, though."

A delighted but secret excitement seized on Mrs. Harvey. Even if this girl did not prove to be the ultimately desirable daughter-in-law, she might at least serve to awaken an interest in women in his son, and thus lead toward the supreme event. She assumed as steady and unconcerned a voice as she could muster, and enquired: "Is she a lady?"

"Oh, rather! Yes, of course."

His mother smiled. "In these democratic days it is not 'of course' my dear, that a student is a lady — from your account of some of the junior students."

"Oh, *they'll* never do anything," he said with scorn. "A lot of bumkins, thinking only of bread and butter. Will you tell me what they are allowed to come to college at all for?"

She would not allow him to divert her from her new interest and lead her astray in the mazes of a discussion they had had many times before over the meaning and the true place of the uncultured type of perfunctory junior student that frequented his and many other courses in all the London colleges.

"How old is she?"

"Lord! How do I know?" he replied. "She hasn't any wrinkles."

"But surely you must have a more definite idea than that. Does she massage the wrinkles away?" his mother asked.

"Goodness, no. I tell you she's got work in her. She really does seem keen, and she knows what she is after. There's that little to be said for her."

"*Little* to be said for her!" his mother replied, in pretended indignation. "You tell me she's a lady, young, beautiful in the style of Lady Hamilton, and intellectual in addition. My dear laddie, what more do you expect of flesh and blood?"

"Let's hope she doesn't smoke and giggle," he muttered.

His mother let the subject drop. She was far too wise to express her delight in the advent of a girl within the sacred precincts of her son's professional enclosure. For a week Kenneth did not mention the invader, and Mrs. Harvey curbed her desire to know more of the personality which might have so potent an influence. At the end of the week she did not re-open the subject directly, but said to her son, with innocent guile:

"Kenneth, my dear, you have not asked me to tea for a good many weeks."

"My darling Mum, you know I very seldom ask you. I expect you to drop in whenever you are shopping in Tottenham Court Road."

"Well, my dear, I have to go to Shoolbred's[14] to-morrow, so expect me at five o'clock."

Kenneth's eyes twinkled. "Am I to have the unknown equation on show?"

His mother dissembled. "Certainly, if she will come and you think she will not disturb our tea together."

Consequently, next day, without any preparation, and while she was all unconscious of the penetrating gaze that rested upon her, Lilian was subjected to a minute analytical investigation. Her dress was disposed of in a moment. It was simple and girlish, pretty and suitable, but it did not reveal any special indication of her character. Her hair, her nails, her shoes, her accent all united in satisfying Kenneth's mother as to the girl's breeding. After an hour's conversation with her, Mrs. Harvey thankfully came to the conclusion that Lilian Rullford might safely be trusted to spend solitary hours of study with her precious and beloved son; that is to say, if the solitary hours led to far from solitary kisses, she would be content in the anticipation of a wedding to follow.

Lilian did not suspect that Mrs. Harvey regarded her with any particular interest. Dr. Harvey's mother excited in her but a momentary feeling of curiosity. Lilian, however, felt the charm of her gracious personality, and she was attracted by so perfect an example of the flower of the passing generation. Had Mrs. Harvey ever come across a crowd of hooligans — which she never did — she would have won them to gallantry by the gracious gentleness of her voice.

Before leaving, Mrs. Harvey said to Lilian, "You know my son's students always interest me and I am delighted to see them. You must must come and visit me one day."

"Thanks so much," said Lilian, "but the daylight is *so* precious for my work, you must excuse me from coming early in the afternoon."

For one moment Mrs. Harvey wondered whether the girl was using subtlety, for she had herself been seeking how to ask her immediately to dinner without an appearance of excessive eagerness. Was Lilian consciously playing into her hands? She looked for a moment into the soft young eyes and then cast the thought away as being unworthy. She answered with a winning smile.

"Then you must come to dinner. I know research people like to work late; I never see my son to tea now save on Saturdays and Sundays. Dinner is by far our most sociable meal. When can you come?

Lilian smiled. "Any night; we hardly ever go out now, you know, and we are so busy and so happy over our work that it has resulted in our slipping into solitude."

The cordiality of Mrs. Harvey's response suggested to Lilian that her frankness might be understood as appealing for friendliness, and mentally she reproved herself. "There I am, always blurting out the truth when there is no call for it!"

"We live in St. John's Wood, the Finchley Road end, so it will be easy for you to come from Hampstead. I shall look forward to seeing you."

Lilian thanked Mrs. Harvey with rather prim formality and did not remain chatting, as she might easily have done, but explained that her sections were waiting for her and slipped away at once. After she had gone, Mrs. Harvey smiled and nodded in answer to her son's questioning eyebrows. "Your description was not so bad, Kenny, but she can't be more than nineteen."

"Must be," he said, laconically. "She's got her degree and didn't begin studying till she was nineteen, so there you are — a clear twenty-two at the very least."

"Just the right age," thought Mrs. Harvey to herself.

CHAPTER
5

TENDERNESS
TOUCHES HELL

AFTER Vera's appearance at the Opera, Rose Amber told her sister one day that she was going to call on her. Lilian tried to dissuade her, but not very effectively.

"Your warm charity dislocates my standards," she said.

That evening at dinner Rose Amber recounted the simple facts that she had been, that she had stayed only an hour, and had left before Sir Harry returned.

Lilian breathed a sigh of relief.

"Why?" Rose enquired.

"I don't know," Lilian answered. "It seems so awfully — so really improper, you know, in a way, only something bigger than that, that you and his wife, or rather his divorced wife should be there together; it is so frightfully unnatural."

"I do not feel that way at all," Rose Amber tried to explain. "It is like this. He is tenderly pitiful to her, trying hard to do the best and kindest thing he can to help her through her terrible time. The pain of it has wrought great lines on his face and turned his hair a little bit grey, and made him something almost super-human in his power of endurance and tenderness; and their relationship has not *anything* of that thing you call awfulness about it. Harry Granville is not the hero of a silly novel, Lilian."

Lilian flushed at the rebuke, and Rose was all compunction.

"That does sound horrid of me, doesn't it?" she confessed, putting her arm round her sister tenderly. "But you know real human life gives me a sense of greatness in man's unexpected potentialities, and this affects me somehow in the way your science does you. It is so big and wonderful to be human."

"Yes, oh, yes," said Lilian. "But you are so young and so pretty, and I suppose, after all, conventional ideas *are* based on something true — and I am — I ought to be your guardian"; a grim smile overspread Lilian's face. Rose affected a solemn, mocking air.

"Yes, my dear sister. You are rather like a dear little maiden aunt with a skittish young niece to look after, though, aren't you?"

They slipped away from the greatness and terror of life into the easy and tender realms of cheerful jest.

Lilian's work increasingly absorbed her; she piled up heavy books and bent her head to read.

"The horizon expands and the problems grow bigger," she said with awe, "till it doesn't seem wonderful to be human at all, but pitiful."

Rose took up her sewing. "But you know more and more — "

"But I get further and further off my goal — "

"You're tired," said Rose.

"The labour of studying for a degree in comparison with the *real* work which comes after it is trivial."

Rose Amber protested against her absorption and forced Lilian to put down her books and take a rest. Lilian, stretched on the springy sofa, talked of her science, and wove half fantastic theories which she would not have dared to consider in the technical and impersonal atmosphere of the University. Rose entered into all her ideas with such interest and understanding that Lilian forgot that she was not in any real way concerned in the work, and expanded her themes freely. These irresponsible weavings would not all collapse at a touch, but would remain the weft and woof of a sound idea which she took down for serious discussion to the University.

One afternoon Lilian tiptoed in to startle a solitary Rose. "Halloo! I've come home to be petted instead of to work. I'm suddenly tired of sitting in that museum, and I want a walk, to be soothed and made much of."

The maternal Rose, instantly touched, put her arms about her, "My poor darling, you do. You're white, even for you. Put on a furry coat and we will go up to the pine trees and from them see the last glow in the sky. It is so clear that I'm quite sure it will be beautiful."

As their footsteps echoed up the dull street, Rose turned to Lilian and said, "What luck we have to live so near the Heath. I really don't know what I should have done without it. Just two streets away and we get to the beginning of it! To feel that there are trees, sweet air and wild creatures near makes the loss of our old home less awful than if we lived in the bricked horror of the city."

Lilian squeezed her hand, but said nothing. They went quickly over the bare fields, where the willows were shedding their leaves and down the broad gravel path to the Vale of Health. When they got into the curve of the Spaniard's Road they looked back into the valley in which London lay as under a gauzy veil, through which a few lights in the main streets were twinkling like glow-worms caught in spiders' webs. They turned to the west, where the glow of the sunset lit a wide expanse of sky. In silence they stood for a moment, then followed the high crescent of the asphalt road to their favourite point under the group of ancient pine trees. No one was on the rustic seat, and they sat watching the last glow left by the autumn sun in the clear sky. The dark pines overhead whispered the day's story to the shy stars. The wind gently stirred the brown bracken-fronds in the valley and fluttered the golden lockets of the birch in the little copse beneath them. Billows of grey and purple mounted in the distance beneath the dull gold of the western sky. Right overhead a few of the brightest stars were shining through the dark and heavy tracery of the pine trees, which interlocked like a design cut by a master hand.

Lilian sighed. "I am glad I came back early this afternoon, in time to see this. Though I am very keen on my work, I do sometimes get tired of the bare deal boards, and the outlook of bricks and mortar down at the University."

"Of course you do," sympathised Rose.

"You shouldn't work so hard."

Lilian, thus spurred, was eager. "But I don't work hard enough! The subject I am tackling is *so* immense. Men have spent their whole lives, and only then begun to get a few results, and I have not only my own job to do, but I have to read all the miles of print which tell me what other people have done before me. It is like being an explorer, setting out into the unknown, through miles and miles of partly-beaten track that weary him first, before his real explorations can begin."

"You're lucky," said Rose, enviously. "At any rate, you have a single direction to follow, but I feel that *my* problems are a tremendous maze, too difficult to unravel, and I go backwards and forwards on them, and never seem to advance."

"*Your* problems?" Lilian smiled indulgently. "I didn't know that you had any."

"Didn't you know, little big sister," asked Rose Amber, "that I am studying just as much as you are?"

"You were the social one, not the student."

"At home, yes. There it was easy to live a social life. But don't imagine you inherited *all* father's brains. I am coming to the conclusion I got just a few myself, only they are mingled with mother's temperament. If we had remained rich I should have danced and flirted and influenced men as girls of our class generally do and no one would ever have guessed I had any brains till I was grey and wrinkled."

"Poor child, what you have lost," sighed Lilian.

"No." Rose Amber's voice was joyous. "I have found — myself. It is really very delightful to be intimate with oneself. In the old days there was no solitude. I did not have a chance to know myself at all. Now, for want of more obvious occupation, I have been fishing into myself and discovered that I am just like you — a student really."

"Rubbish," laughed Lilian. "You seem to me always to be petting people, making them happy and comfortable, playing with babies, nursing sick people, and letting middle-aged gentlemen confess their sins to you."

Rose exulted. "Exactly — but that's my *practical* work. That corresponds to your dissecting and laboratory experiments, Lilian."

"You horrid thing. You are not dissecting their souls, are you? Or are you only making fun of me? I thought this was a serious conversation."

"So it is. Is not human life and love as big a problem as the evolution of rabbits, or whatever it is you are working at? And as worth careful study?"

"Don't be revolting," Lilian protested.

"But you look at it wrongly," Rose answered gravely. "Of course I do not do it in the cold-blooded way you do your dissecting. But if anybody *does* tell me their own private troubles I think about them and try to find their real place in the general scheme of things. It seems to me," she went on, the dusk helping her for the first time to open her mind to her sister, "almost as though I were beginning to see something — something like what *you* would call a general theory."

"You? But how — ?"

"Well, it looks to me very much as though each generation has its own *great* problem. A couple of generations ago everybody was arguing about the literal interpretation of the Bible. Now most people have left that to theological specialists, and humanity is facing another problem, in quite another way."

"And what do you think that is?" Lilian was curious.

"*Biological science.* Just think what *unrealities* people were fighting about when Darwin[15] came along! And see how he changed the face of everything by getting people to accept the conception of the evolution of our bodies!"

"Do *you* think of that?"

"Of course! It is not only the scientists and biologists who are affected. All classes are influenced by his work. Even the most ignorant man who knows nothing about science yet has to thank Darwin for the atmosphere in which his mind can grow toward truth if it wants to."

Lilian was surprised at this unexpected revelation of a new side to her sister, but so interested that she only interjected the encouraging remark, "Yes, go on."

"Well, since this discovery the actual *literal* interpretation of the Bible does not matter any more to most of us — even to clergymen — and now — " Rose Amber's words glowed, "humanity is on another quest."

"Another? Oh, can't we ever *rest?*"

"No! We now have another, a fresh immense problem to fight out, and I feel as though *my* generation is going to tackle it. Having learned about our bodies, it is now the turn again of people's souls, or personalities, or selves — whatever you like to call them and *their* relation to social development. It seems to me at present that nearly everyone is unhappy, and yet if we only *understood* I am sure people could be really happy, and at the same time fit into a proper social scheme. That seems to be the work of *my* generation, and I do so want to begin to do it."

"But it is all too vague. What can you, or anyone do?"

"You know, Lilian, you often speak of yourself as exploring far away and apart from us all, finding out things that you will bring back and give to humanity. Now in your work you are essentially cut off from mixing with the great mass of people." She smiled tenderly, and cuddled her sister's arm. "That is why you are such a romantic, absurd duckling and think that when people are once married everything is settled once and for all, and they are happy for life. Now I am in the thick of the present generation and I *know* — they are *not.*"

This sister who was talking as an investigator and thinker was unknown to Lilian. She felt once more that faint bewilderment which she had experienced that day weeks ago, when Harry Granville was with her sister unexpectedly as she came in; it felt to her as though there were unexplained labyrinths in ordinary people's lives with which she was unacquainted. Her sister became for her mysterious and baffling. Was it possible that her own little sister, whom she had always thought so delightfully simple and human, was really exploring into an Unknown even more subtle, more elusive than her own scientific fields of research? She spoke almost petulantly:

"But, Rose, what *has* that to do with the fact that everybody confides their love affairs and their domestic difficulties and every kind of trouble to you? People wouldn't if they thought you were studying them."

"Of course, I don't let them feel that," said Rose Amber, "and I don't feel it myself at all at the time, only afterwards, when I see how dreadfully, dreadfully everybody has got tangled up in all kinds of ways that can only be straightened out by something fundamental, something that would affect our whole social system. I don't know *what* it is they need! That is what I am trying to find out."

"Divorce reform?"[16] asked Lilian, scornfully.

"I don't think so," sighed Rose. "It is not nearly so simple as that. Our whole social life is built up of the idea of an old-fashioned novel, in which people fall in love, marry and live happily ever after. Our happiness and our very ideas of what is decent and proper are built up on that, and it jolly well isn't true. But that is only one of the things that are wrong."

"Oh!" cried Lilian, in astonishment. "I had no idea you were so serious on a subject like that. It isn't suitable, it isn't really, for you to be thinking such things. It must be that wretched Harry; I suppose he has all this time been confiding his woes to you?'

Rose nodded. "Perhaps he has; why not?"

Lilian was really angry. "But, Rose, surely you know that a young girl does not talk of things like that with a middle-aged man."

"See here, Lily-sweet," said Rose, "you live in an imaginary, fantastically beautiful world which is only materialized now and then in exceptional people. You, yourself, are an exceptional person, and your happiness may materialize for you. I do hope it will, I hope awfully that you will marry somebody and be happy ever after, so that you can leave our ignorant world to behave itself or not behave itself, just as it likes, and go on with your own scientific work. Only I have not inherited the same kind of exceptionalness that you have, and when I see so many people hurt and unhappy, I can't help trying to think of a way out."

"But, Rose, how can you — " Lilian stopped.

"Do anything? Of course not yet. I am only feeling out towards what I want. In all the biographies of people who have done anything you will always find it said how they dreamt about it for years and years before they did it." The old mischievous, audacious Rose laughed at her for a moment but was swiftly serious again.

"What are you going to do?" asked Lilian, timidly.

"I can't put it into words exactly, but it seems to me what the world needs, at any rate what England needs, is someone to sympathize and understand the real *insides* of people's private troubles. We need some great person — big enough to be able to weld all the yearnings of all the people who are unhappy into something new, into some kind of new social conscience that will put things straight and bring happiness to everybody."

Lilian sighed. "That kind of thing is so intangible."

"I know," said Rose. "That is why everyone has muddled along without anybody doing it." She stood up. "Come along home, Lily-sweet, it is getting cold. It is no good putting these things into words. I only tried to spread out my little ideas in a serious sort of way to make you understand, because you are so dreadfully technical about things. Why should we be able to harness electricity and talk across miles and miles of distance and yet not bother even to try to understand people enough to make them happy?"

Qualms of compunction assailed Lilian sometimes when she realized how little interest she was showing in her sister's life. Then she would lay her cheek on Rose Amber's shoulder and say, "Now, what have *you* been doing to-day, Baby?" Rose would tell her some amusing incident of her work at the Secretarial College where she was still erratically studying with the avowed object of qualifying herself to be a first-rate secretary. Sometimes, but not often, Rose would have more serious things to say. Of the visits to Vera she had little to tell, though she always mentioned how Vera was getting on.

Vera failed more quickly than they had anticipated. Rose Amber maintained she was doing it on purpose, generously, to match Harry's generosity in surrounding her with the material comforts of life.

One day, when they were quite alone, Rose Amber encouraged Vera to talk. "I sometimes wonder what is the use of people like me. If I had been faithful to him, should I always have made him happy? Probably I should have deadened him, and we should never, either of us, have really lived; just gone from the season in town to a round of country visits. But now, as things are, see how strong and beautiful he has become!"

"You helped there," whispered Rose.

"I wonder if there is a God? And if so, if he has a purpose with us? It is hard on me if he has only used me to strengthen Harry's character. But, of course, I was given my little fling first — I had my success and my little worldly pleasures — then I was broken, and perhaps used up to serve him." Rose Amber saw then that Vera did not need to be answered; the pent-up musings only sought an outlet. She encouraged her to talk all the afternoon. Another day she said to Rose, "I do not believe in Hell, you know, do you?"

"Of course not," Rose Amber's tone was comfortably certain.

"I mean I do not believe in the Bible kind of Hell, after we are dead," Vera explained. "There *is* a Hell, I know, only people put it in the wrong place. We are in Hell now; this world is Hell. Why should it not be? If I could see any real good in it, I should not mind, even being in Hell. But I prefer purgatory. I rather like the idea of purgatory, don't you? It seems more sensible to have a purgatory that fits people up for Heaven than to have a world which spoils them for Hell. But if *this* is purgatory these souls of ours must be complicated things, not only made of one person's. Perhaps lots of people's souls have to be broken up to make one really good person's one? I was not fit to be a whole soul myself, I suppose, so I have just been used up in making other characters. The result of our life together is that Harry comes out of it far stronger and nobler and more beautiful than anyone would have thought a worldly man like that could ever have been, and I emerge — nothing — used up

— finished, because I was born a little thing, without any possibilities to start with — "

Rose would not allow her to continue in this strain.

"You goosie," she said quickly, "when you know you are only going ahead a step quicker than we are, and you have got heaps of good things to your credit to hand to St. Peter when he rattles the keys at you. You have taught Harry to love in a wonderful way, in a way one would never have dreamt of at first, and me too." Rose smiled and touched her hands. "You know, you have made me love you such a lot."

Vera leant over and kissed the girl's fingers. "You dear, sweet girl. You don't mean to say you are coming here out of anything but charity?"

Rose Amber's stout denial that charity had ever entered into her head, and the warmth and sincerity with which she urged her affection, temporarily convinced Vera.

"If you and Harry are both so good, perhaps God, if there is a God, won't be hard."

She half sat up, suddenly eager. "Do you know, the extraordinary thing is I am scarcely at all sorry for my really bad sins, things the world would blame me for, but I am dreadfully, dreadfully ashamed of the oddest things. I remember when Harry and I had only been married about three months and the dear, stupid darling had gone to the wrong shop to buy a box of chocolates for me and got a kind I did not like, and I was so sharp with him and threw them into the waste-paper basket; he had a look in his eyes somehow as if he was a child and I had slapped him. Do you know, really, I think I have repented of that a hundred times more than of anything else I have ever done to him?" She lay back and laughed hysterically, coughing as she laughed. "I never can understand why the little things of life are so dreadfully important and the big things so comparatively easy to get on with."

Rose nodded comprehendingly. "Yes, I know. Some absurd little *faux pas* or chance word that hurts somebody makes one wake up in the night, hot and cold with shame, for months afterwards."

Vera was coughing so much that Rose had to ring for the nurse, who was never very far away now. She brought a soothing drink, and in passing it whispered to Rose that she could not allow Lady Granville to talk so much. In a shrill voice Vera answered her.

"I heard you, nurse. None of that sick-room whispering goes down with me. You know I always hear what you say. It is so absurd," she protested, "that you cannot understand that I am not a patient to be deceived. I know quite well that I ought not to talk so much from your point of view, but if I choose to talk I shall talk, so there!"

"But, my lady," said the nurse, reproachfully, "you know only this morning Sir Harry told me to look after you more carefully."

But Vera tossed impatiently. "Oh, don't bother me, nurse, go away," she said.

As the nurse closed the door behind her with professional quietness, Vera smiled a little scornfully.

"Harry insists on her calling me *Lady* Granville, the ridiculous, considerate darling."

A queer feeling in her throat prevented Rose from answering, and Vera said, eagerly, "I say, darling, do read to me a little, won't you; something jolly and cheerful. Harry was reading an awfully funny story to me this morning, but I am sure if he knew *you* were finishing it up he wouldn't mind. It's over there somewhere, do look." Rose found it in a corner of a luxurious sofa where satin cushions and books were piled indiscriminately. When Rose had finished, Vera laughed heartily.

"Now that was too funny for anything. I am not going to tell Harry that you finished it, I am going to let him read it to me again." Her laughter made her cough with a spasm of choking, and as she took Rose Amber's hand to say goodbye she broke once more into laughter, saying, between quick sobs of breath — "I hope I shall die laughing — it is the one good end I could come to, isn't it?"

CHAPTER
6

A MODERN IDYLL

THE June skies were so blue that even the grimy windows of the College could not hide their colour altogether. The work which Kenneth and Lilian had shared for months suddenly palled. Talks on ideas, theories, results, seemed arid and wearisome. Yet without them they fretted for discussion — of what?

Kenneth was alone in the laboratory mounting sections; his fingers were all thumbs and he dropped a valuable specimen.

"Hang it — that girl will have to do it! Why isn't she here?"

He was irritated more by her absence than he had originally been by her threatened advent.

Dr. Nicholson came in, smoking as usual, and leant over his microscope. A flicker of tobacco ash fell into the clear jar of xylol.

"Drat you — keep off," groaned Kenneth.

"I wanted to see Miss Rullford," said Nicholson mildly.

"So do I," growled Kenneth.

"Where is she?"

"God knows."

"Quarrelled?"

"*What*? Idiotic fool!"

"Well, it's about time, ain't it? You've been thick with each other and collaborating for five months or so. People always split or splice after that.

"Rats! And clear out."

Nicholson shrugged his shoulders. "I'll nab her myself before you say 'Jack Robinson.' Just the sort of colleague my research waits for."

"Blast!" said Kenneth.

"All right, bye, bye."

The spring weather held and Hampstead quivered into colour. Lilian, too, was uneasy.

Much to their own surprise Lilian and Kenneth mutually and suddenly wearied of their stuffy little laboratory in Gower Street. On a particularly glorious morning in June both looked out of the window instead of working.

"Let's go into the country."

"Let's."

"Where?"

"Anywhere."

"When?"

"Now."

"These days are *too* beautiful to waste," they said to one another, apologetically. So they got out their bicycles and set forth toward the beauty for which their youth had been hungering.

Gone from the highways are the sleek sides and beautiful curves of prancing, well-fed horses. Nearly gone the sturdy strength of the endearing cart-horse. They, like the gracious, billowing beauty of a ship full set with sail, are giving place to the angular, sinister contrivances impelled by a power whose breath is a vomit of foul smoke created by an ingenuity which is without heart. There is no joyous, leisurely pilgrimage along the streets now. The lovers sped through the raucous ugliness of the byways of the town.

Once they reached the outskirts of the city the roads became freer from nightmares; the air less polluted by filthy fumes, and they had to endure only an occasional hooting and skurry of dust and petrol.

Near Stanmore Common they entrusted their bicycles to a waiter at an inn, and progressed as Nature intended lovers to progress, on winged feet, skimming the grass. Once on the Common they forsook the paths and sauntered under the arching trees towards the centre of the wood-land where the sunken, grassy hollows open to the sky are hedged by banks of wild rose bushes. Lapped in the sun and the sweet air was this grassy valley where scented herbs and wild forget-me-nots border the tiny stream that wanders through it. On every hand were billowing masses of wild rose, great stars of white, or of ethereal pink, decking the long, lithe red-thorned stems sprawling over the lower branches of the trees and waving their long trailers across the blue sky.

"Here," said Kenneth, indicating the grass.

Lilian threw off her hat. "Right."

Kenneth and Lilian stretched upon the grass, more intensely aware of the beauties of this rose show of Dame Nature's than they had ever been of the June flowers before, and yet they formed but the background to intenser perceptions of delight and loveliness. Kenneth, half reclining on his elbow, watched the girl near him, and the obvious thought that the sight of her delicate face with the faint flush upon it was like the sweetest of the roses surged through his veins with a novel thrill. Had anyone *ever* seen a woman's face like a wild rose before? Never! He was sure.

Kenneth, unread in the poetry of passion, unlearned in the arts of love, felt and said all the obvious things which a young man feels when he first personally realizes the acute beauty of a woman. To him the discovery of each charm in Lilian, the experiencing of each fresh sensation of delight seemed a wondrous adventure. He stamped no new impress upon the coinage of love words.

"Dash it," he said, "I can't even find words for what I want to say to you. I want some new ones."

"Old words are sweet."

"Like bride and love and home."

"Hallowed by all the love of other lovers."

"But I want new ones, for you are new and our love is unique."

Beside them a bush of pink roses, with its deeper, almost crimson buds, intensified the blue of the sky.

Lilian plucked one. "Look at its burning heart," she whispered, and softly leant towards him so that its petals touched his lips.

"Feel mine." He pressed her hand to feel the throbs he longed for her to share.

"Does it beat for me?" she asked.

His response to her was so sweet that after it had sunk to silence some mingling of placid, neutral talk was needed to hold her to the earth. She endeavoured to return to their scientific discussions.

"What a lot of varieties of these roses there are!" she volunteered. "Look, some of them have thick stems with little prickles all over them, and some have smooth stems with great crimson thorns; the petals of the flowers on the different bushes vary so. I wonder how many each ever so far apart; and the shape of true species of wild rose there are altogether?"

Kenneth half sat up. "*Species*! There you have hit the nail on the head, haven't you? If you can tell me what a species is I shall be obliged to you, and so will the scientists, for not one of 'em knows."

"That is one of the problems *our* work will help to solve," Lilian replied.

"I hope so," Kenneth doubtfully agreed, "though I am afraid it is too big and complex a job for us. Funny idea it is, isn't it, that most people think that science has settled what species *are*? I suppose in actual fact there is no idea really more vague and disputed. They are always talking about species. Even newspapers nowadays — and — "

"It is like most other human conceptions, a name fixed on to an incomplete idea and kept long after the idea itself has been utterly changed out of recognition. Old Linnaeus,[17] I suppose, thought that species were units of a fixed creation, and even after Darwin came along with his idea of evolution and perpetual flux the old idea of what a species *was* remained so strong that in lots of cases even to-day it is difficult to realize that we simply do not know where species either begin or end."[14]

"It's a horrid nuisance."

"I think the philosophic idea of discontinuity,[18] which is so fruitful in ordinary life, has a lot to answer for in creating some of the worst muddles we scientists have got into. Now we cannot think of *time* without cutting it up into minutes and seconds, but most of us have the sense to realize that it is perpetually flowing — flowing on without a break. I'm beginning to wonder whether perhaps life is really something like time — a perpetual stream, yet, of course, the fact that there are individual things like pussy-cats and dicky-birds, and you and me, seems such a strong argument for life being fundamentally cut up into separate bits that it is not surprising that we cling to the old idea of species."

"Don't you suppose it is really only because we see things too near and for too short a time?" asked Lilian, showing that she, too, had thought of this, perhaps the profoundest problem of biology.

Kenneth put his hand on her knee. "I wonder how far our work will take us!"

"Us," repeated Lilian.

"For everything," said Kenneth deeply.

"Both work and play."

"It'll help the work."

"Even if we fail to get hold of a real fundamental principle we will have a jolly sight better life for having attempted it than if we had never made a shot at it."

Lilian threw out her arm to be caressed by the soft, deep grass and looked up at the blue sky between the roses. "We will have such a perfectly lovely human life that to better it we should have to be angels."

"I am a lucky beggar to have got you, both for my work and for my life," said Kenneth, looking down at her with eyes almost incredulous of the grace they beheld.

He was impatient of his own vocabulary.

"Hitherto girls have always seemed to me such conscienceless little creatures somehow, but you — "

Lilian teased him. "You know you didn't want me to come to college a bit. Don't you remember the first day that I came to see you about entering how you tried to put me off?"

"How on earth was I to know that you were *you*, and not like the others," he protested.

"Are you glad I came?" She asked the eternal question to which he gave the only reply possible for a man in love. Larks sang in the blue sky, and the field mice sat up under the arches of the grass to watch the great intruders who seemed so little concerned with anything but themselves. When Lilian looked up again her cheek was flushed as the pinkest of the wild roses.

Kenneth said to her, "I feel so safe, you know. It is like having found a haven. Both my happiness and career are safe now — with you. So many men have their capacities frittered away by impossible human relations, but with each to help the other we shall be able to do *great* work."

"You have no idea, darling, what tremendous luck we have!"

"Oh, you angel." He buried his head upon her knee. "Who could have imagined anything so perfect and so sweet as you."

"Perfect *for each other*, and that is all that matters," whispered Lilian.

CHAPTER

7

"What is Love"

MRS. Harvey came into her dining-room half an hour before dinner in order herself to put the last touches to the flowers before the betrothed pair arrived for their first meal after they had entered their new and blissful state.

She was alone and her thoughts were all radiant within. Pink and white roses . . . simple . . . but sweetly old-fashioned . . . symbolic of the purity and joy she brings. Sanctified as a wedding day . . . even more sweet . . . happier for being without that dash of tears which so often sparkle on a wedding gown. . . . But no tears for this . . . all joy.

"The radiance in my boy's eyes — magic faltering words seem to be gifted with special magnetic power . . . *his* words — *his* love. What had he said? 'Lilian is so different from other women,' he had whispered between the long puffs at his pipe. 'It is extraordinary how she fits into me — how she seems to understand all that I want to say almost before I have said it. It is not only in our work, it is her attitude towards life. She takes life seriously — she has never frittered her love away on anyone else before me. She is like a mountain flower that has budded in the snow, and the moment the sun has melted the rim of the snow field it is there ready to bloom in perfection. She is so cool, sweet and fragrant — she does not rush a man's senses and yet she can satisfy him. She — ' he had stopped and remained silent; then got up and stooped and kissed me — his mother."

"I'm *thankful*."

"So am I! I dreaded the unknown her."

"Why?"

"Well, I've seen so many good men spoiled, either by the perpetual strain of enforced celibacy, or by having their energies sapped by a brainless vampire in the home. Thank God for Lilian — and that she'll have me!"

"You understand, little mother, I know; for you have been wanting this experience, this unique experience for me all along. You knew me better than I knew myself."

44

In all Mrs. Harvey's life the sweet, deep love in her heart had never been roused and shared with passion or with a poet's frenzy, and to her, the tender romantic love of her son seemed a thing of infinite grandeur. Her secret touchstone would not have recognized the dumb burning of a frenzied passion. It rejoiced her that he did not falter inarticulately or affect a common nonchalance as the modern young man so often does. Her ideal son had stepped up to be her ideal lover. And she knew no bigger brand of love. After a last glance round the table, she stooped and kissed the back of her son's chair, and stood for a moment of prayer beside Lilian's.

"Dear God," she whispered, "use me to minister to those to whom I hand on the torch of life."

Just as she was leaving the dining-room her eyes fell on a thumb-mark blurring a silver cover. She rang the bell.

"Jane," her voice was stern and reproachful, "have I not told you that you are *never* to touch the silver without wearing gloves?"

"Yes, Mum, and I always do."

"Look at that thumb-mark on that cover! And to-day, too! Take it away and clean it. The meal is symbolic."

Through dinner the young people spoke chiefly of their plans and hopes.

"Kenneth is going to be very famous," Mrs. Harvey naively explained to Lilian.

The girl answered with an understanding smile. "Of course. He is really, already, among those who know, though the outer world has not had time to learn of it yet."

"Bother the outer world," protested Kenneth.

"It does not count at all." Lilian agreed with him.

"Oh, but it does," Mrs. Harvey insisted gently. What is the good of work that the outer world knows nothing about?"

"It is the best sort," Kenneth maintained.

"It is really," Lilian backed him up. "You see, Mrs. Harvey, what we are working for is not at all the sort of thing the world understands. You see science advances by her disciples making discoveries, but they are hardly the kind that *can* interest humanity; ordinary people don't know enough of the technical jargon even to know what they are about. At the best, most real scientific discoveries are like little stones dropped into a pond and the tiny ripples they make take ever so long to expand before they come to the edge, and by the time they have reached it the pebble is at the bottom of the pond and forgotten.

"We won't either of us be famous in the popular way — ever. We don't want to be."

"Hear, hear!" shouted Kenneth from the depths of his armchair.

"What do you want then, my dears?" Mrs. Harvey smiled.

"Freedom to work at the kind of work we like; tackling all the big problems that are vaguely forming in our minds, but," she added with a sigh, "to do that we will have to keep alive. We need just enough, but we don't want more success than will just keep us going."

Kenneth grunted. Lilian turned, questioning him with her eyes. Was her exposition of their ambitions right?

Understanding her unspoken question, he nodded.

"Go on, little girl. You are telling mother what I have been trying to make her understand for years."

"Well, you see; we want to do, I suppose, what all true scientists want to do, work that nobody but ourselves understands or really cares at all about! The real thing is the finding out things for ourselves which fit into the theories we are trying so hard to complete. To be able to do work like that, of course, we have to live somewhere convenient, and we have to have just enough other enjoyment and comfort to keep really fit — "

"As we are human beings, we can't help needing that," interjected Kenneth from his chair, "we would if we could — "

"Oh, no, we would not," interrupted Lilian. "Not *now*. Now I enjoy being a human being more than I ever thought I should."

Mrs. Harvey laughed tenderly. "Well, as you are human beings for the present, I suppose you will have to live in a house. Where is it going to be?"

"Hampstead," said Kenneth promptly. "It is the only place high enough to get out of the smoke and dirt of the city, and near enough not to waste an infernal amount of time travelling."

"Quite a little house," interjected Lilian. "We are not going to start an 'establishment,' you know. Kenneth will only be an assistant professor at college for years to come."

"But he might be head professor in another college."

"Of course he might; but it is better to live in London as an assistant than to be a chief in the provinces. London is the centre of everything. All the learned societies, all the meetings, everything that matters is in London."

"I have told you that often, haven't I, mother?" said Kenneth. "You'll never see me leaving London for the provinces or the colonies, or any other of the places they lure young scientists to with the bait of a decent screw."

"Well, it is a mercy that you children have the same theories about managing your lives, otherwise one of you might have a sad time. It is a relief to me that you are going to live in a house," she said, playfully. "I was afraid that with all your high aspirations and your ideals about being dedicated to Science that you would want to live on a peak in the Himalayas."

"But that would not do at all." Lilian laughed. "We need laboratories, libraries and confabulations with our fellow scientists. The Himalayas would do for us if we were philosophers, for a philosopher does not need anything but himself."

"A philosopher can make plans of the universe," grumbled Kenneth, "with no elusive facts to hinder him. He can imagine it all any way he likes, and is respected the more the longer the words he invents and the more muddled his mind is."

"Not like us — we try to *clear up* things."

"And are you going to work *all* the time?" wistfully asked Mrs. Harvey. Kenneth looked a little shame-faced and Lilian smiled.

"But, you know, we have both discovered recently there is something very fascinating about poetry. A queer thing, isn't it?" Kenneth asked as casually as he could. "Even that Tennyson[19] fellow's stuff contains a lot of observation and ideas not badly put. There must be some psychological effect in the incompleteness of poets' thought and the rhythm into which they put it."

Kenneth assumed his air of condescension to cover his so recent change of front.

"He has never heard of 'Georgians,'[20] and probably never will," laughed Lilian.

"I used to adore poetry," cooed Mrs. Harvey, "but modern poets don't seem to me so good as the older ones. I suppose really all the best and most beautiful things have been said?"

Lilian took this up. "I am sure they have not, for we are always evolving, and there must always be new things to be said about human relations, just as there are always new discoveries to make in science."

"Why has not somebody written a poem about modern marriage?" asked Kenneth. "How can all the old poems about love and all that fit on to Lilian and me? Do you mean to tell me that a thousand years ago, or a hundred years ago, or even a generation ago a husband and wife would feel for each other just the way that Lilian and I do?"

"But you are happy because you *love*, and the love is the deep eternal thing which poets have always sung, seeing through its superficial circumstances."

"That's just the point," challenged Kenneth. "We go on calling it the same love because the poets have not redescribed it for us, but it is *not* the same thing, any more than Lilian and I are like our prehistoric ancestors."

"But your love makes you happy, and it is love's sweet, primitive sense of comradeship and union you also have."

Kenneth grinned. "There must be some magic in it, anyway," he conceded. "Here have I spent an evening thinking about poetry and feeling instead of scientific facts."

"An interlude," smiled Lilian, "to brace us up to work all the harder."

"By jove! Yes," chorused Kenneth. "Lilian and I have got big things to do together, no time to waste."

CHAPTER

8

WELCOME DEATH

ITH a maternal tenderness Rose watched her sister blooming in the joy of love. They spoke little. One day Rose announced the conclusion of her musings. "You are very lucky, Lilian, that your theories and your practices are able to fit in so well together."

"How?" Lilian asked.

"Why, you are a Puritan, you know, and you have actually been given a Puritan's love affair! You have not had to face some awful situation. Supposing the man you loved had been another woman's husband, or a murderer, or a man three times your age who wanted you to go on the stage. What would you have done then?"

Lilian laughed. "I simply should not have loved him."

"But you might," threatened Rose. "That is where you make your mistake. I know women who have had to face things as preposterous as that."

"Then it must be their own fault." Lilian was callous. "They have allowed themselves to be carried away by unrestrained feelings. Surely first of all the intellect must be appealed to; one must respect before one can love, and anybody so ridiculously impossible or irresponsible as you describe would never have made any headway with me in the beginning."

"But sometimes," persisted Rose, sagely, "there *is* no beginning — or it is all beginning and finished in a moment, and then a whole life is tangled up. I really know people whose stories are like that, and you can read of them often in the divorce court proceedings, let alone in novels and plays."

"That is so curious," Lilian sighed patiently, "and it seems to me quite unreal. Purposeful, intellectual people *don't* get mixed up in affairs like that."

"They do."

"It's a sign of weakness then — flaws."

"Look at Harry. Look how poor Harry Granville has had *his* life muddled up for him."

"But he has had exceptionally bad luck," allowed Lilian, compassionately. "I never felt so sorry for Harry as I do now — now that I understand better what he might have had."

"But most people are in the same kind of a fix, in a greater or less degree," explained Rose Amber. "I am sorry for nearly everybody round me. You and Kenneth have really *terrific* luck."

"You absurd baby." Lilian assumed her elder-sister air. "You are a whole year younger than I am. A year hence, when you are engaged too, you will feel quite different."

Rose saw less of Lilian than ever, but her days were very full. She was now secretary to an elderly author, Mr. Joshua Mompson, in the mornings, and though she had only been with him a few weeks, he was already expecting her to smooth out all his troubles. They seemed to her very trivial — an announcement from a publisher who sent his proofs late and then objected to what the author considered very reasonable corrections; the incorrigible housemaid, who in dusting always re-arranged or mislaid his papers; the persistent little kitten, which would slip in every time the door was opened and originate an Alpine expedition up his knees while he was trying to write.

Rose Amber had not yet discovered what had withered her author's heart, but she assumed that he must have had one. He had so long lived with people who were convinced he never had had one that he felt the change in the atmosphere as inconvenient as a draught of warm air. He looked at her over his spectacles and asked himself: "Am I being mothered by a child in my old age?"

But Rose Amber's ministrations to him were more those of an institutional nurse to a rather troublesome child. Her mind was alive elsewhere. Many afternoons she spent with Vera Granville, who was now confined to her room and saw no one else but Harry and the two nurses. Rose Amber often revolted at the social convention which forced the frail creature to continue her long struggle with death. So often now Vera moaned, "Why on earth can't they kill me and have done with it, instead of keeping me alive to worry everybody? Why should I waste the time of two healthy women to nurse me when I must die, anyway, so soon? Why should poor Harry have any more of it? It isn't as though I was any earthly use!"

She listened eagerly to Rose Amber's tender assurances of affection, but they left no lasting impression on her mind. Her plaint was that Rose Amber was so good and kind that she did not tell her the truth.

One day Rose received a note from Harry Granville saying, "I know you always come to Vera when you can; she is asking for you very insistently just now and the doctor thinks it may only be a few days, so if you can manage it, do try and come this afternoon."

Rose showed the letter to Lilian at breakfast.

"How dreadful!"

"Not more than usual," Rose mused.

"It is dreadful; the whole thing is terrible."

"Perhaps the *whole* thing, yes. But why is it terrible that it should be so near the end, when ages ago she prayed for the end to come quickly?"

Lilian shuddered. "I don't know how you can bear to see her; it is so embarrassing and painful."

The silence that followed the clatter of their knives and forks on the plates seemed artificial. Lilian broke the tension by saying, "I suppose you will go? Oh, but you can't. I have just remembered. You promised to go with Mrs. Harvey and me to a matinee. You said that you especially wanted to see that play, and it is only on this week."

"You will find somebody down at the College to give my ticket to," Rose answered quietly. It was characteristic of her that she wasted no words in explaining that she really would not go.

Lilian sighed. "It does seem a pity to waste the ticket when you wanted to go so much. Wouldn't it do for you to see her after the theatre was over?"

"No." Rose Amber was inflexible. "I shall stay a good while to-day; long enough to let Harry go out for a walk; he is sure to have been in the house too long. She doesn't talk very much any more — there is nothing more to say — but he hates to feel that she is alone with the nurses, so he has been stopping in the sick room far too much."

"It strikes me that she is selfish." Lilian was incisive.

"Not a bit," said Rose, indignantly. "She does not want to keep him there; he insists. And sometimes she is weak and frightened. They won't let her have the chloral.[21] She wanted to get it over at once and set Harry free."

"Why doesn't she get hold of some? I should," Lilian announced calmly.

"She did try one day, but I stopped her. She had a lot of chloral in a bottle under her pillow. I came across it quite accidentally and I made her promise not to use it as she was going to."

"Why?" enquired Lilian. "I don't understand you at all. You are always so compassionate and want to help people, and yet there you go, in the ordinary human way, keeping alive someone who is longing to be dead; and when it would be such a relief to everybody if she *were* dead. It is only cruelty to keep her alive, cruelty to Harry and everyone concerned."

"I do not think so," Rose flashed. "If I had thought that it had really been best I should have given her the chloral myself; but Harry would be sure to know that she had taken it, and it would be just the very last thing too much for him to bear. He would always imagine that he had not been kind enough to her. He is rather more old-fashioned than we are, anyway, and to have his wife take chloral is a thing no decent man could ever forget."

"You are awfully queer," Lilian sighed. "I do not think I understand you a bit about the whole thing. From the beginning to the end it is incomprehensible to me. I cannot understand how she could ever have left him and gone with that other man in the first instance after she had married him and had loved him. Even if she hated him, they were *married* — and then to go back to him UNMARRIED! I still hate the idea of your going to see her. I have to concentrate my mind as much as possible on the thought that she is an old friend and that she is ill, and try to forget everything else, or else I should have to *forbid* you to go. I really don't know what Mrs. Harvey would think; I hope sincerely that she will never know."

"I did not mention names, of course, but I have already told her quite a lot about it," Rose remarked quietly.

Lilian put down her knife and fork and looked at her sister with amazement. "You told her! When?"

"The last time she was here to tea and you and Kenneth were in the garden, we were having a talk about life."

"But you have only seen her about half a dozen times!"

"Yes, but she is a kind, sweet-hearted woman, you know. And we have something of the same kind of way of thinking about some things." Rose laughed, half in amazement, half apologetically. "We both feel as though we were mothers to half the race and were responsible for nearly everybody."

Lilian still looked at her sister curiously. "I remember now that she did say what a charming girl you were and how unusually wise for your age. It's simply extraordinary, Rose Amber, the intimate relations into which you get with people! And at such a rate. Now, though Mrs. Harvey is going to be my mother-in-law, and though I have seen her ten times for every once that you have, I simply could not have talked to her about Harry Granville. It does not seem to me to *bear* talking about."

"Why?" asked Rose. "The greatest tragedies of history have been talked about."

"But did not Mrs. Harvey think it was *dreadful* for you to be mixed up in it all?"

"I do not think so," Rose answered simply. "She said she was very glad the poor thing had someone to go and see her."

"But didn't she think of *your* side of the position?" asked Lilian, a little petulantly.

"*My* side?" Rose questioned.

52

"I mean the harm it might do you — socially, you know."

Rose remonstrated gently. "It is too absurd how you never forget that. I am sure that Mrs. Harvey would never have thought of it any more than I would. A thing like that cannot harm one."

Lilian got up and kissed her sister goodbye for the day.

"I really believe, Rose Amber, that it may not harm you. There is something extraordinarily simple about you with all your complexity; things that make people blush you pick up tenderly and put straight; I really believe that you are a kind of soul-doctor."

After Lilian had gone Rose stayed behind for a few moments to do the day's ordering before going round to take care of her old gentleman. She remembered Lilian's last words, "A soul-doctor!" "How lovely of Lilian to find that idea!" she thought. "It explains me to myself. That's exactly what I hope to be."

She got up and put on her hat, smiling at herself in the glass. "I believe Lilian has hit on my profession. How the poor world seems to be in need of soul-doctors! I only wish I knew some professor of the subject to whom I could go to study. I'd take my degree with him like Lilian with her professor of animals' bodies. Why do they have hundreds of professors of bodies and no professors of hearts? Clergymen, I suppose, might *claim* to be soul-doctors, but I'm afraid I have never met one who would be any good! I must try to gather together all I can from the people I meet, the little scraps of knowledge to be found all over the place; here a word and there a hint. I shall just have to piece it all together and make a textbook for myself."

A mocking voice within her seemed to say, "Physician, heal thyself!"[22]

She sighed, then laughed. "Yes, I'm just the one to make a blighting mess of my own affairs. Heigh-ho!"

A day soon came when in the Granville's hall the nurse shook her head gravely when she saw Rose. "Her ladyship is very low indeed to-day, Miss. She has been asking for you all the morning, though she knew you could not come."

The luxurious beauty of her dress and surroundings which had always seemed so essential a part of Vera still lent their grace to her tragic part. There had always been an air of exquisite delicacy about her, so that even in the midst of the most abject humiliation which can overtake a woman she had never been touched by sordidness. To-day she lay dying — but dying with a grace to which the wan eyes of lace-makers and the weary fingers of weavers of the fairest silks and linens had contributed. Her ravaged face and deep burning eyes looked up from a pillow of the softest down, and the neck, too weary any longer to carry the head, was caressed and covered by the filmy delicacy of lace. Rose noticed as she crossed the room towards the bed what an exquisite artist Vera was to the very last, and how she had spared everyone the cruel home-thrust of sordid misery, and had made herself a centre of beauty for all who served her. To Rose Amber this was more than an extenuating circumstance; it was, in a way, an achievement.

As she took the wasted hands Vera faltered, "I am glad — you — have — come — I — wanted — you."

"I came the moment I could." Rose Amber bent her head and kissed her cheek.

"He will be free to-night, I hope," Vera whispered.

Rose stooped low to say, "You also will be free; free from worldly mistakes and full of the happiness of understanding."

Vera moved her head restlessly. "For me neither understanding nor happiness," she moaned.

"Yes there is," Rose answered, comforting her with a tender, warm hand-clasp and a tone of certainty. "It is always harder to forgive ourselves than to forgive anybody else, but even for ourselves it must be true that to understand everything is to forgive everything. You will see perhaps, then, how your suffering has in some strange way helped Harry. And I myself, *I owe you much!* I know I should have been blinder and harder without you. Dear Vera, long after you have passed through the Valley of the Shadow, we will both always love you."

"Dear girl," Vera stretched out her hand; "when you are here you almost persuade me . . . I am tired."

She turned her head on the pillow and for a long time did not speak. She opened her eyes later, and when she saw Rose Amber sitting by her bed, she said, "Oh, I was forgetting. Look, I want you to have this."

She took off her finger the glittering hoop of diamonds which she had always worn. Rose gently forced it back, but the sick woman insisted with all the vehemence that was left in her. "You must; I should not be happy if you did not."

"No, no." Rose Amber protested. "Wasn't it — ?" She stopped, and Vera nodded faintly. "Yes, my engagement ring — to Harry — that is why — *you* must have it."

Tears filled Rose Amber's eyes, and coursing down her cheeks, sprang on to the soft silk ribbon on Vera's night-gown and lay glittering near the diamonds. Vera once more took off the ring laboriously and, fumbling for her hand, placed it on Rose Amber's finger.

Rose was about to take it off again, but Vera was so distressed that the nurse interjected, whispering, "Humour her for the present. It is wonderful how much she has talked of you to-day. She was prostrated all the morning, but she was determined to see you." The door opened softly and Harry Granville put his head into the room. Vera, seeing him, beckoned to him and gasped, "Harry, she has got — got — to keep the ring — hasn't she?"

"Just as you wish, dear," he soothed her wistfully.

When Vera slept, Rose Amber slipped away. She took the sparkling ring from her finger and placed it in Harry's hand.

He came into the hall with her.

"Poor Vera," she sighed. "I wonder if I shall see her again."

"You must keep the ring, she wanted you to," urged Harry. He did not hint at his longing to toss it into the sea — to drown the glitter of the hard, cruel symbol of the will o' the wisp he had thought was passionate love light.

"No," she said, "it was yours."

"Please."

Rose Amber insisted no more on its return.

That evening, when the two girls were resting after dinner, a telegram came saying that Vera had died at seven.

"How sad," sighed Lilian. "But it is a good thing that it is all over at last. Harry will be thankful."

"One can be thankful and heart-broken, too," suggested Rose Amber.

CHAPTER
9

EXTINCT MONSTERS

"I MUST be a born biologist," Lilian remarked at the University one day. "No familiarity seems to dim my joy in seeing through the microscope the ordered details of tissue-structure."

"I know," said Kenneth. "A good section of the commonest plant stem or the nucleus of a well-known animal cell fascinates the eye perpetually by its exquisite detailed perfection. I feel it every term with the same old students' demonstrations."

"When, in addition to the ordinary beauties of tissues there is the fresh interest of the discovery of new structures — well — it intoxicates me."

"We live removed from the ordinary sphere of humanity!"

"We do."

"They think us stupid."

"Mad."

"It seems to double the interest of each new detail that comes to light, seeing it from two slightly different angles like this — now we are — us."

"Are we exceptions, or shall we come a cropper over this one day?" asked Kenneth of Lilian on an afternoon when they had made strides in their work together.

"Rose Amber says we are exceptions," answered Lilian with a smile which gently indicated how mistaken she thought Rose Amber was.

"*You* are an exception, of course. So as a pair we must be," said Kenneth. "Yet I have hardly heard of a case of collaboration where the two people did not quarrel some time or other before it was over, and wished to Heaven they had tackled the subject alone and had not messed their time away arguing with some blankety-blank fool who could not understand what he was looking at."

Lilian laughed infectiously. "When that happens, my dear, we will each write a paper to show how mistaken the view of the other is — " but the sentence was broken across by something she observed, and she called out to him, "I say! Come and look at this!" He leant across her shoulder with his cheek touching hers, to peer at a new conformation of little spots and wriggles on a glass slide, which they both recognized was a clinching proof of one of their latest ideas. There seemed no likelihood of an immediate disruption of the partnership.

Kenneth and Lilian, in pursuit of their great ideas, grew into discontent with the evidence obtainable from living creatures alone. I don't see how we can possibly know all we ought to know about these living animals unless we know their pedigree back to the very beginnings of things," pronounced Lilian one day.

"That is just what I was thinking."

"How are we ever going to find out?" sighed Lilian.

"From the people who study fossils."

"Are there any fossils of any use to us?"

"Must be. Palaeontologists[23] are getting quite uncanny. They seem to know the very insides of creatures dead millions of years ago."

"Yet how many zoologists and botanists bother to know what the ancestors of their own particular living specimens have been up to?" asked Lilian.

"I suppose palaeontology is a whole science, but that need not prevent us taking it in at a gulp!" She looked round mischievously, and she and Kenneth laughed and laughed again for sheer joy in the expanses opening out before them. What a realm to explore and what a mate for the expedition!

The plaster walls echoed with their mirth, and the attendant in the corridor skinning rabbits for a class muttered to himself: "Wimmin! There'll be no more work out of Dr. Harvey with a pack of wimmin about. They should never ha' been let *in* the colledge, spoilin' a young man as 'ad somethin' in 'im." The attendant had not learnt the difference in tone between empty-headed laughter and the high mirth of Olympus.

"We are not undergraduates; we won't begin at the beginning," exulted Kenneth, unconscious of the needlessly embittered janitor without. "We will plunge into the middle of the subject and snatch the heart out of it. I suppose we had better go along to the old Natural History Museum and have a look at the fossils."

"Fossils are mostly bones and teeth, aren't they? And seeing that our creatures have very little backbones and are mostly squashy stuff, I don't think there will be much hope for us in the rocks."

"I don't know," said Kenneth. "Think of jelly-fish, they are still squashier, and yet look what stunning jelly-fish Dr. Walcott[24] has got in the Silurian[25] rocks which are millions and millions of years older than anything we need worry about. We modern zoologists gas far too much of what we *think* evolution *may* have done, and jaw about species, arguing which comes from which, and why one of them lives in the North Pole and the other in Timbuctoo, as the case may be, but we don't bother half enough about what *evolution actually did do*. It is only the Palaeontologists who get the fossils out of the rocks who can say what the ancestor of any particular precious creature really was like. Let us be Palaeontologists."

"When shall we begin?" Lilian agreed with acclamation.

"To-day, of course." He came across the room and kissed her. "Why not this minute? Get your hat and coat and let's go and see what they can do for us at our national emporium of extinct monsters."

Lilian stood up and ruffled his hair. "This is not like your sober, intellectual self, is it? We do not know in the least how to look at fossils yet."

"Let's branch out into our new line while we have the impetus and the zest to do it. We can deal with the details later. When the dreary days of November come we can be plodding enough in all conscience. We have got to take our inspiration when it comes."

"Come along then." She was as eager as he. "Let's tap on the silent hearts of the fossils and say: "Hullo, you are a missing link; tell us what you linked up?"

In this playful mood they set out on a serious professional excursion, entering on a field so bristling with difficulties and technicalities that many a worker who should have learnt to know his way about its paths has been deterred from even entering the domain.

When the two came out of the college into Gower Street, Lilian turned towards the Metropolitan Railway Station, but Kenneth took her arm and led her across a side street into Tottenham Court Road.

"Let's walk," he said laconically.

"I thought you were in a hurry?"

"A hurry to *start*. Now we have started there isn't any hurry. We have got lots to think about; my mind is full of all sorts of ideas."

They cut through the back streets, dodging their way round little Jewish children dancing to barrel-organs, their sentences disjointed and hurried by their sudden descents from the curb in their endeavours to circumvent loiterers on the pavement. At last they came out into the park. There they sauntered and talked more seriously; and suddenly Kenneth seized Lilian by the shoulder and pressed her on to a small green chair under a tree. There they talked during the whole afternoon until the rays of the journeying sun sparkled and danced through Lilian's hair, and Kenneth, suddenly aware of its beauty, remarked on it. Lilian realized that it was tea-time, and that they had never got to the Natural History Museum after all. Laughing, they went into Piccadilly for their tea, and over hot tea-cakes continued the weaving of their scientific dream. The waitress came back several times to their table, and hovered discreetly, but they paid no attention to her. From time to time Kenneth stretched out his hand and with a couple of bites demolished a cake in an absent-minded fashion. An hour after they had first sat down at the little table Kenneth reached for another dainty, but when he felt that the plate was empty, without comment drew back his hand to enforce some point in his argument and did not ask for another supply. The attendant waitress, huffed by the way they ignored her volunteered ministrations, decided that nothing would induce her to bring more cakes unless the customers did ask for them. Among her fellows she contemptuously described them:

"Lovers you would think," she said, tossing her head, "if it wasn't for the way they're jawing. But they must be Fenians[26] or burglars or something from the plans they're making on a bit of paper."

Lilian at last became aware that they had been there long enough and looked at her watch.

"Ken! What do you think the time is?"

"Eternity," he was confident.

"Exactly," she smiled. "Eternity plus quarter to seven in the evening, and dinner at seven o'clock!"

"We'll do it"; he took up his hat. "You are not going to dress, are you? Let's take a taxi; then we will get a few minutes' quiet. I haven't seen anything of you to-day."

In the course of the next week they really did get to the Museum, armed this time with a more exact knowledge of what they wished to see. Lilian managed to lure Kenneth past the fossil turtles, but he pulled her up in front of the Triceratops,[27] whose great skull, with its armour-plate-like projections and its three horns, fascinated him.

"What did the beast *eat*?" was his question.

"He had far too much backbone for us to take any interest in him," Lilian reminded him. "He must have had an extra strong one, I should think, to support all that skull."

"But what did he *eat*?" repeated Kenneth. "What on earth is the good of the way we scientists jaw about environment and evolution when we don't even know what the ancestors of our living beasts ate? Talk about environment! Isn't the thing you take from it and put inside you the closest environment you can have?"

"Come along," wheedled Lilian.

He could not pass the great bones of Ichthyosaurus and Plesiosaurus[28] fastened up on the wall like stoats nailed round a game-keeper's shelter.

"By jove! Those fellows had backbones all right," he exclaimed.

"Come *along*," insisted Lilian, pulling at his coat.

"Shockingly utilitarian creatures women are; won't mouch for the pure fun of it, but must have an object in view."

In one of the remote galleries, where the lowlier animal fossils are now separated from the great monsters among whom they disported long ago while they were all alive, Lilian and Kenneth opened the text-book they had brought with them and began to be serious.

They were alone in the gallery save for the solitary attendant who stood disconsolately at the very far end, his reflection dimly repeated in the glass doors. The noise their entering feet made filled them with shame. They tried walking on tiptoe, but then the echoes seemed even more obstinately persistent than when they boldly trod the floor. Seeking their particular family of creatures they walked right up the length of the gallery, and the attendant, with his back toward them, knew just which exhibit they had reached by the sound their footsteps made. A large, square case on legs broke the echo with a different tone from the solid cases filled with drawers to the floor.

They reached the exhibit near him and stood for a moment reading the labels on it. The galleries were still, and in their silence, the old soldier, now serving his country as guardian of animals which could never run away, felt once more the long oppression of vacancy closing down on him in these silent galleries. He looked curiously at the two, intent upon their specimens.

"Not ordinary lovers, they aren't," he said to himself, "if they be lovers at all. Some of these 'ere new-fangled students, only they don't look young 'n untidy enough. Perhaps they're some as really know wot they are looking at?"

He drew nearer to them. The idea that they really knew what they were looking at grew upon him. He came up beside them.

"Beg pardon, Sir, beg pardon, Miss; do you mind me askin' a question?"

"Please do," responded Lilian.

"It's like this; I spends 'ours in this 'ere gallery and it's empty most all the time. It isn't like the crowded galleries outside there, where the flies and fleas and all them interestin' things are; no one comes 'ere, 'ardly, 'n I have nothing to do, so I reads the labels."

"Dull reading, are they?" enquired Kenneth, with interest.

"'Orrible, 'orrible," he continued, intensely. "It's their 'orribleness wot upsets me, not their dullness. Dullness I'm used to, 'avin' been a working man all me life, but this 'orribleness is too much for me."

Lilian felt vaguely uncomfortable; the man was evidently distressed.

"What was it you wanted to ask?" she said gently.

"It's like this 'ere," he hesitated. "If them labels is true the Bible's a lie, and what I wants ter ask you is, *are* them labels true?"

"Yes, certainly," replied Lilian, promptly. "Each is written by the chief specialist on the subject."

"'N the Bible's a lie?" The man looked uncomfortably white, as though it mattered to him.

"Oh," began Lilian. Then she stopped, wondering what to say.

"I ask you, be them labels true? — and you say yes. I thought myself they must be true, or they wouldn't be allowed to be stuck up here; and if they're true the Bible's a lie, and what is the good of being alive?"

The man turned and went slowly away from them, and Lilian and Kenneth, both distressed by his emotion, did not know what to do, so they pretended that they had finished with that room, and that the families of fossils they particularly wanted to see were in another gallery. They tried to slip out quietly, but the sheets of glass and the boards of the floor played their usual tricks upon their footsteps and they crashed their way out like Megatheriums[29] out of a thicket.

"Fancy," repeated Lilian, when she told Rose and Mrs. Harvey at dinner of the incident. "Just fancy finding in these days anyone who believes *literally* in the Bible! I suppose he thought that the whale really swallowed Jonah and that the world was really made in seven days. I thought his type was as extinct as the Dodo; why, even the Salvation Army preachers know about evolution and the poetry of Genesis now. The really right place for him was the Museum of Fossils. The poor man was dreadfully upset, and we didn't know what to do!"

"Which gallery was it?" asked Rose.

"The one on the left when you get past the Ichthyosauruses."

"Is he always there?"

"I don't know. . . . He said he spent most of his time reading the labels."

"The poor man," said Mrs. Harvey, compassionately. "Couldn't you give him some books to read while he is there?"

"I guess it's against the regulations," said Kenneth.

"What was he like?" asked Rose Amber.

"Oh, rather a short little man," Lilian explained, "Very upright, with a reddish-coloured moustache. Not at all the kind of man one would expect to be so sentimental."

Rose Amber said nothing more on the subject, but began to talk about the flat which was being furnished for the lovers.

The next morning Rose told old Mr. Mompson that he would have to do without her for two hours in the middle of the day. She had been his secretary long enough for him to lean upon her already.

"I can't, my dear," Joshua Mompson grumbled, "I have to write a letter to *The Times* about the way the boys whistle in the streets. I want it to be biting and sharp and not too long; it will take me all the morning to compose it."

"I am sorry"; Rose Amber was gentle but firm, "but if you will compose it in the morning, I will type it out before tea and it will catch the same post. I *must* get off for two hours to-day — please." She smiled winningly.

"Oh, dear; oh dear," moaned her old gentleman. "This world is a very difficult place for anybody with susceptibilities. Even you, my dear, are not so considerate as I had hoped, but, of course, you are very young."

Rose Amber laid out a large pad of writing paper and several sharp pencils, placed his chair and left him.

She found her way down to the Natural History Museum, asked for the fossil tortoises; then asked another attendant for the Ichthyosaurus, and found the gallery haunted by the melancholy veteran. She looked in and saw no one there but an upright figure in a dark uniform. She went forward slowly, pretending to glance at the cases; the echoes would have shamed her had she attempted haste. When she was near the attendant she bent over a case intently. He watched her, and she suddenly looked up and caught his gaze fixed upon her. She smiled, but his smile in return was wan.

"He seems to be the man," she said to herself. "Here goes! If it's the wrong one, I can't help it."

Aloud she remarked: "How interesting this place is; do many people come to see the collections?"

"Mighty few," he responded briefly and sarcastically.

"You can't have much to do then," she suggested with a smile. "It must be awfully dull."

He sighed. "Dullness I don't complain about," he said. "A working man is used to dullness."

She waited for him to continue, but as he did not she ventured: "The labels are all very interesting; do you read them?"

He started. "Read them?" His tone was bitter. "What else 'ave I to read? Books and papers ain't allowed."

"Then you must learn a good deal about the fossils," ventured Rose Amber.

"I learn more than is good for folks." His expansiveness had cost him so dearly yesterday that to-day he was taciturn. Rose found it a more difficult business than she had expected.

"But," she bravely persisted, "I don't think the truth can ever be bad for people, do you? Tell me," she continued, "were you here when my sister was looking at this case yesterday. She told me someone had asked her if the labels were true?"

He looked at her suspiciously, not ready to face a further undermining of his belief. "Yes," he said, after an interval.

Rose Amber saw the uselessness of beating about the bush, so she plunged.

"My sister said that when she told you the labels were true you said that the Bible must be lies, and she didn't think of explaining something to you that makes a lot of difference"; she paused, but he did not answer.

"The Bible isn't lies," she continued eagerly, "It's true, beautifully true, only in another kind of way — just as though you were looking at another side of the same thing. You know a penny has a king's head on one side and Britannia on the other — they are different pictures and they are both sides of a penny."

The man's face grew eager. "But — " he protested, "but all the same, Miss, if these 'ere labels is true — "

"Yes, they are," boldly asserted Rose Amber, but her smile softened the assertion which yesterday had been so devastating.

"Well, then, the Bible *is* lies. The Bible says quite clear that the world was made in seven days and the labels make it out millions of years."

"Oh," Rose Amber met him brightly. "Have you forgotten that the Bible was not written in English?"

The man started. Rose Amber followed up this attack.

"It was first written in Hebrew, you know. You must have seen the part in front of the Bible, telling you that King James had it translated."

"Yes, Miss," the eager face was an illuminating encouragement.

"Well, you couldn't expect those old-fashioned English people to know Hebrew so very well, could you? And the truth is that the word that they translated *days* has two meanings in Hebrew, so that it really can mean *periods*, and it might just as well have been translated as periods, and then the first chapter of Genesis would read in your Bible 'And God made the world in seven periods,' and that is just what these labels are saying! These geological records really do correspond very well to short poetical descriptions of the seven periods in the beginning of the Bible."

The man's face cleared and a look of intense joy spread over it. "Is what you say *true*, Miss?"

"Yes, really it is true," affirmed Rose Amber. "You know yourself the bible was not written in England."

"That's right, Miss; that's quite true." He leant forward suddenly. "God bless you, Miss," he said, and turned away to take out a red spotted handkerchief.

"Good-bye," said Rose Amber quickly, unable to brave an anti-climax. "I find the labels awfully interesting: I must come and see them again."

The man's gruff good-bye was muffled in the reverberations of her retreating footsteps.

Some days later Lilian and Mrs. Harvey were surprised at Rose Amber's vehemence on the subject of religion for the working-classes.

"Why should some cruel bits of truth be rammed down their throats and none of the beautiful, comforting bits that would help them to keep their God and learn something as well?" she asked indignantly.

The others had forgotten the attendant in the Museum and they teased

Rose about her sophistries, but she saw only eyes in which the light of hope had been re-lit.

CHAPTER

10

THE ENDOWED CHAIR

TIME sped so swiftly and happily for Lilian that she did not realize
that nearly two months had passed since Vera's death. One day a
visit from Harry Granville awakened Lilian's dormant sense of
responsibility for Rose. After he had left them she protested. "Why don't
you make him travel?"

"I did," asserted Rose. "I packed him off to Switzerland with strict
instructions to send me a picture post-card from a different place every
three days and to walk from one place to the other, and he *has* been away
for nearly six weeks."

"Six weeks! Is it so long?"

"Time flies when you are happy. *His* six weeks seemed long."

"Not long enough. He ought to go for six months."

"I have tried to make him;" Rose was plaintive. "Harry said he had
nothing whatever to do with all the energy he was storing up in the
mountains, and he couldn't be responsible for himself if he got much
more vitalized."

"Can't you make him go to Canada? He has big estates there, hasn't
he? Let him go and look after them for a bit."

"I have tried that, too," smiled Rose at her sister. "It's no use. Besides
the poor man has had pretty nearly two years of an almost mourning existence and he is strong and well and rich; it is only natural that he should
want to come back among his fellows."

Lilian sighed helplessly. Rose Amber knew perfectly well why her
sister sighed and she thought it rather pathetically funny. "We have
known Harry Granville since we were babies," she reminded Lilian.

"Umph."

"I have ridden on his back."

"Umph — but — "

"And even you yourself have run races with him."

"Those days have vanished with your baby shoes;" Lilian suddenly
assumed a conventional air. "It isn't right for a young girl like you to see
so much of Harry Granville without — a chaperone."

"Lilian, you are the dearest thing!" Rose Amber threw herself on the sofa laughing. "Chaperones for working girls are as extinct as the Dodo, so perhaps the right and proper place for you *is* the fossil department of the Natural History Museum."

Lilian, vaguely conscious that Rose was using one of her own arguments against her, could not recall exactly which.

"Well," she remarked, consoling herself, I shall soon be married and Mrs. Harvey will have charge of you, and when I am married you will be able to see something of people at my house. I am sure it *is* hard for you to have no social life at all."

"Not a bit," Rose was cheerful. "I see all the people I have time to. Only I am not going to discourage Harry Granville, who is an *old* friend — fifteen years older than myself — just because you think he would be a bad match!"

"I didn't say so," protested Lilian, indignant at this frank expression in words of what had, in truth, shamefacedly crept into her mind.

"But you thought it," asserted Rose, light-heartedly.

"No."

"Why not say it?"

"I didn't — "

"It's much better to have a bogie materialized in words and bowled over than for ever hovering and immense. Now let's settle it. Harry Granville would no more think of making love to me than he would to you; and, secondly, if he *did*, I don't see that there would be the slightest bit of harm in it. He has nearly sixteen thousand a year," she reminded her sister, mockingly.

"Rose, don't joke; it is too dreadful to be joked about."

"Bogies treated *seriously* are more dangerous than if joked about."

"I *am* glad I am going to be married soon," averred Lilian, helplessly.

"So am I, dear," cooed Rose Amber, suddenly serious. She put her arm round her sister. "Your marriage is such a wonderfully perfect thing that I can hardly believe it!"

"Yours must be just as lovely, Rose, darling, and it will be, if you don't play with fire and let people like Harry Granville grow fond of you."

Lilian, trembling with dislike of her theme, asked Kenneth's mother what she thought about it. "I agree with you, he is by no means so unlikely a lover as Rose herself believes."

"What can I *do*?"

"Lilian — do nothing — perhaps the stress and pain he has gone through in the last two years make him feel old and worn, and as though life's springtime has passed. It may be safe."

"But I think that as the relations with Vera are now finished completely, and with as little self-reproach as the tragic circumstances allow, he is beginning to be conscious of the possibilities of — a new force in his life."

"But is he not the type of man who will be romantically faithful to one love throughout life?"

"He told me that the Vera he had loved in the past — had — snuffed — out — become phantasmal. The love which he *had* felt appeared now only homage to the reality of LOVE."

"Dangerous!"

"I think so!"

"His friendship for Rose Amber seems to him at present the only true and sincere human relation he has."

"She's been cut off so much from everything, she's quite unspoiled."

"He even reads Jane Austen, or poetry to Rose in the afternoon while she sews. She's busy sewing for my wedding cushion covers, embroidered pillow-cases and pretty things of many kinds with Harry Granville spending whole afternoons talking, with a book open on his knees unread!" It was true, and Harry Granville was enchanted by her version of her sister's work, sketched with a mixture of tolerant humour and the suggestion of a mysterious wonderland into which ordinary mortals could only peep.

One day he said to her, "I should like to meet that chap she is marrying."

"Of course you shall," cried Rose Amber. "I will give a dinner party, and invite the bride and bridegroom-to-be. We will have the party here, if we can electrify our Mrs. Potter sufficiently to give us any food."

"Let *me* give the party," volunteered Harry Granville eagerly.

"Another one later," Rose allowed. "Not this one; this one is for me."

So delighted was she with the idea of her party that she sent Harry away very early that day, and interviewed the landlady immediately. Mrs. Potter's promises had too often withered for Rose to trust her cooking. "Everything must be cold," she said, "except the soup. She *can't* spoil that, surely!"

The party was aided by the fact that the two men thoroughly liked each other at once. Lilian suddenly realized that parties of this kind were much safer than tete-à-tete afternoon sewings and readings, and felt as pleased with herself as though she had arranged it all.

"I say," remarked Harry Granville to Kenneth, "do you mean to tell me that the University uses men with brains like yours at the rate of four hundred a year? Good Lord, it's a scandal."

"Universities not many years ago had the impudence to start young men holding the highest degrees in this country and abroad too perhaps at a hundred and twenty."

"Good Lord! Why do they go? They could get more in a bank or as a butler."

"They go because they love their work," Kenneth shrugged. "That's how the community sponges on us scientific chaps. Everyone knows we always *would* do our work with no salary at all so long as we can keep alive somehow. So, with a few exceptions here and there, where wealthy men have endowed chairs, we are all of us living within sight of the starvation line. It has always been like that. Look at Lavoisier[30] — he burnt his last kitchen chair to keep his chemical retorts going for discoveries from which the whole world has benefitted."

"That is so long ago," objected Harry. "Things are different now, surely! What about all these endowments of research? We are always seeing that someone has left a hundred thousand pounds to endow something or other."

"Mighty little of it finds its way as salaries for junior men! No, I am lucky to be getting four hundred at my age, doing nothing but a little University teaching and a lot of research."

"But you are one of the chief authorities on your own subject, aren't you?" inquired Granville.

"Humph!" said Kenneth thoughtfully,

"He is," Rose Amber averred eagerly. "Lilian knows, and she told me there are only three or four men in the whole world who know as much as he does in his special line."

"It's monstrous!" Granville was emphatic. "Why doesn't the University pay you decently?"

"Don't blame the University." Kenneth was placid. "It's shockingly in debt, poor thing, and has a frightful struggle to live. Blame the pork butchers and the brewers and the rotters on the Stock Exchange, who put forty or fifty thousand a year into their fat pockets and never ask what an intelligent man would do with it."

"But we so often hear of endowments."

"If you heard of an endowment every week of the year, what would it amount to?" asked Kenneth impetuously, of everyone. "How many Sciences are there — let alone Literature and History and other things — how many Sciences alone? Twenty or thirty, according to the way you split them up, and in each of these sciences, a dozen special branches, each needing teachers of great erudition, though I say it as shouldn't. And how many colleges and Universities and Institutions up and down the country are teaching some of these various branches? Figure it all out; you will find that an endowment a week for ten years wouldn't be too much to put things decently straight, and as things are there is nothing like a decent endowment more than once or so in a year."

"I am amazed"; Granville was serious, almost incredulous. "I always thought Universities were awfully well off. Oxford and Cambridge have lots of fat lands."

"I knew a specialist at Cambridge just before the war," announced Kenneth, calmly, "whose official salary was one hundred pounds a year, plus a few pickings here and there, tutoring, a minor fellowship and so on, but for one hundred pounds a year he not only taught advanced students, but he had to carry on researches into the unknown."

"Good Lord! But the professors do themselves pretty decently; I knew a professor once, Sir — "

"Oh, *professors!*" interposed Lilian, scornfully. "It is the junior men who are doing most of the real work, you know and it is only one professorship here and there with a decent salary attached."

"You had better be a professor," suggested Granville.

Lilian laughed and Kenneth gave a sudden short grunt.

"There is no professorship that just fits my line, and if there were there would be twenty or thirty men, though not quite in my own line, ahead of me in seniority for it."

"Oh, hang it all!" said Granville. "I suppose the University would make a professorship if some chap left the money for it? Why don't you get up a Lord Mayor's Fund for it?"

"You try," taunted Kenneth with a grin.

"Why not, eh?" queried Granville.

Lilian and Kenneth raised their glasses of cider and mockingly drank his health.

"But, I say, more difficult things than that have been accomplished. What?"

"Have they?" asked Kenneth sarcastically. "Try it and talk to me a year hence, and we will see if your opinions remain the same."

"How much does it cost to make a new professorship?" enquired Granville, not inclined to be so lightly diverted from what seemed to him an excellent idea.

"Not long ago the University of London had the decency to decide that nobody should be a professor without a minimum of six hundred a year. Before that, some of the poor wretches were keeping up a dignified appearance, with a wife and family, on three hundred, and trying to do researches at the same time on which they ought to have been able to spend a thousand a year on apparatus."

"Good Lord!" muttered Granville. "Six hundred pounds seems mighty little."

"I could name men," said Kenneth, quietly, "whose names are known in every civilized country in the world who would feel they were in clover had they got it."

"Humph," said Granville, humorously. "I see my heroic part, rousing up the Lord Mayor to start a fund to make a new professorship every year, as a beginning."

"Bravo," they all shouted. Rose started "For he's a jolly good fellow."

"You don't take me seriously," he protested.

"We don't," agreed Lilian. "You are unbelievable."

Before they parted, Granville had invited himself down to see Kenneth's laboratory, and Lilian promised to show him some slides. He undertook not to smash them while looking at them through the microscope.

A few days after his excursion into the scientific world he came up to Hampstead to read with Rose.

"Look here," he began eagerly, closing the book she laid open, "you and I have got to concoct a plan together. I ran across the Lord Mayor at a fool-function last night and said something about starting a fund for the Universities, and I confess he didn't seem keen. Beastly bounder! It makes one sick to have to do with a man like that. But in the meantime, I don't see why people like your sister and Kenneth should be scrimping and screwing at home and in their scientific work for the want of a paltry six hundred a year, when a rotter like me has the use of about sixteen thousand. Would you mind if I had six hundred a year less than that, Rose? I mean — er — would you mind if you were me?" he hastily covered up his first question with its too obvious suggestion. His enthusiasm for the ill-paid scientists was quickened only by their being linked indirectly to Rose Amber.

"I don't see how you *can* spend all that money;" teasingly Rose Amber gave him the answer he wanted, unconscious of his thought.

"Not so difficult with a wife," he answered, "but, of course, now — I did not feel justified — ." He hesitated. Rose encouraged him.

"I can't go to the University and say 'Make Kenneth Harvey a professor;' that would not do at all, but I have thought of a plan, and *you* have got to help me. I am going to be one of the repentant rich and my conscience-money is going to take the form of an anonymous gift to the University of six hundred a year. My lawyers can see to the anonymous part — gas vaguely about a will or something. But the real difficulty will be to find out exactly how we can get *Kenneth* to benefit by it. I suppose they are more likely to give it to him if I am supposed to be dead and leave an endowment mentioning the great young scientist? Eh? I don't know whether my solicitors will be willing to fake it — they are a very respectable firm."

Rose laughed. I don't expect you will find any difficulty in getting the University to accept six hundred a year."

"No," he allowed; "but all public bodies rather hate gifts with conditions attached."

"I don't know," Rose considered the subject. "It depends on the conditions. They accepted Galton's[31] money to found a department, and ever since there have been Universities at all different benefactors have founded professorships according to their own fancies."

"You think it can be worked? Eh?" he asked eagerly.

"I don't know," encouraged Rose, "but I should think so."

"You mustn't let Lilian or Kenneth have an inkling," said he. "They would only refuse, or feel uncomfortable or something, and that would be fatal. Mind, it's *our* secret, and you mustn't give it away on any account!"

"*Our* secret." A phrase well worth six hundred a year, the rich man thought.

CHAPTER

11

A WEDDING AND LOVE

EVEN the simple wedding, which was all Lilian and Kenneth allowed their two mothers, as they now laughingly designated Rose and Mrs. Harvey, was sufficient to create an intriguing sensation. The flat was filled with the sound of fairy silks, lifted and rustled by scented airs of mystery. To enthrone the happy day a pile had to be raised of airy nothings, radiant with colour like the iridescence of blown soap bubbles.

The actual preparations permitted by the calmly reasonable lovers, who protested against a "fuss," were so unassuming, so simple, that the real work entailed, spread as it was over several weeks, had to be spun out by Mrs. Harvey into a fine web of illusion to fill the time with enchantment. Rose Amber, enjoying it with a zest scarcely less keen than Mrs. Harvey's own, yet perceived the unsubstantiality of their assumption of overwork.

"What is the *feel* of a marriage?" she enquired mischievously one day. Mrs. Harvey, delighted to listen to Rose Amber's chatter, encouraged her.

"It is like a handful of the loveliest white soap-suds, or like a mouthful of white of egg when you grind it between your tongue and teeth. I love the *feel* of things, don't you?" she continued, leaning back and curling her feet up in the corner of the soft sofa. "It is the feel of shortbread and of almond paste, and the tickling of bubbles which break on the top of champagne and the nice stickiness of cherries in plum cake and all the things like that which make food worth eating."

"You funny child, it is the way the food *tastes* that matters."

"Not half as much as the way it feels," maintained Rose Amber, "and contrariwise, that is why I hate with an unspeakable hatred tapioca pudding and spaghetti and oysters and half-cooked eggs. I wish I had known that when I was a child, so that I could have explained to nurse what was the peculiar loathsomeness of tapioca pudding. Once these darling lovers are off our hands, and their flat furnished for them, I am going in for propaganda work."

72

"Oh, no!" Mrs. Harvey was serious.

"I am going to start a Society for the Informing of Infants of the Fundamental Psychological Reasons for their Inherent Instincts. Will you join the I.I.F.P.R.I.I.?"

"Not unless you work harder than you are doing now," Mrs. Harvey smiled. "I want those white satin bows tied very nicely. Jane did some but they were not half pretty enough; she has a clumsy hand, so now you do them."

By the wedding day everything was ready, down to the very last white satin bow. Not a single shimmering tear slipped from the bride's eyes to her wedding dress.

"How calm they are!"

"Our marriage is not like the usual frail barque[32] of ignorant senti-ment, swayed by gusts of instinctive feeling, to and fro along the waves of emotion! We're *rocks*," said Lilian.

Rose half reproachfully said, "No. Be like a steady lighthouse built upon the rock, illuminated by an understanding of mind and body — but — "

"Oh my dear, don't — no buts — "

"I won't. They *are* happy and will always be."

The shakings and flutterings of emotion dwelt far more in the bride-groom's mother than in the bride. Mrs. Harvey said to Rose, "I feel as though the love of all my years of widowhood is concentrated on this day!"

Then came the reaction. As Rose Amber explained it, "the time *after* you had pinched your froth of bubbles."

After the wedding, Harry Granville called to complain that he had been neglected.

"It is weeks since you took me for a walk," he wailed to Rose, "and more since you took me to a theatre, and it is absolutely ages since I have seen anything except fragmentary scraps of you."

Rose Amber laughed at him mercilessly. "A man like you cannot be lonely; go to the club."

"Hang it all, I am not lonely *miscellaneously*! I have got a particular kind of loneliness for a particular kind of person, and you are the only person of that kind I know."

"What is the good of being grown up if you can't get along without someone to look after you?" asked Rose.

"Men never grow up. Isn't that what every woman knows?"

Rose was now living with Mrs. Harvey, and Harry Granville

wandered round her drawing room looking at pictures and picking up pretty trifles while he talked. Rose was half lying back on the couch watching him and eating the chocolates he had brought.

"I feel particularly light-hearted now," she sighed luxuriously, "having got those two darling people nicely married."

"All the more reason for taking on a fresh job."

"I want a rest," said Rose Amber, looking the embodiment of radiant strength.

"Of course you do," he assented quickly. "Let us go out to the country."

His peregrinations had led him to the other end of the room. After glancing at her across it, he turned his back towards her and stood picking up silver trifles from a table. When he spoke his voice sounded quite different from the tones of mocking banter he had just been using, and without turning he said to her: "This is an awfully pretty room, and it suits Mrs. Harvey to perfection; she merges into it like a grey-blue shadow of an island in the hazy, blue horizon, but you stand out of its back-ground vividly, like a white and rosy Venus rising from the waves. I — "

Even the echo of the light banter had died away, the air of the room was hushed and Rose Amber felt within her brain the singing of a thousand distant larks in an infinitely high and remote blue sky.

Harry Granville stood there without moving, but it seemed as though he were the centre of flooding waves of light and song; intangible, unheard, that leapt round her and through her, and set the joy and laughter rippling and dancing in her veins. Harry Granville stood there without moving, but the hands of the clock ticked softly, marking seconds during which these two stood entranced. His back was towards her, but he felt the change in her feelings. He was conscious of every soft beauty of her, and the attitude of lovely startled surprise with which her spirit stood to await the onrush of his feeling. His hands yearned to touch and caress her, and the skin of his fingers felt the rippling waves of her hair and the soft smoothness of her cheek; his lips trembled to touch hers, and every cell of the epithelia[33] of his body quivered and sang to its fellows "we are near; we are near to one whose touch completes us." The pent up vitality of his manhood surged through him, radiating toward her, and she, startled and still unaware of its significance, was lapped in its magnetic waves, poised on the brink of time where it merges into eternity.

Harry Granville stood motionless, with his back toward her, and his eyes observed and his automatic brain recorded a little scratch on the silver ornament in his hand, while his heart echoed with the orchestra of sweet sound made of every nerve in his body vibrating, "This is She." "This is She is whose body is the soul that completes my soul! This is She without whom I am nothing! This is She on whom my eternal life depends!"

The laughter which had bubbled up in Rose Amber's throat when he first began to speak slipped away and seemed to leave a golden vacuum. Before she answered him she had to command and coerce the muscles of her throat, and then she gravely and quietly said: "I shall have more time next week. Let us go into the country."

And Harry Granville turned, as the door opened and Mrs. Harvey came in.

"Good," he replied in his normal voice. "I will keep you to it. I must run now; I have an appointment;" and he left her without shaking hands.

The commonplace words which had passed between them did not shatter that sudden sense of fusion which had united them for a brief space with eternity. Their personalities, sensitive, shy, subtle as spirits of the woodland, had ventured out across the space of the room and met in a plane above their bodies; had met unafraid, because they had never yet hurt each other, and neither knew anything to fear from the other; there had been as yet no misunderstandings, no blindness, no regrets between them. Their laughter and comradeship had been but a cloak, a shell, from which they had joyously burst, seeking each other, in each other seeking that exquisite completeness of union in which only the spirit of a man and woman can meet, completing each other, creating by their union a new and wonderful individual. This mystic union can only know the radiant perfection of its rapture before either has even subtly wounded the other.

Rose Amber had never yet spoken of love, and the exquisite sense of anticipation that it was about to reveal itself in her own life kept her heart singing wordless music.

This day, though neither of them had spoken to each other, they together entered that marvellous region whose air is mutual joy; that region which, unclogged by the material aspects of life is perhaps the pinnacle of the paradises known on earth.

CHAPTER

12

THE KNOCK-OUT

THE bridal pair gilded the autumnal term at the University with their bright honeymoon joy, working and playing: living and loving in harmony.

"Have you never had even the smallest tiff?" asked Mrs. Harvey one evening.

"No, why should we?"

Kenneth puffed luxuriously at his pipe.

"Settling in with each other is sometimes a difficult business — living at close quarters — "

"Not for us, we are exceptions, you see."

His mother delightedly teased him.

"Oh, you're trying to keep up your old dignity. You have got to be exceptions, haven't you, to justify your former scorn of all other women?"

"I'm right, aren't I?"

"Supremely."

Lilian arranged her work so as to take one afternoon a week off for domestic duties and enjoyment. She played like a child in her tiny flat; made out the week's menu for their housekeeper-maid-of-all work, and entertained friends to tea.

"You're never going on with your work now you are married!" was the usual refrain.

"Rather, my work's only just beginning."

"There's fog outside, and yet the sun seems to be shining in here. How do you do it?"

"Gold silk curtains, yellow walls — "

"And happiness."

"That's it."

"You look clear, like a crystalline spring, quite different from most married people. They so often look dull and soggy."

"That's the difference between Love and — the other thing that begins with 'L' and leads to 'ell.'"

"Lilian, I never heard you so naughty."

"Oh, it won't last," confidently exclaimed the visitors, either in the drawing room to her face or on the path behind her back. Rose and Mrs. Harvey often talked over the bridal pair.

"I always did think Lilian the most delicious, old-fashioned darling," said Rose Amber confidentially. "I never dared hope she would find the right man to marry her. When one thinks of the appalling possibilities of unhappiness, it is too wonderful that those two should have found each other. Do you think Kenneth will stay like that always?" she asked. "I can't imagine how *your* son should have so little subtlety — be so extra-ordinarily simple."

"Men take a long time to grow up," smiled Mrs. Harvey, "and none of the tragedies of life have touched him." That gave him a charm, but even his mother, who utterly trusted him, knew he had not yet been tempered in the fire.

"He rather despises people who make a mess of their lives, doesn't he?"

Mrs. Harvey smiled indulgently. "I often think that the Universities are so shut away from the realities of life that a young man who goes straight into University teaching after taking a degree is apt to become narrowed, or at any rate to develop human sympathies *later* than a man of the world."

"Later!" Rose Amber was less than half serious, but she proclaimed: "If Kenneth turns into a man of the world, Lilian will die broken-hearted on the spot."

Mrs. Harvey said hastily, "Oh, my dear, don't think such things; they will both grow older and wiser together, and I would not for the world have them different from what they are now; it is *too beautiful* to see anything so simple and sincere. If only it could last for ever."

One Sunday Kenneth and Lilian rode on their bicycles towards the country. The road was smooth with fresh asphalt and a light rain had fallen recently. The many motors travelling over it dripping grease on the surface had painted it with skins of iridescent colour.

"Some of the spots are lovely!" Lilian called out, "like riding on a road of peacocks feathers."

"Unlucky things," said Kenneth.

"Nonsense! And you a scientist!"

"Unlucky."

"Beautiful, you're superstitious. Fancy *you*."

"Oh!"

There was a swirl, a rush — a swift passing motor had overtaken her. The safe margin between the kerb and the wheels of the car vanished as the car suddenly skidded and swerved, colliding with the front wheel of her bicycle.

"Oh!"

She was thrown against the lamp-post; her temple struck the cold-rimmed iron of the post. It was the last sensation she felt in this world before she collapsed upon the kerb and slipped into the gutter, splashed with mud, beneath her bicycle.

The shout raised by the driver made Kenneth turn.

"What's that?"

A cold sword pierced his heart. His breath felt like ice in his lungs. Dizzily he rode back shouting over and over again:

"You're not hurt, Lilian, are you? You're not hurt? You're not hurt?"

He knew death when he saw it. It had been often before him on the dissecting board.

He turned savagely to the policeman who came up: "What devil has been using her for his experiments?"

The policeman took the number of the car.

"What am I to do?" asked Mrs. Harvey of Rose Amber, "what can I do? For three days he has sat in that armchair like a log, his pipe, unfilled, in his mouth. He won't open a letter, he won't speak. I can hardly force enough food down his throat to keep him alive."

Rose Amber, though she had lost a sister, forgot her own grief in sympathetic anguish. "I'm no good, I'm no good, for I — I don't know what to do to help him."

"What *can* we do?" reiterated Mrs. Harvey.

"Talk to him about the college."

"You try."

The telephone helped her. The professor rang up to say that until the end of the week Kenneth Harvey was not to return; his colleagues had taken all his work upon their own shoulders,

Rose tentatively suggested to him an idea which she thought might move him — consideration of the extra burden which had fallen upon others already doing their full share of work.

"Why should I care? Old fools helping young fools to swot for their degrees. Fools blindly mauling at life's secrets and calling it science."

"Your work — "

"What's it all to do with me — now?"

Rose Amber timidly asked him: "Could you get away for a few weeks in term time?"

"If I hanged myself."

Rose took his wrists in her warm grasp.

"Kenneth, Kenneth," she shook him. "Don't be so mad, so cruel."

"Cruel?"

"Yes, to mother, to me."

"To mother?"

"Of course. Let me arrange with the professor. Let's all go away together — the sea — Cornwall — a voyage."

She flew to the telephone and rang up the University. The action seemed to stimulate some numbed cells in his brain. He took the receiver out of her hands and put it back.

"No, my dear, stop it."

It was as though he had suddenly seen his duty in that empty laboratory.

"I can't leave them in the lurch in the middle of the term."

"I am sure they could manage for another week or two if you would only go away," she suggested. She could not tell him how his strained features cried aloud for rest.

"There are a lot of examinations to prepare. There is a crowd of students this year. Term stops before Christmas. Then I will be done with it. I'll get away then."

He said no more, but his tone rather than his words made Mrs. Harvey anxious.

"Away for a holiday?" she said, tentatively. "You will need it badly; you must not put too much strain upon yourself now. Even though the grief may never pass, dear boy," she said tenderly, "by the spring term you will be able to take up your work normally."

He lit his pipe and looked out of the window; he inhaled the smoke and slowly puffed it out in long, straight clouds; and his eyes saw much farther than the glimpse of the trees beyond the garden wall. Mrs. Harvey waited eagerly, anxiously for him to break the silence.

"I will *never* take up my work." His decree, with an air of finality, was at last pronounced.

"Oh, darling!" Anxiety and pleading were in Mrs. Harvey's voice.

"I am done," he said, laconically. "Something has smashed in my brain. I *could not* do scientific work now, even if I wanted to. Oh, I can teach a bit, the old routine. Enough to see it through to the end of the term all right. That much is automatic. But there is no more — no more in me."

"Yes, yes, my dear boy! You are mistaken." Mrs. Harvey held out her hands blindly. There was a long silence between them.

"My son! Your work has always been your very life. Go on with it for — for Lilian. Finish what you and she would have done together. It is your life now, more than ever it was."

"My life is finished," he said quite quietly.

As he spoke, everything looked black to him, and at the end of the long, black tunnel he saw no more than the immediate duty of not leaving his colleagues in the lurch. All was utter darkness, a darkness in which he had not even the hope of joining Lilian, of meeting her if he plunged through the gloom to follow her. It was as though his spirit was already coffined in a small black box with six intangible sides.

"No, my dear," he slowly became aware that his mother was saying, "of course you feel like that just now, but later — you must think of other people. Consider what your life, your work in the world, means. You are thinking now so splendidly for others that you are going back to college to take up your work at once, because you can't leave it on other people's shoulders. It is the same with everything. Your whole life is important to other people; you can't just drop it."

He shook his head without a word.

She spoke imploringly. "Don't feel now as though you will always feel like that, my dearest boy. But — but don't let us talk of it now. You will come and stay with me again, won't you? Several friends have asked Rose Amber, if you would rather not have her here. Perhaps it pains you to see her?"

"No, not at all," he replied politely. Then his heart added, "But I won't come to you just now, little mother; I would rather stay in the flat."

Mrs. Harvey did not urge her invitation. She herself knew some of the mystic joys of love, and would not rob him of his dream memories, alone with his wife in the empty bridal home. But she took care to see him every day and to take him out as much as possible.

So he finished his term's work.

Down at the University, in the professor's smoke-room, his chief said, "Extraordinary, how little Harvey seems to feel the appalling loss of his young wife. One of the most tragic things I ever heard. Why, they had hardly finished their honeymoon, and they seemed made for each other. One never knows, though, of course. It is extraordinary the way he can laugh and talk about almost anything. Callous, I call it." Nicholson agreed.

"The students say his lectures were never better," he added.

The professor was astounded when Kenneth told him he was sending in his resignation. He kindly remonstrated with him.

"Of course it is natural that you should feel like that just now, but don't do anything hasty. Take a term off, and go to the mountains. Or join some scientific expedition to the tropics. Something of that sort will make a break, you know, and you will be able to pull yourself together. We can't afford to lose you."

But all that he said was in vain. Kenneth answered that his determination to resign was final.

The professor felt regret at having misjudged him and nodded his head wisely. "Look here, Harvey," he said kindly. "I simply won't accept your resignation. I will get a temporary supply in your place and you will find your job waiting here for you at the end of next term, or even at the end of a year if you like. I can't let you do this thing seriously, when you tell me you are chucking University life. It is a mistake, and a mistake you will repent a year or two hence. I know young Duncan was wanting a temporary job before he goes out to India. I'll get him in. That will suit both of you."

Kenneth, to avoid argument, pretended to acquiesce, but he could say no more than, "It's awfully good of you," and he wrung his chief's hand. "But, mind, if any good man comes along, fill my billet. I mean it. I shall never lecture here again."

The chief laid a kind hand on his shoulder. "Now, now, my boy, we won't talk about it just at present, but you will find this place open for you a year hence, when your work calls you again, as it is sure to do."

CHAPTER
13

THE WIDOWER

KENNETH confirmed his resignation to the University. He told his mother that he had done so, and that it was irrevocable. She, with the command of herself that such a woman always possesses, concealed her dismay. "Perhaps you are wise: a change will do you good: you will come back later on."

"Never." He shook his head. "This is not a change; it is final."

His mother stifled a sigh. "Well, you know best, dear. A man's career is a very complex thing, and often takes him away from his mother."

Looking into his set eyes she saw it was useless to argue or complain.

In the old days Kenneth would have been unaware of the anxiety, amounting almost to dismay, which his mother's tender, placid smile concealed; but in these days his senses seemed to be more acute. It was as though his own anguish had broken through and removed an outer layer of the covering of his spirit, leaving him sensitive almost to rawness.

Like most sufferers, the acuteness of his perception was chiefly developed in relation to his own feelings, but as a by-product of this, his realization of the sufferings of others had been quickened. He divined that his mother's heart ached. He cared so little what he did with his life now that had it been possible he would have yielded to please her, but a force more powerful than his filial love and gratitude impelled him to set himself free from the old trammels, to go out into the world, his ambitions floating like a rudderless barque awaiting direction. Tenderly he tried to explain to his mother this feeling, this intense longing, but his words failed. For all her sweet acquiescence he was conscious of her veiled disappointment, aware that she did not — could not understand.

Kenneth began to see that it might be necessary to call in Rose Amber to strengthen his position. He relied on her not only to understand, but to succeed in making Mrs. Harvey realize that her son's life would no longer develop along the lines she anticipated. Kenneth knew this would not be easy, for he had so often described to his mother his hopes and his ambitions that his future stood proudly, like a firm citadel, in her mind. He now found his words, his hands, too weak to shatter the fine structure his airy hopes had reared.

Mrs. Harvey, fearing that perhaps Rose Amber's presence must recall so many poignant memories that Kenneth would shrink from seeing her, had hesitated to bring them together. This Kenneth noticed, and told her that on the contrary he would like to see the dear girl. Lilian and her sister had always been unlike in their personal traits; and Rose Amber was one of the few people with whom he was intimate. Kenneth even arranged to come to his mother's house one day when he knew she would be out to tea, so that he could have an undisturbed hour in which to secure Rose Amber's assistance.

The girl felt that he had something to say to her, and beside the warm comfort of a glowing fire she waited encouragingly. Her beauty, tear-dimmed and pale, shone slenderly above its black draperies. She said nothing, but in the undisturbed quiet of the room the soft current of her good-will streamed towards him and soothed his heart. After the perpetual effort to meet and baffle the hard incomprehension of his colleagues, and of his struggle to disarm the tender but resilient opposition of his mother Kenneth found Rose Amber's air of quiet endeavour to understand him as refreshing as a battle-weary warrior finds the cool, dewy grass. After he had lit his pipe and stretched out a hand to shield his eyes from the fire, he told her frankly the difficulties of his position.

"It is simply impossible to make mother see."

"She has planned success and happiness for you ever since you were little — "

"I know," he conceded. "It's rough on her, but it is no good letting her go on hoping that after a bit I shall swing back into the old ways again. I can't. I have not taken either my science or my love as easily as some people do, and just because they were my whole life, I cannot go back to them now; I have simply done with my University work — finished completely."

"Kenneth, have you explained this to your professor yet?"

Rose Amber wished to know whether he had eased his soul by endeavouring to explain its new, sad phase to anyone.

She realized how the mind becomes obsessed by ideas acutely felt, to which all expression has been denied. So many times had she seen a distracted heart eased by the telling of its woe that she felt that if Kenneth had not had at least one good talk about his position she must win him to speech.

"No; no good." Kenneth stopped to take a long pull at his pipe. He spoke slowly. "Mother simply wouldn't believe that I *do* mean it and that I know what I am about."

"There must be somebody to understand. Someone who could make your mother see."

"There isn't anyone," asserted Kenneth, gruffly. "I haven't a lot of intimate friends. I could not maul myself about in front of them if I had. There is no living soul who really could understand what this thing has done to me."

Rose longed for the power to voice her tender compassion, but said nothing. She stirred the fire gently.

"I wish *I* could understand, but I am not a scientist, you see," she half whispered at length.

"You might understand the human side, perhaps, all the better for that," he responded. "Look here! I want to *talk*. I have not really talked to a human being since — since it happened."

"I wish you would," she said, softly. "Lilian used often to talk to me." Two big tears gathered in her eyes, welled over their lids and ran down her cheeks. In the dusk she did not stop their progress. Kenneth must not be disturbed by the flutter of a handkerchief.

"Yes. I expect perhaps sisters do understand each other, and living with Lilian you must have got to know what real scientific work means when one takes it up in earnest. She was supremely a scientist; the best kind. Seeking the real truth; not caring a farthing whether it made some bloated aristocrat richer or added to the paraphernalia of civilization; working only to find out what life *is*, what life has come through and what it is; not because humanity cares — but just because one is after a great fundamental truth. That is what we were after together, but this knock-down blow has sent me off at a tangent."

"Perhaps toward new truths?"

"Dunno. I have been thinking lately that Truth has a myriad facets. One can only rub up a bit of one of them in a lifetime. Lilian and I had got all our life work planned out, our own special job to do. All sorts of schemes. I suppose the fact that we were to do it *together* brought us into relation with the big essential things of life, though we did not understand how it was. Didn't even have an idea that it was so. But now; when she's — given up — all these details and gone into the bigger things beyond," he turned suddenly in his chair, "I — can't — I'll be damned if I can stand the finnicking trivialities of all that academic work in the University."

"But outside."

"Whatever it may be that has happened to Lilian, she has fused with something immense and impersonal, and have I got to go on with my paltry, regulated little time-table? Lectures at ten in the morning, demonstrations from two-thirty to five, tea at ten minutes to four, a stupid boy to scold if he is late, papers to be read before the Linnean Society, finicky, idiotic jobs of correcting proofs, seeing that they have spelt the words properly and that the lines run straight, piffling little discussions on somebody else's work, gradually and laboriously working myself up past the petty jealousies of my fellows to the supreme height of being an F.R.S.[34] and a head professor. So the weary round would go on, with no enlightenment, no freedom, a few hours of recreation now and then, just enough to keep myself alive. Bah! Damn!" he said, thumping the arms of the upholstered chair. "I'll be damned if I'll go on with it."

"But it's a good life — it — "

"Before ever I met Lilian I was content enough with the prospect. Certain adventures were to come, quite unconsciously I reckoned on the outlet of love — she came and widened and sweetened and balanced the whole thing. We planned to work together, she and I; and now *she* is free from the paltry routine, so will I be!"

"But academic posts give one more freedom than most men get — they — "

"What, after all, is the University set like? Oh, this last few weeks have opened my eyes to them, to the absurd inanity of the whole business. A great man came to dine at 'high' the other day. He has spent his whole life on some problem on the Immensity of Space. He spent the whole hour at the lunch table in a furious temper because the secretary of one of the learned societies had the hour of his lecture printed wrong. There is another professor who is always snapping and snarling at a distinguished colleague, simply because, when they were lads, they had both loved the same woman and the other one got her. Another was sneering at a foreigner's work and openly saying that he had not read it! The few who really care for the Truth as I care for it, are growing sad-eyed, drab, soured by the endless struggle with routine trivialities and sweated labour. None of them seem to have got hold of the *great* things of life."

The vehemence in his tone died away. He puffed his pipe for a few minutes, then said, in his ordinary conventional voice, "I shall never go back to college again, you know; now do you understand at all why?"

Rose nodded.

"I felt as though perhaps you would get the hang of it. You will try to make my mother understand as much as you can, won't you?"

"I'll try, but I would rather have more than that to tell her."

He looked up quickly. "More, how?"

"I should like to be able to show her that you are not just throwing everything away, but that you have *grown through* some of the things and are going into something bigger."

He looked down into the fire. "God knows."

"With your scientific experience behind you, with your keen, trained brain, and with all that you have suffered and begun to understand, you ought to be able to do something big," urged Rose Amber gently.

"God knows," he repeated slowly.

Then he shook his shoulders and straightened himself. "I must leave all that for a bit; at present I only want to go away; right away, out of the University, out of the city, out of England."

"Your mother — "

"To prevent hurting my mother too much, I thought I would cover my escape perhaps by volunteering as a naturalist for one of these tropical expeditions. There are some of the sort on at present and my professor suggested that I could probably get a billet in one of them. Some chap has fallen through and they want a man in a hurry in the South Seas somewhere. There would be solitude there perhaps. I might find my feet."

Rose nodded. "I will tell your mother that you are going on an important scientific expedition, and remind her that that was what Darwin did when he was a young man, and it helped him ever so much to be the famous man he was."

"But that will only be keeping her hoping," he objected. "I shall never be famous now."

"You may be *great*, which is far better," said Rose Amber. "I hope to see you a great man."

Kenneth stood up.

"See here, dear girl," he said huskily. "My mother loves having you here; you will stay on as long as you can, won't you?"

"Of course," Rose Amber agreed.

He ended abruptly. "I'll be going, I think; it is time I was at the University. We have got some fool meeting or other to discuss whether we will have the word 'this' or 'that' in regulation five hundred and forty-seven. Good night."

The next day Rose Amber called in Harry Granville to her assistance.

"See here, Harry," she explained. "It may be all right. If he is a genius or a saint it *will* be all right, but I am not quite sure whether he is! And, anyway, one oughtn't to take risks. His mother cares so awfully about his success in life and it looks to me as though it's touch and go now, whether he isn't going to chuck it all up. Let him go on his expedition for a year — that's all right. But we must have something to induce him to come back at the end of it, and that is where *you* come in. How is your scheme for founding a professorship? How are you getting on with it?"

"Getting on like a house on fire," replied Harry proudly. "The college says it will be graciously pleased to accept *nine* hundred a year."

"Well, then," said Rose Amber, the conspirator, "you must see his professor and get *him* to talk to Kenneth about it. It might interest Kenneth to feel he could start a thing on new lines. Or you might talk about it yourself and let him know frankly that you are doing it. It is the human interest he *really* wants at present, though he doesn't know it."

"It is no earthly good *my* coming into it," objected Harry Granville. "I will see his professor, if you like, on condition that he is bound to secrecy, but not otherwise."

"Yes, I expect," sighed Rose, "that it would be no use letting Kenneth know *we* were doing it for him; it would probably make him refuse it all the more."

"You adorable angel! How I love you for that 'we,'" exclaimed Harry.

Rose Amber blushed. "That *was* a slip. Why didn't you call me a forward hussy?" The kindly professor, pleased not only that his department should have this additional foundation, but delighted at the thought that here was really a tempting bait to lure back the errant spirit of his best assistant to its academic confines, used all the little subtlety he had. He spoke glowingly of the prospects of the splendid opening for Kenneth.

"Twelve months in the tropics, my lad, and the almost certain chance of your being elected to this thing when you come back, puts you head and shoulders above most men of your age. Ah! What would I have given for a chance like that when I was your age?"

Kenneth looked at him curiously, as though for the first time observing a new specimen. "Does he think only of worldly and scientific success," he wondered. Can't he *feel* that I am done with it? Why should he reckon so surely on the average recoil and expect *me* to do what most people would do in the circumstances?"

When the professor had finished speaking, Kenneth hesitated. "I congratulate you and the department tremendously, Sir," he said, at length. "There are lots of good chaps who ought to have a post and salary like that, and I am delighted that anyone has the public spirit to give the endowment, but don't think that I shall ever apply for that professorship or any other. I am going out to join that expedition to please my mother and to get away without too much fuss, and as I have joined it, I will collect the beetles and corals and anything else they want; but when the twelve months' agreement is up I will not come home, I will see the world for a bit."

"Well, we'll see, we'll see," acquiesced the professor soothingly.

"You are very good, Sir," said Kenneth, "but don't penalize the other men who ought to be having a chance."

The fact that Kenneth smiled as he said this made the professor think to himself, "The young cub has something up his sleeve. No man could afford to throw up a chance like this unless he had something better in view."

Harry Granville, some weeks later, came humorously to Rose Amber. "The darned professorship is accepted by the University all right. The bally thing is in their hands now, and it seems to me that we are spending our money on Lord knows who, from Lord knows where, for the bird we set out to catch has flown."

"Oh, dear," sighed Rose Amber, and then she laughed. "Well, it has made *you* into a first-rate, public-spirited benefactor, and that's something of an achievement, for you used to belong to the unimaginative, unrepentant rich!"

CHAPTER
14

THE TROPIC SKIES

KENNETH went out as zoologist to a tropical expedition which had been cruising already for a year. The zoologist who had gone originally with the party had been invalided home, and the organizers were delighted to have a man of Kenneth's capacity to replace him. Their yacht, fitted with collecting apparatus and a small laboratory, was now going from island to island in the southern seas east of the Indian Ocean, amassing insects, bottled and dried plankton, examples of new species and the rarer specimens of the marine fauna and flora, and anything else that attracted the various collectors aboard.

Kenneth hoped for respite from thought in this varied life, so free from routine, so full of possible distractions, among a set of men who would not remind him as did all his old colleagues of the innumerable ramifications of his sorrow. He hoped his mind could ship oars and drift for a bit till it ran into a new course — or foundered. He did not then care which.

The expedition was stationed at a certain island for two months. Here he would pick up his colleagues. A trading steamer was to make the connection from the nearest port to which a main line of passenger steamers would take him.

Aboard the liner Kenneth definitely hedged himself about, shutting out the other passengers. He wanted to think, to rest — to be passive. The strain of carrying on his job at the University in the midst of his anguish had almost broken him. So he pulled his deck chair out of the sheltering awning where diaphanous lady passengers congregated and giggled or flirted with the men, and he sat in the bright sunshine in the fresher air of the prow.

An imposing-looking book on his knee allayed curiosity; but for hours at a time he never turned a page. Often half a day would pass without either thought or conscious feeling; his mind dreamed, and floated with the rippling water through which he was carried, danced with the bubbles, swirled up with the flying fish, quivered with the hot air above the machinery on deck. He did not heed the chatter and laughter of the

89

passengers playing under the awning which cut them off from the blue sky, and he was but vaguely conscious of the sibilant swirl of the waters round the prow during his long, luxurious rest.

The white-clad steward, tinkling round with lemonade at eleven o'clock, made a point of speaking a word to him. His isolation seemed unnatural in a good-looking, young male passenger. Kenneth's mechanically reiterated thanks at last dried up the flow of conversation, and the steward, shrugging his shoulders, put him down as a crank.

In the dining saloon Kenneth's manoeuvres placed him next to an extremely deaf old lady at the end of the table. Though he paid so little attention to them, the trivial details of the surfaces of his companions projected themselves into his mind. His eyes were so trained in observation that it was impossible for him to avoid seeing what came into his line of vision. The black letters K.L.M. on a canvas trunk registered themselves.

He took for granted, but was annoyed by the opacity of most of the people on the ship. But one of the girls, a plain little thing, startled him by having in her eyes a look which he had learned to associate with Rose Amber. "Queer," he thought, "the same eyes, but what a different setting, what a pale shadow of Rose!"

Now and then, on deck, he would glance at the girl. Her writing case bore K.L.M. in gold. He was secretly annoyed by her tolerance of the inane young men who, unaccustomed to being too numerous for the available girls, preened themselves and swaggered in the most primitive fashion. "She hasn't had a chance like this before," he thought. He had no desire to speak to the girl, but now, in the midst of his aimless musing, he found himself thinking of her as the only one who was real on board the ship, and even she was fragmentary — nothing but deep eyes which danced and the letters, K.L.M.

The ship made its way down the Suez Canal at dinner time. Hence all the passengers missed the mysterious beauty of the oncoming sunset across the desert. Kenneth alone stayed on deck, and the clear, translucent, penetrating beauty of the colour-laden breath of the desert swept through him. He felt as though something clogging had been swept out of him and melted into the rose and gold.

Turning at the end of the deck in his pacing, he saw K.L.M. glide up on deck for a moment between the courses and stand gazing at the clear gold and apricot of the western sky.

"I thought so," he said to himself. "The only one who isn't swilling like a hog all the time — and even she only comes up for a minute." The crimson glow diffused itself into her hair, and over her eyes so that they looked like burning pools. He did not speak and she went downstairs.

When the purple night hid his doings from the other passengers and crew, he slipped up with his sleeping bag and lay down among the machinery on the upper deck, where no passengers were allowed. His head was almost on a level with the rail of the truncated deck, and as he lay he could look down on the chatterers or, by turning his head, could gaze straight up into the starry space above him.

As he stretched out, with his arms bent under his head, the stars seemed to slip down from the purple deeps and sway almost within reach of his hand. Never before had he seen *space*. Our northern sky, which looks like the inverted surface of a hollow dome with the stars stuck on it like the painted stars in the ceiling of a cathedral, all flat and on the same level. Our stars had never oppressed him with the deeps of distance. But here, in the misty miracle of space the peerless stars hung each at different levels. Some seemed to swing so low that a flying sea-gull might reach them and others glowed in abysses infinities away. The mysterious qualities of space, space in three dimensions, rich in its deeps, over-arched him with an incommunicable sense of comfort. He had never before so clearly visualised himself as hanging on a planet, whirling through incredible distances. Suddenly the Universes of the stars became for him profound realities.

His mental state was like that of an infant for the first time gazing at the ceiling, and aware that it is out of reach. He brooded in surprised delight through aeons while the tropic stars danced and wheeled within the immensities of the sky.

Between such brooding silences, however, he had times of torment, times when body and soul were racked with uncontrollable longing.

One night of burning heat he flung himself against the solid iron of the winches, clasping his arms around the machinery in the hope of staying the fever of his senses — but the iron was warm — warm as the flesh of a woman. All day long in the scorching tropical sun it had absorbed swift rays of heat, and the air round it was still heat-laden. He drew back quivering; it was the thought of woman he sought to escape.

Kenneth discovered what it is to be a young widower, a man checked in the first rapturous expression of his love. Pulled up mid-flight in their first satisfaction, his thwarted desires haunted him. His own unruliness amazed him. Human nature as well as the starry heavens revealed deeps he had not conceived that they possessed. Looking back on his earlier self, it seemed to his present self like a figure flat as painted cardboard.

Many of the hard things he had said in judging others echoed mockingly in his ears. "Did I then appear to other men as inane and futile as I do now to myself?" he asked himself. "Did my judgement seem to others as hard and ignorant as it really was? There was Carson of my own year who had got ploughed in his medical examinations and went on the

Stock Exchange — yes, old chap — asking me now what I had meant by dropping him because he had married an actress from the variety stage. You're grinning, Carson. Don't say the words 'prig and narrow-minded imbecile!' Those words are in the air. Yes, I know my old self called you a rotter who deserved all the contempt I had felt for you!"

Under the stars, pillowing his head on the bend of his arm, Kenneth told himself that life would take some looking into if he was ever to get the hang of it.

At Aden only one passenger joined the ship, just before dinner-time, and he was placed by the steward in the vacant seat at the end of Kenneth's table.

Kenneth Harvey watched the stranger curiously. "Six months ago," he said to himself, "I should have called him simply a drunken swine. But I see he is not *only* that, thought he is one of those expert drinkers — brandy secretly — bottles of it already in his cabin, I expect. That sometimes goes with temperament. What is he? And why is his right hand in a sling?"

The man spoke to no one during the meal, but with quick, keen glances seemed to be sampling the atmosphere which each of the passengers created.

Kenneth went to bed early that night. His retreat still undiscovered, the passengers did not shun the corner of the balustrade and awning on the deck beneath him, so that sometimes their heads were within a foot or two of his recumbent head. He cursed when they stopped there to chatter or kiss. To-night he noticed with annoyance that K.L.M. was sitting on the edge of the balustrade looking at the broad band of silvered gold which rippled between her and the moon. Soon the new passenger came along the deck. Even in the darkness, it was clear from the white sling that it was he who came up without hesitation to the girl on the balustrade. He stopped beside her.

"Good evening," he said. "That's a jolly moon."

"Good evening," she answered, looking gravely at him for a moment.

"Haven't had time to get introduced yet," said the new-comer.

"I don't think we ever do get properly introduced on board ship," the girl answered. "Time does it, somehow."

"And I am rushing it?"

The girl smiled. "Well, I don't think I noticed you had come on board."

"I noticed you. I want you to do something for me." His tones were so frank and appealing that the girl smiled again. "I am in a hurry for it," the man went on, as though his request had been granted. "And I believe you are the only one on board this ship who can do it."

The girl was intrigued. "Really! What is it?"

"I want you to write a love-letter for me," said the man calmly, as though he requested, "Please pass the salt."

The man saw the girl's eyes, startled, reproachful.

"I say, I am not joking," he said, quickly. "But I haven't been able to write for weeks and my sweetheart will be nearly crazy. I was ill up-country with a lot of beastly niggers, and down at Aden there was not a decent person I knew, and I was only there a few hours, anyway. My girl must have a proper letter; it's weeks overdue — won't you write it?"

"Oh," said the girl, with a note of compassion in her voice, "of course I will write it. I will get some paper and you must dictate."

"No, that's just it," objected the man. "I asked you to *write* it. Hanged if I'm going to dictate it to anybody. I can't talk about love in front of anybody else, and I asked *you* because I thought you could write it yourself."

The girl's laughter bubbled with amusement. "I don't know what you are like and I don't know what the lady is like; how can I write a letter that will fit into anything you would have written?"

"You can," he maintained. "Just you write as if you were me, with my hand torn to shreds by a beastly mad monkey, blood-poisoning, too, after being for the last six months up-country alone with a lot of beastly niggers.[35] Write like me, thinking all that four weeks [of] hell that she will be feeling I have forgotten her. I have never missed the mail before. You will write that letter?" He spoke confidently.

The balustrade raised her face to the level of his. The girl's eyes looked straight across to meet his face, lit by the moonlight, which revealed only the best of him. She studied him slowly and without embarrassment.

"Yes, I will write it," she agreed, jumping off the rail. "That's if I can do it."

"If you can't there is nobody else on board who can," he said, helping her down the companion way.

Kenneth, within a yard of them, not daring to move, for to do so would have cost him the secret of his precious open-air sleeping place and only embarrassed them, said to himself, "Well, I'll be damned. How on earth did that drunken brute take only half an hour to pick out K.L.M. as the only girl on board who could write a love-letter? Yet he is right and I, a trained observer, have watched her for a week without spotting it! I'm a blind puppy."

15

MIDNIGHT IN PENANG

KENNETH affected boredom at Port Said; despised the sunbaked, arid earth at Aden; but at Colombo he abandoned his over-supercilious isolation. Colombo's palms; its glorious surf beach, and long, proud lines of advancing breakers, rearing together in their united charge, dashing themselves to one wide crescent-surge of foam as they bent in homage before the smiling land; its opals; the voluptuous beauty of its brown-skinned women, laughing beneath the clustered riot of vivid flowers — all awoke in Kenneth that delighted curiosity as of a child in a new house.

Anchor was cast in Penang just after dinner one evening. So much cargo was expected for shipment that the steward told the passengers they could count on twenty-four hours at least in which to enjoy themselves ashore. His manner of making the announcement, however, minimized the influence of the cargo and insinuated that they ought to believe that he had personally interceded with the captain to grant them this holiday. He mesmerized a few of the less accustomed travellers into giving him a special tip. He had never known this method entirely to fail.

The coteries which had formed themselves on board crystallized round their various centres and set off to explore the town.

Kenneth found himself with the group of people whom he least disliked. They were K.L.M., the "Girl with the Eyes," the secret drinker, and another very neutral-tinted lady. Kenneth now knew what it was to live in bodily fear of the oversexed woman to be found wherever there is money to pay for idle leisure. There were three at least on board, between them well-endowed by nature, wealth and blood, but he shunned the parties which centred round them. Kenneth and his three chance companions set off in rickshaws to visit the chief café on the outskirts of the town, a café celebrated both for its tropical gardens and the quality of its ice cream.

The rickshaws in Penang are large and comfortable, and the strong coolies[36] who draw them run with such an easy swing that for some time Kenneth was not conscious that a human being was his draught-horse.

As the shafts were lowered and he stepped down, the brown streaming face and patient human eyes of the coolie whose strong muscles had transported him suddenly pierced his heart; but he could not speak to the fellow. He did not know his language. Through coin alone could he communicate his repentant goodwill.

The crowds in the café and the great palms and tropical, blazing flowers illuminated both by the moon and the curiously "civilized" electric light, kept his companions chattering and exclaiming with interest. But behind and through all, he saw the wrinkled, brown face of his coolie, as enigmatic, as remote as that of a monkey behind the bars of a cage.

Some of the wealthier passengers decided to spend the night in the hotel, but Kenneth's party took rickshaws to return to the ship. It was already late, nearly eleven o'clock, and the broad road leading to the quay was quiet.

Rickshaw coolies have a rooted objection to running side by side, so that a party of people are drawn in single file, with two or three yards between each rickshaw. A large number going out together, however wide the road, do not form an irregular cloud as cyclists do in this country, but are spun out in one long tandem line. When the occupants of the rickshaws have anything to say to one another the whole line has to be summoned by a chain of calls from one driver to the next, till all the shafts are lowered and all the brown, perspiring faces of the drivers turn to hear what is amiss.

Leaving the hotel Kenneth told the waiter the name of the ship to which they were returning, and he instructed the leading of the four coolies, the others had no responsibility but to follow the man in front.

Then, by chance, at a turn of the road another stream of rickshaws cut across the little procession. Kenneth and K.L.M. found themselves for a moment out of sight of the leaders. Their coolies did not hesitate, but ran swiftly on down the road. Neither Kenneth nor the girl felt any uneasiness at first when they did not catch up with the others for the ship but continued to follow the chain of strangers. Then they began to feel that they were taking twice as long to return as they had done to reach the café in the first instance. Kenneth tried to attract the attention of his coolie, but he shouted in vain. He jerked in his seat, even kicked the rickshaw shafts, but the man ran on with his dogged, swift stride, his head bent, following the strange rickshaw in front of him. At last Kenneth precariously leaned forward and, stretching out his foot, kicked the glistening back of the runner with his toe. The coolie called out to his fellow in front and they both stopped.

"Where are you taking us?" Kenneth asked loudly. "I am sure we don't go this long way round to get to the ship."

The brown men, wiping aside with the backs of their hands the perspiration which streamed from their foreheads, stared dumbly.

"Where are you taking us?" repeated Kenneth sternly.

The man in front slowly backed his rickshaw till the two were side by side. They shook their heads and made no answer to Kenneth's repeated enquiries.

"I say!" He called out to K.L.M., "what are we going to do? The fools don't understand us."

The girl leaned forward. "Are — you — going — to — the ship?" she slowly projected her words towards the staring depths of the brown eyes.

"Umppph?" the man grunted.

Kenneth and the girl decided that the only thing to do was to make them drive on. "Of course they know," the girl reassured him.

He shrugged his shoulders and impelled them to drive on by moving his hands forward as though he were shooing chickens. The two coolies took up the shafts and settled into their long, steady strides.

Later, the roads through which they were passing being still stranger, Kenneth called another halt.

"See here," he said despondently to the girl, "I believe these idiots don't know where we are wanting to go."

The two men, with impassive curiosity, watched the Englishman's antics as he essayed again to ask them if they knew where they were going.

"Ship — Boat — Steamer; Shoo-shoo; Puff — puff." He tried in vain every way of conveying the concept of a steamer to them. At last the girl spied through the darkness a man in uniform recalling to mind a British policeman.

"Hooray!" she announced. "Penang is a British Colony; the law will speak English."

"Hi! Please come and help us," they shouted; but when the policeman came over to them, the moonlight showed that his face, too, was brown.

"Will you tell these men, please, that we want to go to the quay, back to the ship?"

The policeman was as uncomprehending as the coolies. The girl tried French and German, and Kenneth tried Cockney and Billingsgate, but without conveying the faintest impression of their meaning.

"Good Lord!" muttered Kenneth. "They have gone and lost us irretrievably now. How on earth can we make these idiots understand?"

"Had we better go back to the hotel?" suggested the girl.

"Back, yes, that's a good idea," agreed Kenneth, with relief. "HOTEL, where we came from."

But this, too, was unintelligible. Despairing of being understood,

Kenneth descended and turned round the shafts of the rickshaws. With resigned meekness the coolies took them up and started running again in the opposite direction. But they did not even understand that they were to go back to the hotel where they had taken up their fares, and they waited for directions at the first cross roads.

"Hang it all," shouted Kenneth to the Girl with the Eyes. "Did we go round this corner or did we run on straight? Do you remember?"

"I don't." Her tone was one of placid resignation.

"Get along," shouted Kenneth to his coolie.

Feeling a touch on his right shoulder the fellow turned to the right. The simple code among many Europeans is to give a kick on the side on which the turning should be made.

After another half hour, Kenneth and the girls decided they had better get down and walk.

"We can't get *more* lost so quickly walking, anyway," the girl remarked with an adventurous air. A handful of small silver made the men happy and invisible.

"I remember the moon was on the right when we left the ship," remarked the girl.

"You do?" asked Kenneth eagerly. "Well, right about face, then. This road seems familiar, doesn't it?"

"The coolies have brought us along it twice, but I don't see that it is much good to us."

"If the worst comes to the worst, we will have to knock up one of these houses. They look very big and respectable and must have some Europeans in them."

"They are all asleep," decided the girl after they had stopped for a moment and peered into the darkness of shuttered windows. "Why, even the trees seem to be asleep. Look at this acacia, with its leaflets all folded up neatly, and their heads tucked up in their wings. Oh, and look where that great electric light has its fizzling blue glare in the middle of the tree; the leaves just round it have stayed awake while the others a little way off have gone to sleep . . . "

"Well, it's no good making scientific observations in the middle of the night in an unknown city," interrupted Kenneth, "interesting as they may be. Come along."

They walked down the long, paved road, past bungalows wreathed in vivid masses of blossoms without seeing a light in any of the windows, and without meeting a human being.

"This is getting uncanny," suggested Kenneth. "I'm half sorry I got rid of those niggers now."

"Penang isn't a *big* town," the girl reassured him. "If we walk on we *must* come to the sea, and if we walk round the edge of the sea we *must* come to the boat."

"Umph," demurred Kenneth, "and you with slippers and a white muslin dress." He looked at his watch. "I say! K.L.M., it's after twelve. A nice escapade. I'm frightfully sorry." His tone was apologetic.

"Well, it isn't your fault in the very least. I suppose at the café they gave the order to the leading coolie and the others followed like sheep and once they were lost they were completely lost."

They came to cross-roads. "Which shall we take?" she said. Neither of them knew which direction would lead to the sea.

"Toss," suggested Kenneth, drawing out a large silver coin. In the luminous moonlight the difference between heads and tails was clear.

"Right O! Left about wheel," was the verdict.

The girl began to laugh. "What would you do if I had a fit of hysterics?" she enquired.

"That might be the solution of the difficulty. We should *have* to knock up some of these people then."

"You assume they speak English; what would you do if they couldn't?"

"Don't make it a nightmare."

"Shall we keep on going to the left? It would be more logical to keep on going to the left," she said, as one beaten by fate.

The next turning to the left brought them to a road of smaller houses, and when they came to the end of these the street suddenly opened on to an amazing spectacle. From the unfrequented silence they plunged into the middle of a seething multitude. The small road opened into an enormous square, packed with people. Their first astonishment mingled with relief. Among these myriads they would surely find some who could speak the Master-language of the place.

Half-way across the square they realized the strangeness of their progress. Though the crowds were so thick that there did not seem to be space even for a child to wedge its way in among them, they had penetrated and found their way through that crush of people without having to push or even to touch a human being. Always between them and their thickly-packed neighbours there seemed to be a space of two or three inches.

No one spoke to them; no one seemed conscious that they were there, but at their coming a way was made for them. It was like walking through a wall in a dream. It was like the progress of a drop of oil through water.

Kenneth and the girl stopped. "How queer it is," the girl murmured, suddenly shivering, "Let's speak to someone."

They addressed several people, but beyond a quiet, impassive, curious look, no one took any notice of them, no one answered a word.

"Hang it all," said Kenneth. "The whole bally crowd are Chinese!"

At the end of the square was a great platform, and on it actors were performing part of an endless play. Noisy cries and the sharp reverberations of taut drums drowned the words on the stage. With the throng of onlookers, Kenneth and the girl gazed curiously for a few minutes, the crowd around them straining to see over each other's heads — but still that impenetrable cloak of two inches of air separated Kenneth and the girl from every contact.

"This is positively uncanny," protested Kenneth. "There must be a real policeman in all this crowd somewhere."

"Policemen are not much good," said the girl sarcastically.

"But hang it all," Kenneth verged on blustering, "this is an English colony."

There was a movement in the crowd and a carriage drove through.

"A carriage!" he sighed with relief. "That must mean some decent people."

They could just see the smart horses with their jingling harness and a couple of men in livery on the box.

"We'll have to stop the horses," said Kenneth, and he went forward preparing to call out in English and ask for help when he fell back a step, disconcerted by a cold shiver down his spine. The occupants of the carriage were two Chinese ladies, as impassive as images in a temple. Each with hair smooth as carved ebony, jewelled as are rich relics in a shrine, had a face chalk-white with thick powder. They sat bolt upright and even their eyelids did not flicker.

A sudden and simultaneous revulsion of feeling swept over the two stranded Britons. The adventure had in the fraction of a second become a nightmare.

"We must get out of this," said Kenneth, his lips met in a hard line. He took the girl by the arm.

"Which way?" asked the girl, weakly. "We *were* going to the left with the moon, but — "

"Any way."

There was a narrow street leading out of the square, and down this they went. The low, wooden houses had balconies, and most of them were gaily lit.

"Perhaps they will know English in some of these shops," tentatively suggested the girl.

Kenneth barely heard the voice and did not grasp the meaning of her question. The bewilderment caused by a realization of his personal insignificance was upon him. Since his school days he had often heard that there were six hundred million Chinese alive in China. The crowd in the square through which he had passed as though he had been imperceptible to them made him for the first time realize what it might mean to be among six hundred million Chinese. Suddenly he saw the self-importance of his academic colleagues in that queer perspective, distorted, unrelated to reality. He tried to shake himself free from the obsession of the realization that there were living myriads from whom he was cut off by something as intangible as two inches of space and as impenetrable as the barrier of language.

The girl persisted. "These don't look like ordinary shops, do they?"

He glanced at the houses on either side of the road. Many of them were widely open to the street, as shops or restaurants might be, but they were barred. In the brilliantly-lit interiors were women, some fair, some dark, of many types, and half a hundred different nationalities. Dressed vividly, with flashing teeth and laughing eyes, they jested with the passers-by. A white arm came through the bars of a balcony waving a flower; dark brown eyes burned passionately from dusky faces.

The girl in white beside him gazed around her curiously. Kenneth's lips met like a line of steel. Taking her arm he told her to hurry as it was getting late. She half turned back, looking inquisitively into a room as they passed.

"How curious it is," she said. "Why are those shops open so late at night? And I don't see what they are selling."

Kenneth pinched his own arm and wondered if he really were awake.

He had known of all this before, but a traffic in women so garishly open he had never pictured. He did not tell the girl what it was they were selling in these open houses; he did not exactly like to tell himself. He prevaricated, "I should think they are some kind of native restaurant — birds-nest soup — eggs a hundred years old — and that sort of thing, you know."

The girl laughed, but suddenly stood still and shuddered. "How queer it is" — her startled eyes looked into his for a brief glimpse. "Oh, how queer it is! What is it? The air feels choking somehow. Let's get away."

Kenneth, with immense relief, spied a rickshaw. It was one of the big, comfortable Penang rickshaws which can easily hold two.

"Here, let's get into this and have another try," he urged. His arm impelled her to mount swiftly. K.L.M. had never been to him a *girl*. She was no more than a chance and fragmentary reflection of Rose Amber's look: but she was a feminine thing and he was her transient guardian. His the responsibility for her safety; he must get her out of this — if it were real, that is, if it were not a nightmare. He stumbled on the rickshaw step. The acute shaft of pain in his toe asserted the reality of the experience, for it did not wake him.

He sat beside the girl, and the coolie took up the shafts and turned for directions; once more the World's Master-language was no good to them. But the girl, quickened by acute distress, suddenly remembered that the day before the purser of the ship had given all the passengers (by way of mingling compliment with advertisement) a black silk ribbon with a picture of the ship embroidered on it, with its name in colours. She had it in her little handbag, and, feeling that it was like a light held aloft in an accident in a black tunnel, she brought it out and showed it to the rickshaw driver. He could not read the name of the ship, but the picture conveyed to him the direction in which they wished to go. He nodded and trotted quickly off.

He took them back to the quay, where Kenneth and the girl soon recognized their vessel. Others were there late ashore that night and no notice was taken of their return.

The girl's brave laughter was a little tremulous when Kenneth told her she had behaved like a brick. She shook his hand and gave him one swift, inscrutable look.

In his cabin the battle in the field of sex between Kenneth's body and his mind resulted in a draw. The body, thwarted, had its revenge and Kenneth could not sleep. Inarticulate thoughts surged through his brain; amorphous conceptions dominated his spirit; a portentous chaos reigned. With the cooler sanity of the dawn words disentangled themselves and he thought grotesquely, "It's beastly — being so unimportant, being ignored by myriads in that kind of way. One doesn't realize it at home, where however big the crowd, however little one may be known, there is always within reach the *Post Office Directory* or the University calendar or something to identify oneself by. All these myriads of Chinamen — living now — and how many more *have* lived and will live? Great Scott, it's horrible!"

He looked out at the stars overpeered by the approaching but invisible sun and paling over his head. "And each of those little things is a sun — perhaps the centre of a planetary system; and in each of the planets perhaps creatures incredibly more different from us than are Chinamen . . . It is brutal to be given the power to know that and not the power to understand. Is it all chaos? Is there *nothing* to connect one on to it at all, no bridge to link me and the Chinamen and the stars that are suns?"

CHAPTER
16

FERINE HEART BEATS

KENNETH left the ship to wait for the trading steamer, due a fortnight later, which would take him on his way to join his expedition. After having made all the necessary arrangements he still had ten days or so which he could fill in as he liked.

For a couple of days he explored the irregular little town built of brown wood in which the low houses, often barn-like in their simplicity, propped each other up in the irregular main streets, or, surrounded by gardens, helped to support themselves by cuddling up against some massive tree. Their low roofs seemed often weighed down by the masses of creepers, smothered with flowers, scarlet, gold and orange, sickly sweet, themselves the busy market place of the bees. The immediate surroundings of the town lacked interest. The great forests near by were said to be monotonous, and certainly lacked pathways. The few European houses, though cordially thrown open to him and providing excellent dinners, were engrossed in local gossip. The big public room of the one European hotel, to which all grades, all colours of mankind seemed attracted, was replete with revolting stories.

A sudden whim decided him to go off on foot on a little expedition through the forest. The Consul was well advised about roads and neighbouring villages, but Kenneth refused all his suggestions, which were based on the taste of previous tourists. Kenneth noticed in his office a map which indicated that near by was a track of virgin forest through which a narrow river ran down from the hills.

He decided that it would be fun to walk through the forest, following the windings of the river till he reached a native town about fifty miles upstream.

"Can't be done," said the Consul; "there is no path that way. This is untouched forest, you know, virgin, full of thick, tangled bushes and lianes. If you're new to it, you'll find it the very devil. If you are prepared to take plenty of coolies and hack your way through it, you won't do more than half a dozen miles a day — and there is nothing to see when you have fought your way in."

"Oh, hacking's no fun," agreed Kenneth; "I'll just follow the river."

"Can't be done," repeated the Consul. "It's not navigable."

"Is it swampy?"

"No, but it's rocky all the way. All right to go up it for a mile or two for fishing, supposing it was worth the effort, but it isn't."

"See here," said Kenneth, "although I'm not much of a geologist, I'm geologist enough to know that a river like that has got sides to it, and that if it is swift and rocky, there is not much chance of the sides being equal, so it will have one steep bank and one shallow, pebbly bank. Consequently I shall walk along the pebbly bank."

"What is the good of that?" objected the Consul, "and anyway, you ought to be geologist enough to know that a pebbly bank dodges about from side to side."

"Then I shall have to cross the river to follow it, and walk on the other side. You say the river is too shallow for a boat."

Kenneth saw that the Consul was beginning to doubt either his honesty or his sanity, so he hastened to offer an explanation for his persistence, the first which might sound plausible. He wanted to get away into the virgin forest; he wanted to feel and smell what it was like. He wanted this in that blind, hungry way that a longing for solitude obsesses certain people at uncertain times; but he did not want to be put to the bother of an elaborate expedition with a pack of coolies. The idea of following the river into the heart of the forest, with just two or three coolies to carry necessaries, attracted him. He peculiarly abhorred the fuss of making himself too conspicuous over it, so he seized upon the first likely excuse that would cover his going. He knew there must be some insects new to science in this forest. In every virgin forest unknown insects hover. So he resolved to take a butterfly net with him, so as to be able to throw down his spoils and defy anyone who questioned the scientific seriousness of his quest.

"See here," he explained gravely to the Consul. "You know I am joining a scientific expedition? Well, some very important insects are known to be in this forest region — awfully rare things they are. I am not sure that there are not even members of a new family; there are some of the rarest genera, anyway. Now I must get hold of some of them for my collection. I ought to be able to scramble up that river's banks and get through the forest that way."

The Consul was visibly impressed. "That's quite possible," he admitted. "The water's drinkable if you boil it, and the stream bed shallow, but you will have to cross the river innumerable times. But it's represented to be really very shallow. Of course you can stick it out if you make up your mind to. A river *does* cut an opening through the trees, that's true. As you have only a few days for it, I daresay it is the best way to get into the middle of the forest if you've set your heart on getting there. You must catch those jiggers if you want them."

Kenneth grinned.

"Now one sees the value of a reputation," he said to himself. "If I want to go up to a tropical river into a virgin forest just because I *want* to, I should probably be stopped as an imbecile or an intruder; but if I go to collect a few butterflies for a national museum thousands of miles away, and give them jaw-cracking names, then I am a perfectly sane member of the community. *Now* I can go up the river just because I want to, and I'm going." Mentally he patted himself on the back while he talked gravely with the Consul, using the longest technical terms he could think of for all the details with which he deliberately wearied the unfortunate man. The Consul was much impressed, and that night as he smoked his after-dinner cigar, he reported that Professor Harvey was an uncommonly clever young fellow, but one of those cranks who were all scientist and nothing else.

"Never had a lark in his life probably," he surmised, watching the smoke rings he was slowly making.

"Not your style, eh, old chap?" The colonel dining with him winked a bibulous eye.

"Thank'ee! Devilish queer it must be," the Consul continued, "to know everything about the world and the insides of things in that uncanny way and not to know the jolly part."

"And so to miss the point of it all, eh?"

Kenneth and his coolies scrambled along the banks of the river, sometimes in the burning sunshine which poured through the openings in the trees; sometimes in the cool shadows of the overhanging vegetation, where the air, filled with green light, was sprayed by the broken mist from the water gurgling against the stones.

After clambering over the rough surfaces of the rocks for half a day, Kenneth began to envy the coolies their straw and thong-bound feet, and when they halted for the midday rest he unrolled his puttees and took off his leather boots and made the coolies improvise for him sandals made of skin and straw, over the rough ends of which he bound his puttees as low as they would go. A foothold was in many places very difficult to obtain and sometimes long, steep ledges of rock cut almost sheer into the water. Along these he had to clamber like a fly, holding on to the shoulder of a coolie who walked beneath him up to the knees in water.

Wherever the bend of the river confronted them with a bank too steep to pass, they forded the stream and travelled along the opposite bank, which was generally flat and edged with water-worn pebbles. At first fording the river was great fun. The men searched with poles for a shallow crossing, and miraculously the coolies seemed to know where the water would not overwhelm them. When the current was swift they joined hands while fording. Kenneth tried to keep his legs dry by riding on the shoulders of two coolies in the way they expected him to do, but early in the day they stumbled mid-stream, tipping him over and plunging him into the river. After that he forded with them. He preferred to know which end of himself was going to get wet, and make preparations accordingly.

Their progress was slow, for now that he had got his desire and was wandering aimlessly, everything interested him.

Had he not brought his net and collecting bottles, the gorgeous insects would have tantalized him beyond endurance. As it was he did not really mind a bit whether he caught them or not. But he pretended it mattered enormously.

He had been warned that the stones on the warm, dry banks would be snake-haunted, but he felt impelled in schoolboy fashion innumerable times to stop and kick over particularly fascinating rounded lumps of rock.

The shadowed depths of the forest on either hand offered vistas of impenetrable mystery. Again and again he pushed head and shoulders in among clambering lianes, to be stopped, either by the cautioning gestures of the coolies, who had an abject fear of unknown animals and snakes, or, more effectively, by the tangled, seething mass of entwining vegetable life. Beyond an occasional scurrying sound and the glimpse of a small fugitive, they met no animals on their clambering progress. Kenneth kept his rifle slung over his back, easily available. It was not needed.

The coolies had been instructed before they set out just what they were to do, and how to set up the light tent which they were carrying. From them Kenneth picked up a dozen of the easier, corrupt Malay words of command which they could understand, and when the fancy took him, late in the afternoon, he told them to pitch the camp. The place he chose attracted him by its suggestion of an even greater remoteness than the side of the river possessed. It was an island. An island a hundred feet long and half that breadth, formed midstream by an accumulation of water-worn pebbles on the lee of a rough piece of rock which stood defiantly resisting the disintegration which had overtaken the strata round it. Some soil had accumulated, and on this little strip above the water-level grew three or four trees, overtopping a few bushes and rough grass. In the comparatively still water down stream trailed a fringe of reed and water plants.

The coolies approved Kenneth's choice of the night's resting-place. Here they could protect themselves more easily than on the banks from possible attacks by the larger animals of the forest. Kenneth's supply of

Malay was insufficient to allow of their conveying to him their anticipations of the coming of terrors of the night; but the little he could understand of all they suggested added to his enjoyment, for he was on adventure bent. Leaving them to make the fire and prepare supper he forded back to the stream edge. Scrambling up the steep bank he found himself out of sight of his men in a narrow opening between the trees and tangled undergrowth. The top of the bank was an open glade, on which the slanting sunbeams still shone. Here the bright green, happy life of plants living in the open formed a joyously insect-haunted noisy border to the still, dark mysteries of the forest beyond.

Kenneth sat down to dream on the thick, epiphyte-clad[37] trunk of a broken tree. He sat so long unmoved that the birds and the lizards, and soon even the monkeys went about their own business and ignored him. Then in the grass he heard a long slender rush of sound, the slow deliberate hurrying of a creature without feet, which loved the sunshine and slithered through the blades growing towards it. Kenneth sat immovable as the lifeless, giant tree, and watched the succulent herbs parted or bent as the five-foot length of a great snake glided out into the warm air. Once the penetrating rays of the sunshine touched the smooth velvet of its back it slowed its speed and crept with voluptuous writhing inch by inch towards Kenneth's foot. His breath was stayed and his hand closed eagerly upon the rifle which lay upon his knee, tilting it so that it was aimed, ready to be fired. The blood sang in his head, and he pictured the shattered reptile's skull on the grass by his feet and the triumph of swinging the long, rippling body over his shoulder. Then suddenly the creature's unawareness pierced him with the revelation of the possibilities of a snake-life of which he had no inkling, and the desire to kill was transmuted into a sudden curiosity to know what the snake would do. He held his breath tensely, watching every movement, and inch by inch the five feet of tapering length thickened itself to the span of his arm and stretched again before thickening, as it slowly luxuriated through the grass to the edge of the steep bank, down which it glided. It slipped past him three inches from his foot.

The snake, like the Chinamen in Penang, had ignored him. He had surprised it in the midst of its own affairs, and he was nothing to it. What had it seen down there as it crept inch by inch forward in the warm vibrating air? An impulse to see the earth as the snake saw it and to view the world within its ferine horizon made him slip down from the tree-trunk and put his face on the leaf-blades, which were still bent over, only half recovered from the weight which had passed over them. Kenneth's cheek touched the soft green tresses of the earth and through their translucent surfaces the sunlight was filtered to a stream of vivid golden-green light. Within this he saw upon the leaves the delicate edging of white translucent hairs. His cheek happened to touch a small, flat pebble, still burning hot with the warmth of the sun's rays, which had been penetrating it the whole day long. Without thought, without conscious feeling, Kenneth crouched, half dreaming, half observing the strange, rich beauty of the tropical undergrowth. He was stung and irritated a hundred times by flies and mosquitoes, but the curious mesmerism of the warm solitude nerved him to stoic disregard of these outer things, and he dreamed, with intensity of enjoyment such as he had never before experienced. His mind seemed loosened from its moorings, agile and buoyant, yet imponderable and inconsequent. He was conscious of many details of his life, most of which stood out as swiftly-happened, curiously futile scrambles in places so over-populated as to be stifling. He particularly remembered the crossing at Piccadilly Circus with the unseeing hurry of all the thousands round him: then the futile concentration of the learned meetings in Burlington House. The hour since the snake had passed had been strangely spacious and long, and in this perfectly passive quiet the mastery of his whole self had seemed to be a sovereign right. Only the sunbeams moving away from him and letting in the blue-green shadows of the dusk made him stir. He rose incredulous, feeling that he had added years to his life. Some few yards away the coolies were awaiting him, and he reached them while the triumphant sense of the sun's majesty was still upon him. He smiled at them, wondering what could be the secret of their lives.

But supper dispelled these dreams, and their ceaseless chatter angered him before he slept.

The next day and the next day they alternately loitered and scrambled up the river, and Kenneth was ever more perfectly entranced by what his fellows would have described as trivial, aimless observations. Now and then, in order to keep the coolies up to the mark, he made a great display of catching a particular insect and killing it in the asphyxiating tubes they carried for him. The capture, whether a treasure in reality, or a mere member of a prolific species, he made a great show of solemnly entrusting to the coolies. They appeared to be enormously impressed. They feared at any rate to take any liberties with him. That was all the insect was used for.

Incongruously the thought of dinner became increasingly interesting, but after two or three days the camp provisions revolted Kenneth by their sameness and by their inappropriateness. It seemed to him that he could taste the preservatives in the tinned meats, and the very depths of something in his being hungered for the fresh, keen odour of frizzling fat and the drip of gravy from flesh browned by an open fire.

Kenneth found himself seated by the camp in the evenings looking across the stream into the shadowed depths of the forest and saying to himself, "Here am I, where scarcely any human foot and probably no white foot has ever trod the ground, in a virgin forest with trees that never felt the axe, with creepers away over there like the hawsers of a ship, which perhaps never met a human eye before, since the seed from which their seedlings sprang was dropped there by a wild parrot screeching through the stillness. That's very impressive. I only wish to Hell I felt it more! But if those blamed niggers haven't caught any fish, and are going to serve me up tinned meat and dry biscuits for dinner again I shall have to murder something!"

He reasoned with himself. He knew that as he had kept the coolies on the trot all day, they had had no time to catch fish; he pointed out to himself that as a city dweller from the heart of civilization, let loose in a virgin forest for the first time, he ought to be overwhelmed by the awe and wonder of it, and never stop to think of what he was eating at all; but it was all of no avail. Nature was tapping him on the shoulder, saying, "Eat, eat, eat!" The daily exertion in the clean air, scrambling over the rocks above the clear stream had put an edge to the health of his body. Food became a paramount interest, and dry biscuits did not satisfy all its composite longings.

Late the next day, on their way upstream, they passed a glade which opened on to the edge of the water. He understood from the coolies' pantomime and the broken fragments of their talk which he could under-stand, that animals came down to it to drink. He crossed, and looking closely at the banks made out the slender footprints of antelopes. The desire to kill and eat overwhelmed him.

He told the coolies to pitch the camp on some flat rocks protected by steep, upstanding sides a little down-stream. Kenneth slipped off alone to watch the drinking-place from the opposite bank. He kept his ambush for hours. The stealthy boldness of the creatures that came down to their accustomed haunt — all grey and silver, or black in the strange dimness of the unearthly light at first enchanted Kenneth and kept him silent, an onlooker. Eyes suddenly gleaming like green phosphorescent balls, or with a flicker of red like bubbles of flame as they met the line of his vision, held him breathless in succession for an hour. Then there came out a bold little antelope, and stood, poised motionless on its slender legs, offering a target which not even a Cockney, accustomed only to aim with coconuts, could miss: a rush of triumph spun through Kenneth's veins.

He aimed and fired, and the unsuspecting little beauty of the forest splashed in the water — dead.

Kenneth, leaping through the shallows towards it, pictured the roasting of its meat by a glowing fire and smelled the rich odour of its frizzling fat. He lugged it home to the encampment, roused the sleeping coolies and stirred the hot embers of the fire. By pantomime he ordered them to cook, and he again raked over the hot ashes on which they roasted strips of the flesh on forked sticks.

By the time he reached his improvised bed, he was prepared for sleep, which fell quickly upon his healthily tired body, deeply, richly dreamless.

CHAPTER

17

BETROTHAL

ONE day in the spring, Mrs. Harvey sat in her quiet drawing-room reading a novel and waiting for Rose Amber's return. The girl had gone to a matinee with Harry Granville, who was to bring her back to the flat in good time to dress before dinner. It was a day of holiday-making and he was taking Rose Amber and Mrs. Harvey to a dance in the evening, the first time since her sister's death.

Dusk filled the room save where the glow of the firelight conquered its creeping shadows, and Mrs. Harvey laid the book down upon her knee, as she could no longer see the printed words which, for the past hour, had carried her into a world of lovers' youthful happiness.

She closed her eyes, thinking of Rose Amber. She saw bright pictures of the girl irradiated by a glowing vitality, richer and more joyously human than her sister's had ever been. It seemed incredible that such attractive radiance could leave the hearts of her satellites unscathed for long. Mrs. Harvey sighed. She knew that inevitably she would soon lose her precious companionship. She had grown to love the girl more dearly than she had ever loved any young creature save her son. The little clock on the mantelpiece chimed six, and Mrs. Harvey, glancing at it, wondered why they were so late when the door opened and Rose slipped in with a glow of light — was it only from the hall lamp? Kneeling beside the older woman, Rose Amber kissed her, and the fire sent a shower of sparkling light-flecks gleaming from the girl's left hand. On the third finger was a hoop of emeralds. Mrs. Harvey touched it.

"My dear!" she whispered.

Rose Amber cuddled her face in the soft neck of her adopted mother. "Isn't it heavenly? Harry and I are going to be married."

Mrs. Harvey had often thought of this so obvious possibility, and reasoned with herself against her instinct that it was a very natural, even desirable match; but, unreasonably, when the obvious thing had been accomplished, she was disappointed.

"We are simply made for each other. That is one of the things I love so about Harry; he doesn't look on marriage in the superficial, common-place way most men do. He says there is no real marriage unless the two souls are halves which fit into each other to make a great, beautiful, dual soul-life — the complete human life. I am sure that it is the real way of looking at marriage."

"It is, my darling." Mrs. Harvey kissed her, "and if you have got that you are indeed blessed. I pray you will have the joy you deserve. If you have that real soul's marriage, you will not lose your happiness even when you are old."

The girl sighed with contented joy. "Yes, I feel that," she said. "He likes me being young and pretty — at least, he *says* I'm pretty"; she looked mischievously up at the older woman.

"So does your mirror, doubtless, eh?"

"But even when I am not pretty any more our innermost beings will keep on loving each other — . Poor Harry! With Vera, you know, he *thought* it was going to be like that, and then they found out she was not fitted into him at all. But that divorce business and everything made him think so much more seriously about marriage than he would have done otherwise. He has read all sorts of serious books about it. One thing he told me I liked so much that that funny old John Milton[38] said — You know he wrote a book in favour of divorce? I did not know, did you?"

"Yes, I knew," Mrs. Harvey conquered a smile. "Properly educated people in my day — had heard of John Milton."

"Well," continued Rose Amber, unabashed, "John Milton says 'That true marriage is the yearning in a man for that which he hath not, to complete himself, and not the mere ridding himself of what he hath in abundance.'"

Mrs. Harvey enquired tentatively, masking a secret anxiety. "You have talked about his love for Vera? It's not — going to be a bricked-up wall between you?"

"Oh, *no*," responded Rose Amber, frankly, "I am not silly like that. Bodies and circumstances hide and smother people's souls so much that it is not surprising that anyone should make a mistake and think he had got his real soul's mate when he hadn't; and I think that Harry behaved so beautifully — afterwards."

Tears filled Mrs. Harvey's eyes. No one with a heart who has known the complex and innumerable sources of Love's unexpected pain can look at radiant joy unmoved.

"My darling girl, I pray that God will bless your marriage in every way." After a moment's silence, she said in a different tone of voice, "Are you going to the dance this evening?"

"Rather!" exulted Rose Amber, springing up.

"Then you will have to hurry to dress in time." Running out of the room, carolling with a gurgling mixture of laughter and song, like a blackbird on a lilac-bush, Rose Amber fluttered into her dancing frock. She tossed off her walking things and pirouetted about the room on her bare toes before slipping into the white silk stockings and satin slippers with big white rosettes which had been laid out for her. Jane came in and fastened her into the floating dress of white chiffon laced with a gold cord and tassels.

"I just hate to wear gloves," she said. She held up her finger for the maid's admiration, and the sparkling beams of light from the emeralds were reflected in the mirror. Mrs. Harvey put her head into the bedroom unobserved, and waited silently for a moment so as to imprint all the details of the pretty figure on her memory before she said, "If you keep dinner waiting, Harry will have to wait afterwards."

When they were seated at the table, Mrs. Harvey asked, "Would you rather I didn't come? Chaperones are nearly obsolete, and now you are engaged — "

"Ma mère!" said Rose Amber, reproachfully. "But of course if you are *tired* don't let us bother you."

"I should love of all things to see you looking as radiant as that and dancing the soles off your shoes. While you dance, Time will stand still for me."

CHAPTER
18

THE CHATELAINE[39]

ROSE Amber had grown accustomed to being addressed as "M'Lady" by her men servants long before Mrs. Harvey was able to fulfil her promise of visiting Harry Granville and his bride in their country home. It was early autumn before she found herself on the platform of the little northern station being eagerly welcomed by Rose Amber in rough tweeds with a pack of barking dogs around her.

Driving up from the Station, Rose Amber, with her hand on Mrs. Harvey's knee, said eagerly, "Now, tell me whether you would rather have a beautiful, comfy, big bedroom on the first floor with nothing to look at out of the window but a lot of pine trees and a magnolia, *or*," Rose paused impressively, "a perfectly scrummy view out of a bedroom window that you have to climb up three pairs of stairs to reach? Out of *that* window you can see a corner of the great black cliff with waves dashing round it, far away, beyond the pine trees which fill up the valley between our house and the sea. I have had them both got ready, so that you can choose freely."

"I had no idea you were so near the sea!"

"A mile only. We ride down to bathe every day when the weather will let us."

"Being married agrees with you?" Mrs. Harvey looked at her long and lovingly.

Rose Amber's eyes did not meet hers. "Rather!" she averred. "Everybody ought to be married, I am sure. You are like a kitten with your eyes shut till you are married. There is the house," she said quickly, "what do you think of it? Isn't it hideous?"

"No. It has a dignified air. It looks as though it had been built long ago, when good solid walls were based on good deep foundations, and the winds and rains could blow and howl outside without anybody in the house being aware of it."

"It looks so like a Round Head." Rose Amber pretended to grumble. "I want to have a veranda and creepers added to it, but Harry points out,

113

what I know perfectly well myself, that they would be horribly unsuitable."

The door opened, and a tall footman took the wraps. Harry was cordial, and Mrs. Harvey was led into the great hall where a fire burned, and silk cushions and vases of lilies and late roses made it so like a drawing-room that she was almost surprised at the two staircases leading from it to the bedrooms beyond.

"You haven't chosen your room yet. Have them both!" wheedled Rose Amber.

"I am a lazy old bones, and if it takes all those stairs to go up to the *first* floor, I think I shall have to do without the view higher up."

"Isn't it awful of us not to have a lift?"

Rose Amber excused the house by her tone, defended it almost, and expected no answer.

"But we *have* got electric light, though we have to make it ourselves, and the machinery goes wrong sometimes. Then we fall back on candles, and there never seem to be enough candlesticks."

Harry Granville's cordiality and Rose Amber's delight in showing everything to her guest set the atmosphere dancing with a certain air of excitement. Everything seemed perfect. After she had been with them for a week, Mrs. Harvey felt that there was some subtle things missing from the chords of love and happiness struck by Rose Amber's life. Yet of Harry's devotion there could be no doubt.

Mrs. Harvey, going into the study unexpectedly, found Harry kneeling on the rug at Rose Amber's feet, sticking sweet-scented little white flowers all over her hair and kissing her while she laughingly protested. As Mrs. Harvey entered, Rose Amber pushed him away, but Harry maintained his ground, demanding, "Isn't she lovely? Wouldn't an artist love to paint her like that?"

"Why don't you have one do it?" inquired Mrs. Harvey. "All your ancestors seem to have had their brides painted; why don't you add to the collection?"

A frown contracted Harry's brow, but he pulled himself together, and answered, "By Jove! I simply must, you know."

"You must get someone who will do it well, though," said Mrs. Harvey.

"I am not going to have rotters like most of the artist chaps dangling about her."

At dinner, Harry Granville asked their guest: "Do you know of any women portrait painters?"

"Not *really* good ones, I'm afraid."

"But women are crying out to do everything nowadays; why shouldn't they be painting portraits?"

Rose Amber looked up with a queer little direct look at her husband, then she dropped her eyes and smiled; it was the smile of a mother who detects a child in an act of which the child himself is a little ashamed.

Mrs. Harvey had not yet the clue which enabled her to interpret this look in Rose Amber's eyes. It was new to her, and she felt vaguely distressed by it, but she continued: "There aren't any really first-rate women painters just at present. For miniatures, yes: there are some awfully good miniaturists, but you ought to have her painted life-size."

"Well, we will see about it some day," said Harry.

Rose Amber laughed and hummed:

"Gather your roses while you may,
Who knows what a hag I shall be some day!"[40]

Next day the post-bag was brought in while they were at breakfast. It was usually earlier, but a trifling accident had delayed the distribution of the letters till they were all at table. The shiny leather case with its brass lock was brought over to Harry, who took the key from the bunch in his pocket and opened it, distributing the letters.

Mrs. Harvey noticed the accentuation of the groove between his eyes as he saw a fat packet in Kenneth's handwriting. It was addressed to his wife.

"News from Kenneth?" enquired Mrs. Harvey, eagerly. "My own mail hasn't had time to be forwarded yet, of course. Does he write often?"

"Awfully seldom," said Rose Amber, "but when he does there are volumes."

"The rest of the expedition he went out to join have come back long ago! Why couldn't he come back sooner?"

"Oh, but he found so many wonderful new fossils, and he has to visit the museums all over the world to compare his new specimens with those already known. He has lots and lots of things unknown before, quite new to science; and then he is not only doing this work for the reports of the expedition, he is hammering out some kind of theory — wonderful new ideas, but they are all his own!"

"It is these new ideas I am afraid of," said Mrs. Harvey; "they seem to lead him so far — ."

"Surely new ideas are just what scientists are always working for?"

"He tells me so little — you tell me — ," murmured Mrs. Harvey.

"He is working out some kind of theory. It seems to take him months at a time to think out a new bit of it, but once he *has* thought it out he has lots to say on the subject."

"A sight too much when his theories are all such nonsense," laughed Harry. "Why you say yourself that he doesn't discuss them with his scientific colleagues."

"No," replied Rose Amber, gaily. "I am the only one honoured by the views in embryo. I will read them out to you, if you like. Only last time I tried it you didn't have enough patience with them to see their beauties."

"Moonshine," he said, petulantly. Then he turned quickly to Mrs. Harvey. "I was so hoping this travel would open his eyes to the advantage of living in London sensibly. You know that professorship can't remain open indefinitely and he seems to wander further and further away."

"Yes," sighed Mrs. Harvey. "And yet — ," she paused, "it isn't quite aimless wandering. And sometimes he writes as though he is so full of his work, and so full of interest in his strange life. To me it feels as though he were a lad again, and going through the phases of growing up all over again."

Rose Amber looked at her, comprehension in her eyes.

"That's how *I* feel," she said. "He feels quite young, somehow, sort of naïve, with a set of new ignorances mingled with the old wisdom and all his scientific knowledge. Such a mêlée. But *so* interesting."

"Men have no business to be interesting," Harry Granville protested, half in earnest.

"Yet lots of the very great people have had that curiously juvenile outlook in some ways, haven't they?" asked Rose Amber seriously. "Why, Newton,[41] you know, was always surprised at quite commonplace things."

"It's a sign of greatness."

Granville went out with the dogs, and the two women were left in the writing-room together. Rose Amber gently tossed the thick pad of Kenneth's letter into Mrs. Harvey's lap. "You will like to read it, though some of it is beyond *my* depth. Perhaps I had better tell you that he is working out his great theory in his letters to me. He says he *must* express his ideas to *somebody*. I'm not much good, I know, but I criticize them now and then. Mostly I just save the letters up, to read to him when he comes back." She laughed. "He often contradicts himself, you know."

"May I read it?"

"Of course."

"Does Harry?"

Rose hesitated for the fraction of a second. "I show him the letters, of course, but he says they are beyond his depth, and he cannot see why he should write so much about it all to me. Read it out, darling."

The letter began soberly enough.

"Dear Rose Amber, — You are right, I expect; I do not know half as much about humanity as I do about frogs; but, all the same, if I find it thrilling to discover the inside works of frogs, *you* can understand how humanity strikes me now! My time will soon be up here, thank the Lord, and then I have an idea. I am not coming home for ages and ages. I am going right away; I am going to see if there *is* any wisdom in the East. I know jolly well that the Eastern skies are very deep.

"You will be glad to hear that my scientific results include the discovery of lots of new species — among other things some jolly fine fossils, though I am not the professional geologist — so that everybody is very satisfied with them, and possibly by the time I come home I may find that their publication has kept my decent, solid reputation going. This may help me to obtain a hearing for the other things I want to say, though I shouldn't be at all surprised if it just didn't.

"Evolution is bothering me a good deal just now. There is something queer about it, something which people don't seem to have begun to suspect, unless it may be a Palaeontologist or two. You know I have long been reading all the Palaeontology I can lay hands on, and there is no doubt about it that there is some queer, unexpected complexity in the whole business which would be *most* disconcerting to the good, old-fashioned Evolutionists if they only had the intelligence to realize it. It keeps me awake at nights sometimes, and the other night I got an idea. All of a sudden, at last, everything clarified. The key had been wandering about in my head for a good long time in a vague, muddling sort of way. Out here in this wilderness, I can't be sure whether other people have had the idea before me or not, and I shall have to come home and read up a lot more before I venture to talk about it. But it is a great idea, one of those glorious, master-key ideas! Quite simple. And it explains a hundred disconnected puzzles. Oh, it is a great idea, and if I can only make humanity see it and *realize* it, as, after his splendid fight, Darwin made humanity see and realize Evolution, I should be a happy man.

"Don't you feel, Rose Amber, as though the world were kind of waiting for a new, big illuminating idea? It wants to shift its focus, somehow, doesn't it? — this old world! Write and tell me how *you* feel. But that is the way it strikes me.

"For long ages, all the time, in fact, since man stepped up from the tree-hanging, ape-like ancestors, right unto the day that fine old philosopher, Copernicus,[42] came along, man (and woman too, God bless her) simply observed that the sun wheeled round the sky and that the earth felt solid under his feet. Consequently he thought that the earth *was* solid and that the sun and moon and stars were set in the heavens and did revolve *round him*. It was so obvious! It tallied with everything that everyone observed!

"And then what happened? We don't know, of course, how many people dreamed it before him and never put it into words, but we do know that old Copernicus came along and maintained in the face of all of them that it was the earth that moved round the sun, the solid, hard, indomitable earth which *moved*. This was for the world of thought the great *change of focus number one*."

"It's *big*, his horizon, isn't it?" said Mrs. Harvey.

"But — ."

"Well, listen, there's lots more. He says: —

"'Just throw your mind back and think what a revolution in human perspective that meant. In my opinion, the only revolution of thought equal to it was when Darwin came along and knocked over the idea that God had specially created each of the separate species just the way they are now and put them on the world. Darwin drove into our silly heads the idea which had been hovering in the minds of his grandfather and *lots* of other people — that all the animals are mighty like ourselves; that in short we get our backbones and our five toes, and our brain-pans and our breathing apparatus by a physical handing on of the ever-modified, ever-evolving matter of life. Then man (and woman too, bless her) at last saw the human race, not as the specially-created Lords of Creation, but as the present end of a long chain of eager, upward trending animal lives. And for the world of thought this was *change of focus number two*.

"'Now do you mean to tell me that that is the end, that we have *now* got the right and final focus? Rats! Of course not. But *where is our change of focus number three*? We'll leave out of consideration established religion. Mrs. Eddyism,[43] Socialism, they are always going on, fuming and seething in the cauldron of man's brain; we want our fundamental or radical change, the change of focus number three! And mark — it must be a scientific one. Observe that the *great* changes of human focus which fundamentally alter man's conception of his *place in the universe* are SCIEN-TIFIC, but not narrow — so profound that they touch all life. Where is the next one after Darwin's? Bergson's?[44] Not radical enough, too blurred. De Vries'[45] idea of Mutations? Too partial — in a way too trivial, only an adjunct of Darwinian Evolution. We want something of wider sweep.

"'Rose Amber, I am quivering with excitement as I write: I have not spoken to a soul about it, but all night (we are at the moment going around making observations on coral atolls,[46] you know) as I lay in my sleeping-bag on the clean, gritty, shelled sand with the palm-trees leaning over my skyline and the regular thud, thud of the great rough breakers dinning in my ears, and the stars leaning down to me and smiling in my face, ideas which have hovered for years suddenly crystallized, and I *saw* where the great change of focus number three must lie! Of course, I may only be the Focus-Changer's grandfather; I myself may never be able to get my great idea said so that people will listen; in my lifetime enough fact to establish it may not turn up, but I know what it has *got* to be. I know it will affect not only scientific work, but every human relation, even as did the changes of focus numbers one and two — and you know that Darwin's Evolution changed the whole trend of human thought, and transformed even religion itself. . . .

"'Send me out — '"

Here followed a list of books he wanted, and the letter finished with details of his daily life.

Mrs. Harvey laid it down: "My dear, is he sane, do you think?" she asked wistfully,

Rose Amber smiled reassuringly: "I believe he is *great*."

Mrs. Harvey sighed. "Everybody who has got a bee in his bonnet thinks he has got a great idea, you know. But just now and then you *do* get a Newton[38] or a Darwin, a man who *does* have a great idea in his head. But how could his relatives tell? Don't encourage Kenneth in it too much; make him come home."

"He will come home himself when he is ready, and if it *is* a great idea you would not have him spoil it by forcing and hurrying it, would you?"

"No, oh, no! But it's queer to think of my little son choosing those lonely places."

"Great people generally do choose lonely places," said Rose Amber. "They are like trees in a forest; if they are packed too closely together their branches cannot spread."

"You believe in him?"

"I think he is the wisest man I know," Rose Amber laughed ruefully. "True, I don't know many. Of course, Harry and I have lots of friends — but one never seems to *talk* of anything very real, somehow, and there are always crowds together. Harry hates having anybody to disturb us, and so do I," she added hastily, "so when we have a party at all we have a whole lot together. It seems to me that we don't get much real talk in that way. I sometimes wonder whether people of our class ever really do talk. I suppose when I was younger it amused people to talk to me because I was so childish and silly. What absurd, wonderful ideas I had about doing something for the whole world."

"That wish is not absurd," Mrs. Harvey's voice was tender with memory and hope.

"But what *can* one do?" asked Rose Amber. "A little sympathy here and there to others and lots of happiness and nice things for oneself seem to be all there is in life. Do you think happy marriage makes people selfish?" she asked suddenly.

"That is the danger, but the want of marriage has worse pitfalls." Mrs. Harvey smiled. "You know, darling, very few human beings ever do even as much as to succeed in being happy themselves and giving

119

sympathy to other people. If that is what your life means, realize that it is an achievement."

Rose Amber sat looking at the elder woman thoughtfully.

"I wonder," she said at last, meditatively, "I wonder! Did you ever expect to do lots of things when you were a girl that you found you never did after all?"

"Of course."

"Well, then, I hate it being 'of course!' Our ambitions ought to *grow*, not wither as we get older and happier."

CHAPTER

19

BEWILDERING
ADORATION

M RS. Harvey's visit was coming to an end, and she was to catch the morning train back to town on the following day. Rose Amber came to her bedroom after they had all said goodnight to see if everything had been arranged for her comfort. She lingered, and before the bright fire she knelt for a moment on the hearthrug beside Mrs. Harvey, who was resting in her padded silk dressing-gown in the armchair.

"You have stayed *such* a little while! You must come back soon."

"I will come whenever you really want me, darling: but you are still in the honeymoon stage, aren't you, and you and Harry don't really need any outsiders."

"I don't believe Harry does," agreed Rose, meditatively, "but he loves you, you know; he is charmed to have you. But — yes — I do feel as though he would like to have a moat and a high wall round the garden and not let anybody in. I — ," she hesitated, "I don't think before I was married that I realized how tremendously he loves me. It — almost frightens me."

"If it will last," said Mrs. Harvey, "and I am sure you will know how to keep it, you will be one of the luckiest of women."

"Oh, yes," agreed Rose Amber slowly, "only it is such a terrific — well — responsibility. You know Harry is not religious, but he has a sort of queer, half-religious belief that men's and women's souls are not complete except when they love their true mates. Of course, if you asked him about it he would deny it. Yet I almost think he believes that the immortality of his own soul depends on keeping his mate's love. It is as though he fancied unmated souls wither when people die, and only the mated souls are complete and strong enough to go into the new life of another world. In lots of ways he makes me feel as though to him our love matters not only for our earthly happiness, but for our very future *existence*. He almost frightens me; it makes him *depend* so on me."

"How strange," said Mrs. Harvey. "One would hardly expect such a romantic idea from such a man of the world as Harry is."

"He has got streaks of mysticism and beautiful chivalry in him," said Rose Amber: "Look at the way he treated Vera."

"Yes; how awful it must have been for him when she failed him."

"That's it," agreed Rose Amber, eagerly sitting up and coming nearer Mrs. Harvey. "In addition to all the natural feelings of a man about a woman he loved who had left him for another man, was the feeling that his very immortal soul was lost. He only consoled himself afterwards by thinking that he had made a mistake in choosing his mate. And he is *so* sure he has chosen right with me! And he is so passionate. I sometimes feel that I can hardly follow it, as though it were a thing I could not understand. And yet I thought I knew so much about everything before I was married." She spoke hesitatingly and almost in a whisper. Mrs. Harvey stroked her hair.

"A man of his build and his freedom from anxiety would naturally be passionate. Thank God that you have his entire devotion."

"Oh, I do! But my body, too, seems to mean so *terribly* much to him, and it is that which I feel I can hardly understand. I didn't realize quite *how* strong men's passions are. Do you know he hates my maid to undress me! Often and often he sends her away and undresses me himself, with a sort of reverent, passionate excitement. He even kisses my feet, and when he is beside me my body seems to stir him so that he quivers and pants and almost groans with the thrill of it, and I — I am frightened: I can't imagine *really* what he is feeling. It is terrible to stir anyone so much and not feel like that too, and not to understand."

"My darling — " Mrs. Harvey did not know what to say. Rose Amber was a wife; how could she tell her that she was a wife bodily unawakened, unstirred? Mrs. Harvey knew well how many women wait for years, or for ever, before they experience and understand the thrilling joys of the body. She longed to tell Rose some of the wisdom she herself had slowly gained, but she hesitated before the difficult task, and the moment passed. Rose looked up at her with wistful, innocent child's eyes. "It is wonderful and terrible to think how dreadfully important we are to men," she said.

"All women are not important to all men," smiled Mrs. Harvey. "Only when a woman is lovable is she important, and only to the man who loves her."

"How funny it is how little people know about love," sighed Rose, meditatively, "I thought I knew lots about it before I was married, but I didn't."

"We all think that."

"Oh, I *wish* I were worthy of it."

Mrs. Harvey's lips were tremulous at the thought of how much Rose Amber, in her tender humility, revealed, unaware of her lack of mated fusion.

"There are things for you to learn yet, dear." Mrs. Harvey's fingers softly touched the curls on her neck.

Rose Amber raised her eyes suddenly, then shrank back, as though repudiating any further burden of knowledge. Unaware of it herself, her vitality was flagging a little, drained by too constant passion. Questions arose almost to her lips, but she suddenly turned, refusing to-day to seek to-morrow's burdens. She gave a little shake to her shoulders, looked up and laughed. "More? I have as much excitement and responsibility as I can undertake at present. There do not seem to be enough minutes in the hours or hours in the day to do all and be all I should like to be for Harry or that he seems really to need me to be for him. I never could have imagined that just one man could be such an entire occupation and leave one feeling that the twenty-four hours in the day or not nearly enough to be all he wants one to be."

She looked at the clock. "What *will* poor Harry be doing! And you, poor darling, have got to travel to-morrow morning."

She slipped for a second on to Mrs. Harvey's knee. "Just one good cuddle," she said. "It's so *nice* to cuddle somebody who doesn't get too excited about it."

Mrs. Harvey smiled, but two tears came into the corners of her eyes at the same time. The slender, vivid, lovely child like a woodland flower in the hot-house of passion, her petals still half folded in the bud. She dreamed of her restlessly.

CHAPTER
20

THE ARTIST FELLOW

ROSE Amber's portrait cried aloud to be painted. A hundred times a day her vivid radiance, some freshly beautiful aspect of her grace and charm, struck Harry anew, and the next time he went to Town he made an effort to find a suitable artist.

He was quite frank with one of his older women friends, and told her that he didn't trust those artist fellows: "They cannot do any harm to her, but they will spoil the atmosphere round her — pawing her with their eyes. And if any of them could be with Rose Amber for the time necessary to paint her portrait and not fall in love with her his picture could not be worth having, for he couldn't be an artist." So he made clear his dilemma.

"An elderly married man?" suggested this mother of daughters.

"Worse than useless," Harry Granville answered; "he would be sure to be tired of his own wife."

"After all, *some* artists are gentlemen," she suggested. "There must be one who, even if he does fall in love with her, won't say anything about it."

"Perhaps, but she would feel it; she is sensitive. And I don't want her to be mixed up in a cloudy atmosphere of that sort."

"She might enjoy it," the friend maliciously suggested. Granville's lips closed, and the woman, seeing his anger, was amused: "Most women would, why shouldn't she?" Granville, having the excuse of a new arrival, turned on his heel.

At last a dowager with a penchant for curiosities procured the man. "The very creature," as she declared in her testimonial; "an Irishman, a wag, entangled hand and foot with an actress; a man of the people who can paint a beauty so that you can see through her the hundred earls of whom she is the daughter. He is so frankly and intentionally vulgar that it becomes amusing. Treat him as a joke," was her advice. "He is not troubled with nerves and he could paint in the middle of the Albert Hall with a lecture going on. He painted — ."

The very man he proved, and Granville arranged for him to come

124

while three or four of his more intimate friends were down for some shooting. He encouraged Rose Amber to invite a few women from whom they had unredeemed promises of intimate and friendly visits.

"Better to have several together; it wastes less of our time."

Rose laughingly agreed, "Some people are rather bores." The other guests were to be safely established before the R.A. made his appearance. Alastair O'Donnahaw, R.A., burst upon the assembled company at tea-time. In the outer hall he had assailed with pleasantries the unresponsive footman, and, uncrushed by his failure to make him smile, came rubbing his hands towards the group around the open hearth in the great hall where the firelight and the masses of blossoms distilled the airs of summer. He had met Granville in town, but he had not yet seen his wife.

"The very setting for a beauty," he proclaimed as he shook hands. "Where is she? The first impression counts." The big voice tumbled out of him in a jolly torrent, and Rose Amber came forward into the magic of the firelight, laughing.

Her little hand was lost in his great hairy one. "Begorrah, I'm in luck at last," he kept her hand, shaking it strenuously up and down. "It's a reduction I'll make on the price this very minute: it's easy to paint *you* looking like a goddess." He sank into the sofa. "This'll not be like some of me jobs at all, at all, when I have had to use up a lot of me priceless imagination to make the picture look fit to hang in a gilt frame. I have made the background a foot bigger than I had planned and charged an extra hundred guineas in me time."

He did not pause for answers: he did not desist while the footman solemnly arranged tea. Irresistibly he drew round him hearers filled with friendly amusement. His large, frank jollity, his unaffected direct appeal were so compelling when uttered in his big resonant voice that even Granville warmed towards him.

"Which part of Ireland do you come from," a lady asked him as he held towards her both hands laden with cake.

"I was not born Irish; I achieved Ireland," he answered the whole company, "and I can assure ye I find it most convenient to be an Irishman. I've got a roll on me tongue that makes it easy enough to do the brogue and so I can get through the world without giving offence. Alastair O'Donnahaw has never given offence yet — because he never pretends. And yet I am all a pretence, for I am not Irish at all, ye know, but I would not for the world have you find that out for yourselves, so I am telling ye."

After tea he was taken for a walk by Granville, and during dinner he was too interested in his plate to spend much time entertaining the company, but after dinner, when he had selected a comfortable corner and pulled up one trouser leg so that an inch of hairy calf showed above the rumpled red silk of his sock, he let himself go.

"It is a ticklish job getting along with a lot of born aristocrats," he began. "They look down on you if you pretend to be a gentleman yourself. That's how my friend, Smithers-Green, can never get more than a hundred guineas for a portrait, and only gets that once a year. He *will* keep his nose in the air and remember he is a gentleman. And he can tip the butler as often as he likes — but you can't deceive a valet with darned socks. Poor Smithers-Green turns pale as a lily when there is any mention of the price of his pictures, tries to pretend he does it for love, and him all the time wondering if the cheque or the bailiffs will arrive first. The very first thing I fix is me price; five hundred guineas for a full-length portrait, and in a few years it'll be a thousand; and a hundred guineas extra for a lady who paints herself before I do her. Anyone will tell ye it's worse to undo bad work than it is to start afresh. Now the last duchess who wanted me to paint her — ."

He kept the drawing-room roaring with laughter at his anecdotes. He was quite brutally frank, and yet with an unexpected dexterity he never actually gave his sitters away. His hearers were always left wondering just which duchess it had been — and if it perhaps had not been a countess after all.

He took the bull by the horns: "If I were you, Sir Harry," he said, "I would be as jealous as a cat with her only kitten. All art is feeling translated into paint. But, begorrah, I would not let any artist fellow stand alone in a studio feeling the beauty of a wife like that all by himself. I wouldn't meself, so I invite you all to come in and watch me painting her to protect me from her."

He was inordinately proud of his technical skill with a brush and loved to show it off. "I'm not one of those self-conscious idiots — who can't paint with anybody watching them; I am like that early Italian johnny, a master craftsman, he was, who could paint circles with one turn of his brush in front of people who came from all over the country to see him do it. It will be a quick job to paint Lady Granville. I have got my inspiration already, though with some sticks I have had to put flesh on to I have been kept dawdling about for a week waiting for a pose. But Lady Granville's picture's here," he tapped his forehead; "I have got her sketched out — did it while I was dressing, with a bit of charcoal I always keep in me waistcoat pocket. That's what accounts for the black smudge on me shirt front." Rubbing it he focused attention on it. "If I had stopped to put on another I would have missed the hors-d'oeuvre, and I couldn't have begun a dinner without a beginning."

Everybody in the house felt as though he was a life-long friend. After dinner he became reminiscent. "Was I really christened Alastair?

You ask. Heaven knows whether I was ever christened at all. I was born in a slum — but I'm not going to tell you where." He grinned tantalizingly: "But when I found meself growing up big I made up me mind to make meself comfortable in the world. If I was to have from Nature lots of flesh and blood inside me big skin and lots of brains inside me big skull, for why shouldn't I have fine lots of money in me pocket? I knew I could paint when I was twenty, so did the master who taught me. I got the prize at the provincial art school at the end of the course, and with me head in the air walked out and said I was going to the continong. But Divil a bit was I really going there; I hadn't a halfpenny to go with. And I wanted to find out how smart folks do things and see the fine houses and parks that I read about in books: so I put some oil and some flour on me head and engaged meself as a footman at a lord's country house."

His hearers gasped: "Whose, whose?" they cried.

He stopped tantalizingly, grinning like a schoolboy at everyone.

"And do you think I am going to give it away to ye? The most beautiful secret that I have! Why, it was at a fine house, one of the finest in the country, that I found out all about ye. Whenever I go to a fine house now I can keep them all agog wondering whether I have seen the back side of it before. Well, I just stayed there as a footman and I learnt a lot. Oh, but I studied you all, otherwise how should I ever have known what ye talked like; how should I ever have known what ye think of a man who deludes himself into thinking he's imposing on ye as a gentleman? How should I ever have known the cruel things you say of folks like yourselves but not quite so good or else better? Oh, I learned many things with ye when I served behind your chairs at table. I learned what cut to a suit makes a man look like a gentleman, and what it is amuses ye. And, by gosh, I made up me mind I would never go stalking behind pretence to ye, making believe I was a gentleman and not a poor devil born in a slum with a genius like that of Michael Angelo.[47] When I had my year of seeing you and learning you and finding out my way about you I went to Ireland to pick up the brogue, with a fine suit I bought cheap from the valet. The lord whose house I was in, ye know, he was about my own figure."

"Who?" they were all agog again. "Who was he?"

"I was a lad of twenty then and I'm forty-three now," he said; "you will none of ye ever know whose house it was."

"Go on, go on," they cried, "what did you do next?"

"Well, I came back from Ireland with a fine brogue on me tongue and me mind full of the beauty of green valleys and rains that drift down from heaven into the hillsides, and golden spring, fit for goddesses to learn to love in. I had saved up all me wages and me gould tips for the year I served with the lord and I spent but a little bit of it in Ireland. So I came to London with the painting of an Irish lassie. She was the daughter of an Irish Earl who was running wild in the bog-land, and whether it was her name or my painting that did it we have never agreed about, but they hung it in the Academy. And a rich lord who wanted to marry her bought it for fifty guineas, and so I was fairly started. But if I couldn't paint like Old Nick himself I should have long ago tumbled out of the saddle."

The fame of the painter spread through the land to the Granvilles' neighbours, the Earl and Countess of Caioran, and Rose Amber received a note from the Countess. "Don't keep your treasures to yourself, my dear, in this howling wilderness."

"Will you behave, if we ask an Earl and Countess to meet you at dinner?" Rose Amber mischievously asked the R.A. that day at breakfast.

"Begorrah, I'll keep me forepaws in me pockets as neatly as a snake does his."

"Dare we risk dinner?" Rose Amber laughed across the table to her husband.

"They have brought it on their own heads if they don't like it," he answered. "Ask them up for to-morrow."

So the tall Earl and the stately Countess came, expecting to be amused, and the Countess smiled while the others laughed. As an ex-vicereine her queenly air had overawed all local climbers.

After dinner O'Donnahaw sat down at the piano: "Shall I sing to ye?" he asked.

"Hooray!" cried Rose Amber. She felt towards him like a child behaves to a big uncle whose pockets are generally stuffed with chocolates: the relationship was inevitable.

Easily his large hands ran up and down the notes of the piano while he roared innumerable parodies of Harry Lauder's songs.[48] The sillier the songs the jollier his voice, jerked sometimes by his cumberous body turning and laughing and accentuating the points by amazing facial contortions. Songs with choruses suited him best. He made everyone sing. It took all his gift of persuasion to get the Countess to join in the hilarious words. The frank jollity with which he filled the air at last thawed her reserve, and her lips curved up in smiles.

"When ma Jenny cried Sandy,
  Prie ma mou!
  Prie ma mou, ou ah ou;
Ma Jenny cried Sandy, Prie ma mou
  And tak' your will o' the whusky."

He had the room echoing with the nonsense. Alastair, hanging on to

the music with one hand, waved his other towards her: "Sing, sing, ladyship," he interrupted the music to say, "Don't look a gifted horse in the
mouth," and before the evening was half way through he had the dignified Countess shouting his ridiculous choruses with the rest.

CHAPTER

21

TEARS IN LOVE

THE sweet, shy confidences of love were whispered by Rose Amber to her lover-husband as she lay cradled in his arms. Everything round her was beautiful, from the keen, salt-sprayed air that rushed over the tops of the pine trees through her gardens, to the soft comfort of the appointments of the house. The ugliness and the sordidness of London and the Carlingford Road lodgings seemed as though they had been but the bareness of the schoolroom. Now she was grown up, and now that Harry was taking care of her everything was beautiful. How lovely she felt it to love, and to know that she, by her very existence, could create in this man's mind and body a rapture which repaid him for all the joy and beauty he had brought into her life. The words of his whispered passion charmed her. "What a strange, beautiful thing love is; I am so glad that my body makes you happy. I wish I understood *why*! Dearest, as you care so much for this side of marriage, it must have been dreadful for you when — you were cut off from it — all that time you — had to do without."

In the darkness her whispering, shy tongue dared at last to clothe her ever-present thoughts: "I think it is so splendid of you to have gone all that time without any woman."

He half roused himself smiling. "Dear baby," he thought, "does she really think I lived like a monk because I was cut off from real love?" He felt it a wise and propitious moment tenderly to make clear the Rights of Man.

"My darling," he said, "bodies, you know, are like machines that need oiling and stoking. You never expected me to do without bread and butter to eat and water to drink because I couldn't share a feast of nectar with you? No, of course not. Now there are other things that a man's body needs to keep him in health as well as good food and drink."

"What do you mean?" Rose Amber's breath came fast.

"My darling! And you have been married nearly a year."

She caught her breath and compelled herself to whisper — it was easier to speak thus without betraying uncontrollable feelings — "Do you

130

mean that you *had* other women's — bodies?" She knew, oh, yes, she knew quite well that men, many men did such things — but Harry, *her* Harry was different. Surely, surely *he* was different, she thought, in agony.

"Don't make any mistake," he said soothingly: "I have never *bought* that sort of thing; I am not that kind. But there are women who need keeping in health as much as I, and if we were kind to each other — surely you would be glad that I should have been well?"

Rose Amber could only whisper, "What kind of women?"

"Oh, women of our own class," he said easily. "Plenty of women whose husbands are old, or abroad, or withered puritans — there are many women who, you know, my darling, would become fretful, bad-tempered and sleepless if they just allowed their husbands to neglect them without taking any steps to make up for it. One or two women like that have been good pals to me, and we have given each other just the meagre diet of — shall we call it bread and water — needed to keep our bodies in health. But that is not *love*. When one has real love all that is forgotten, just as one forgets, when one sits at a banquet with a king, the dry crust one had before. Don't, for heaven's sake, think that now that I have you that I should ever dream of keeping up that relation with any woman. My darling, you are not thinking that?" he asked anxiously.

Her whispered voice did not reveal the extent of her amazement and horror of what seemed to him, as it must to many of his type, the simply obvious common sense of sex.

So accustomed to such ideas was he himself that he did not know that in some minds they inspire disgust, in some a shattering horror. So completely had he felt for so many years that the spiritual side of life and its realization could only be found in the one woman who was *wife*, and something distinct and apart from the purely physiological needs of the body which could be satisfied by other women whose quality was not that of wifehood, that he had not realized the effect of what he said upon a girl so sincere as Rose Amber.

"What is it, my darling?" he cried out in alarm, "you are not *crying*?"

The silent tears that had streamed down Rose Amber's cheeks showered on to his bare arm.

"For God's sake, darling, don't cry; what have I done?" She could no longer restrain her sobs, and lay in his arms, shaken by convulsions of weeping. Protestations, every tenderness of which he could think, failed for a long time to stop her tears.

"It is lovely to have a girl so innocent," he groaned, "but my God, I thought you knew something of a man's nature. You always spoke so wisely of life — surely, you knew what men need."

"I thought *you* were different," she half whispered.

"I'm a *man*, my child — ."

131

Rose Amber did not speak. All her life she had endeavoured never to judge anything until she knew and understood the facts concerning it. Never before had she realized how hard it is to practise one's precepts. All the stray fragments of women's gossip concerning the nature of man flashed through her mind. "Am I at last face to face with the *reality* of this profound and terrible difference between the nature of man and woman which has been the theme of so many novels I hated?" Even novels had sent the tears coursing down her cheeks in sympathy with those whose woes she thought she had understood, but which she now knew she had not realized. She felt that in forgiving and wiping out all thought of Harry's earlier relations with Vera she had made that great concession to his nature which the strange workings of fate demanded of her.

She whispered, "I never felt any jealousy of your marriage to Vera. I wouldn't let myself. However often I longed that my beloved should have been mine alone." She had flattered herself that her experience saved her from the romantic, impossible longings of girls for a virgin spouse.

"But, darling — ." His intense thoughts seemed to penetrate her, though his words failed.

She reasoned with herself, thinking, "What if they had been, those others, in no real sense lovers — merely, as he said, the equivalent of bread and water to a starving man?" Yet they invaded her mind, shattering its security, revealing chasms of ignorance and misconception. "And I, I of all people, thought I understood life!" The very fact that they — the others — held but a secondary place and yet could thus assail her, seemed to degrade the very pinnacle of the crisis of love. She had almost rather he had loved them.

In his arms she lay passive, sobbing through his endearments and re-iterated explanations that she, and she alone, was the only one he *loved*; the only soul who would go with him to eternity.

By mere exhaustion the climax of her weeping passed. She was strangely puzzled to observe that while she could not respond to his kisses and endearments, but lay there motionless, shrinking, repelled by the thought of his lips, yet the mere soft touch of his hand passing tenderly to and fro along her shoulder soothed her and sheltered her from the most savage of the winds of desolation. She did not understand; she only knew that until she understood she must not speak.

Her sobs died away; she stroked his cheek with her finger: "Don't kiss me. I couldn't bear it," she said. "It's at first — the idea — hurts so much. You must tell me all about it some day soon. I want to understand *your* life as well as my own. I've evidently been a fool when I thought I knew enough to help anyone."

CHAPTER
22

MISCELLANEOUS REFLECTIONS

SOME months later Rose Amber was playing the piano to herself in the morning room when Harry brought in her letters. There was once again a thick packet from Kenneth. "What on earth has the chap got to write all that about," said Harry, lingering for want of a definite occupation.

"All his theories mostly. He seems to think I can understand them."

"Do you?"

"I don't know"; she hesitated; "in one way I think I do, but, of course, I don't understand all the scientific part of it."

""When is he coming home?" queried Harry.

Rose had not opened her letter. "The last I heard," she said, "was that he was in Japan for a bit, and then was going to America."

"He's let us down horribly about that professorship, hasn't he?"

Rose laughed merrily.

"You little thought when we hatched the plot that we would be cutting down your dress allowance to provide a salary for that goggle-eyed creature they have put in his place."

Rose Amber got up and put her hand on Harry's shoulder. "I am so glad you did it, though. We could afford it well, you know, and it's monstrous how little people who really can afford things do in the way of endowments. You sneer at the Carnegies[49] of the world, but they seem to be much more awake to that kind of duty than any of their betters."

Harry lingered about the room. "Why don't you open your letters, darling? They may need answering."

Rose Amber sat with them in her lap, opening first the notes addressed in handwritings she knew, and keeping Kenneth's monster packet for the last. An unreasoning irritation grew in Harry's mind. He picked up a newspaper, but was really thinking "Damn the chap! Why should he write half an inch of pages to my wife? She is just as innocent as a babe, but what is *he* doing out there all this time with nobody else to think about?"

Rose Amber, unaware of the gathering storm, dallied over the notes she was reading. An absurd obsession filled Granville's mind: suddenly it appeared to him that she didn't want him to see the letter. At last he said, "What does the wanderer say?"

And Rose opened it. The letter was long and rambling, like all the others from Kenneth. Rose innocently asked, "Shall I read it aloud?"

Harry, feeling himself reproved by her sweetness, and filled with shame, answered roughly, "You haven't recently, why should you this one? I only want to know the news."

Rose looked at him, her eyes wide: a faint tremor passed through her, due to a glimmering of understanding of what he was feeling. Granville turned and looked out of the window: Rose Amber, forgetting to read her letter, looked at him, and with tender pride noticed the fine set of his shoulders and the clear-cut strength of him. "How sensitive men are," she thought; "what dear, silly babies."

She turned to the letter and was just beginning to read it aloud when she noticed the words, "Perhaps *you* will understand; I don't believe anybody else can." She drew herself up in time. Instinctively she felt that with Harry in such a mood, such words would be a match to gunpowder. Skipping the opening sentences, she began to read aloud.

"I have got great things crystallizing in my head now, I can tell you, and I want first of all to have some months utterly undisturbed to think about them, and then I must go to America (which is great shakes for Palaeontology) and verify my facts and see if any new ones have turned up in the meantime. Heaven knows how long I shall be there. For my time of peaceful brooding before my chickens are hatched I am finding Japan excellent. There is a chap here who has set me all agog to see the beauty of their out-of-the-way temples. One can be really peaceful here, and as it is more civilized than the islands we visited, there is less time wasted in the mere getting together the necessities of life than there would be had I remained on one of them, as I once intended to do. It sounds absurd, and I would not dare to tell a scientist, but I feel as though the atmosphere of some of these quiet temples of contemplation is just what I need as an ingredient in my great compound of ideas. I have been reading some of their old Buddhism recently. How awfully true lots of the things they say are. I heard a symbolic thing the other day that encourages me in by belief, that after one has got hold of a bit of really profound truth one must bring it back to the world and mix it in with ordinary affairs, and forget even the thought of the exertions necessary to having captured it. As I see things, the world has got into a beastly priggish way of trying to be virtuous and *consciously* cultivating all sorts of things that ought to have been natural to it. It is because we have got things out of focus and we are diseased in consequence. Do you remember some time ago I wrote to you that the world seemed to me on tiptoe, waiting for the great change of focus number three? Well, I think I said that I feel that it is going to come through an enlargement of our scientific conceptions, but at the same time that it will change all our social problems and everything else: then we may have an era of *healthiness*. No healthy animal is conscious of the functions of its organs in the way we are sociologically conscious. I must tell you the story of the ancient butcher — you can read about him in the book of Chwang Tsze,[50] though I do not suppose you will. I'll tell you in case you don't. He is reported to have had a knife which he used for cutting up his cattle, which he never ground, yet which always remained sharp. Everybody was curious about it, and at last the Duke of Bun asked him his secret. He explained that it was because he knew how to use it. He said 'good butchers want a new knife every year, for they cut the tissues: bad butchers want a new knife every month, for they crush bones, but I have used my knife for nineteen years and it is as sharp as if it had just come from the grinders. It is because I know the inner laws of the cow's body. Between the fibres there are tiny intervals, and the edges of my blade have no thickness, and so it is for me easy to put my blade between the intervals of the tissues of the fibres.' And it is reported that the Duke of Bun exclaimed, 'Now I know the secret of eternal life.'

"Well, what I feel about it is that we ought to get at some of the secrets of the construction of the world so that we need not fret and worry and wear ourselves out as we have been doing: so that we can cleanse ourselves from the nervous diseases of unhappiness, cruelty, fear and all the rest — ."

Granville turned from the window: "I say," he said, interrupting, "what on earth does he write all that drivel to you for? Damned impertinence, I call it, writing in that intimate way about a lot of moonshine. I shall have to write to the fellow myself and tell him that we are none of us heathen Chinese and he had better come home soon if he wants to save a remnant of sanity."

The tension of surprised anger filled the room and Rose Amber felt it vibrating through her. Granville flung himself down into a chair.

"See here, darling, something will have to be done with that chap; there is no knowing what drivel he will write next."

"I don't think it *is* drivel," she answered.

"What!" Harry Granville sat up as though he had been struck. "Do you mean to tel me you *like* the chap writing to you like that?"

"Yes, I do." For a moment Rose Amber too was angry.

Granville sat silently fuming; and, although he did not speak another word, she knew that he was unreasonably wrath. The absurdity, the

MISCELLANEOUS REFLECTIONS

injustice of his wrath set fire to a flame of indignation in her. She rose, prepared to walk out of the room and to remove herself from him until he begged her pardon. She pictured herself doing this and applauded the action as a right and proper maintenance of woman's dignity. She turned, but suddenly there flashed upon her memory the tender appeal which his love had made to her understanding when first they were betrothed. She saw a vision of herself as a mature, wise woman with a fretful child in her arms, and instead of allowing her indignation to grow, she suddenly routed it, remembering how much of the child reappears in a man in his prime — the child who seems lost in the schoolboy and the adolescent, but who returns and dwells in the heart of every man who loves.

Rose Amber quickly crossed the room and sat down upon his knee, taking hold of both his ears in her little hands. She pinched their soft lobes, looked deeply into his eyes, and then kissed him on the top of his nose. "Did he feel a wicked, bad feeling in his heart then?" she crooned, and nestled her cheek against his. Nature told her that the soft touch of her lips would soothe his jangled feelings and scatter the little cloud on the horizon. Rose Amber was too wise, too profoundly a woman, to be offended and on her dignity when the child in her lover had fallen down and bumped his forehead: she knew how to kiss the place and make it well.

CHAPTER
23

THE NICHE DOESN'T FIT

FOR two years Harry Granville and Rose Amber alternated between their town and country houses. In the town they were gay: in the country Harry revelled in his complete possession of Rose Amber. She, like a woodland flower of English springtime, bloomed in the sheltered air of a torrid conservatory, but set no fruit, nor did her nature change, although her tender heart strove to attune itself to Harry's intenser personal passion.

Twice had Rose Amber suffered the agony of losing before its birth the tiny baby that nestled below her heart, and yet neither she nor her husband suspected these losses were the Nemesis which may attend excessive uxoriousness.

In anguish she asked, "Is there to be no son to carry on the Granville tradition?"

Rose Amber felt it strange that this vexed Harry less than she feared it might.

"*You* are everything," he answered. "You make my personal immortality."

"But your line — ."

"Bodies matter less than souls. You are my true mate and counterpart."

"You're kind — ."

"But, dearest, really my father's line can very well be continued by the children of my younger brother."

"Your *father's*, yes — but yours?"

"The world being too full already, it's our immortality that matters."

Rose Amber would have grieved more deeply for him had Harry had a passion for fatherhood, but her own heart ached in a dull, persistent way which he could neither understand nor assuage. She was born to be a mother.

Kenneth, travelling slowly, had now reached America, going from University to University, from famous museum to famous museum, immersed in the collections of wonderful fossils, spending long hours at

Yale with Wieland, at New York with Osborne,[51] and at Washington with all the officials of the State Museum and Survey.

Mrs. Harvey, now that he was within a fortnight's journey, felt as though he were really on his homeward way; but he had much to do in America, and had already been there for more than a year. Since he had been once more in touch with University collections and libraries he was able to finish off and send home more scientific memoirs on the various specimens which he had collected in the course of his travels. These, embodying observations on many new animals, served to revive and increase his reputation as a serious naturalist. Mrs. Harvey, to whom copies of the proofs were always sent, had great hopes that he would return and fill his place in the scientific world once more.

"He must, he surely must," she said to Rose.

"I doubt whether he will ever put himself again into the routine harness of his profession."

"What does he write of now?"

"Generally his theories, foreshadowed rather than put clearly."

"Only?"

"Sometimes of the country or the people with whom he stays. Listen from his last letter. 'But descriptions of America are so hackneyed, and you probably know it all by heart better than if you had been here. Every Englishman has been impressed by the sense of limitless space and the possibilities of the country as well as the wonderful versatility of the people. I don't know whether others have been so impressed as I have by the horribly *unhappy* look of the houses: houses in the country here do not nestle against the cheek of the earth as though they rested there contentedly as they do with us; they look as though they had been stuck in quite recently, as though they were planted there ready-made and would be thankful to be uprooted again. I suppose I notice it all the more coming straight from Japan, where the houses are even more part of the nature and beauty of the country than are our own. In the cities, of course, it is different: the houses are often very handsome, but the streets are dreadfully ruled out, as though ordered by the yard.'

"And this, from Washington: 'This is a city now in the making and a glorious place it will be when they have done with it. I am going to stay here for some time and slowly ruminate my way through the national collection of fossils, which is splendid. I am finishing off these odd jobs of research which are being sent home, but once they are cleared out of the way, I don't think I shall work on much but fossils and the great and wonderful theories I am weaving out of them. I am trying to boil it all down — the main conception that is — to a little pamphlet of a few pages. It would be far easier to write a text-book in six volumes. But I shall never forget my dear old professor when I was a student telling me that each of the important theories of science that really matter can be summarised into ten pages; when they cannot it is because they are not yet clarified enough. We need the thousand-page book of reference for details, so I am trying to write my big text-book first, and when I feel my brain specially clear, I will have a go at the boiling down: it's a tough job."'

At last Kenneth returned; bronzed and strong, but with an air of remoteness and benevolence which his friends had never seen in him before. Mrs. Harvey, who had feared some radical change, was overjoyed to find him so little different from the man who had left England nearly five years ago. When she said this to him he laughed.

"From thirty-two to thirty-seven isn't much of a jump in a man's life; it's not like cutting a first tooth or growing one's first moustache."

It soon became clear that Rose Amber was right. Kenneth refused even to apply for any professorship, though one was open at the time of his return. He only wanted a small lectureship on some special branch of his subject. All entreaties, all representations on the folly of his course were vain. "What I want is time and freedom to develop all the branches of my work, to follow out my ideas, and I could never do that as a head professor."

Harry Granville said to Rose: "Well, a man could never marry without making a position for himself, but Kenneth, I suppose, will never marry again, so he can go off the rails a bit if he wants to."

"Why shouldn't he marry again?" The question was almost tinted by indignation.

Granville was surprised, almost offended. "He and your sister were as perfectly mated as a pair could be," he said.

"They were, but darling Lilian would never be so selfish. If bodies mean so much to *you*, Harry, why shouldn't they mean the same to other men?" she asked.

"But hang it all!" Granville was shocked. "He is a student and an idealist and all that, and anyway, he has had his love and his perfect mating; he can't expect to get it again, and the only thing that justifies *marriage* is the real thing."

"I would rather see him married," said Rose Amber.

"I don't understand you. I should have thought you would rather see him loyal to your sister's memory. He is just as much her mate when she is on the other side as if she were here. Surely, surely . . . "

Harry, a stab of fear piercing his heart, insisted and explained and cajoled till Rose Amber agreed that Lilian could never be replaced in Kenneth's life. She saw how deeply it distressed Harry that there should be any shadow of doubt of this in her mind, and to soothe him she dissimulated a little, while to herself she was puzzled to explain why it seemed to her right and natural that Kenneth should marry once more. All the time he was away, her memory of him had been that of the smitten man who had left them, but as he came into the room the first time she saw him after his return, a sudden sense of the strength and vitality that emanated from him made her realise his renewed and greater manhood. She spoke of it to Mrs. Harvey, to whom the idea had also occurred, but who had striven to quench it for fear that Rose Amber would be sadly hurt if her sister's place were filled. Finding the girl free from even an echo of this jealous thought, Mrs. Harvey talked with her unreservedly about her budding but ill-defined hopes for the future.

"Blue-eyed babies are *so* sweet," whispered Rose Amber one day when she was alone with Mrs. Harvey. Remembering Rose Amber's own disappointment and her thwarted hopes the older woman could not answer, but put her hand on her adopted daughter's knee. In a moment she turned smiling to Mrs. Harvey, her clear brown eyes looking deep into the older woman's.

"You must have a blue-eyed daughter-in-law so as to make certain that Kenneth's babies are blue-eyed like himself."

"You sweet thing!" Then Mrs. Harvey shrugged her shoulders delicately and spread out her fragile hands to indicate her powerlessness in the matter.

"More than ever he will depend on you for the people he meets," Rose Amber suggested.

24

THE GREATER UNIT

*This chapter does not carry on the story
and should only be read by those who **think.***

ROSE Amber sat at her desk in the morning room, looking out through the pines. "I'm inviting both Kenneth and his mother to stay with us. Won't it be nice if they come?"

Granville, being informed of the dispatched invitation, being, in fact, invited to jubilate over the coming visit, made the best of an accomplished fact.

"Oh — yes — yes, rather."

"You're not keen?"

"In some awe of his learning."

"He's nicer now — less academic."

"Well, I'm curious to see what the world has made of the thwarted lover-scientist."

"There'll be interminable discussions about his theories!"

Kenneth, fresh from solitudes companioned by his own ideas; released from his concentrated work in America, had forgotten social perspective, and unabashed by the thought of the possibility of an insincere attention, was ready to talk incessantly. The talk broke his large conceptions into fragments and kept his hearers entangled in a protracted bewilderment.

"I don't know whether it is all utterly beyond me or whether I *could* be made to understand," complained Harry. "If in your views you are trying to meet the man of average intelligence, and if you think I am one, let's have the whole thing out. You can take the whole blessed afternoon and evening to it if you want to. We won't have anybody else present. Just we four. Let's see if you can hammer it into our heads."

"We will sit in a row like a class and only ask questions when we must," added Rose Amber.

Kenneth leaned forward eagerly: "Really?"

"Yes, really."

"Now? Right away?"

"Why not? It's raining, we have all day!"

"Well, there are a lot of very remote things to be fitted in together," he began, after lighting his pipe and slipping down in his chair.

The immensity of his subject at first made him a trifle disjointed and incoherent, but his profession for years had involved lecturing on complicated ideas, and so, given an uninterrupted hearing, his thoughts began to range themselves coherently and words came to his tongue, though not always the perfectly expressive ones.

"First there are a lot of special puzzles which modern discoveries about fossils have brought into prominence — lots of queer, inexplicable things seem to have happened in the past epochs. I will tell you more about those later. Then, secondly, there is the enlargement and change of our view of what Evolution really means, since we have had long vistas of life-histories stretching back millions of years. Those two sides of life yield the chief data for my idea, which is scientific at bottom; but there are also things which may possibly fit into it that anybody may have observed. People are just beginning to notice things about the modern world, hardly definable, not yet definite enough to be included in our ideas of Sociology even — and, Lord knows, that's a vague enough conception, anyway — for instance, all this Internationalism, you know, this linking up of the world by telegraphy, this acting and inter-acting of great masses of people, it has its significance.

"You will see that my idea also has a directly social side. You'll see the way in which it may help the people we call reformers and touch indirectly even on pressing problems like slums and disease and poverty. Our attitude towards all these things must be affected by a general realization of the main truth of my view."

"Then it will be worth hearing. What is it?" enquired Granville.

"As things are at present, the scientific attitude towards life is to believe that it has *evolved*, and that the individuals now living are the results, the survivors of the fittest ancestors who transmitted their qualities only through the offspring who escaped extinction. We know that heaps of kinds of creatures died out completely — the man in the street is inclined to think that they died out to make place for us, their betters. All this gives a background of individual hardness to life, makes it a struggle in which the survival of the fit is the right thing and the weak must go to the wall. That, of course, is not *necessarily* the outcome of Darwin's work on Evolution, but it is practically the outcome of it. I should not be surprised to see this idea developing dangerously as it spreads and takes root in half-educated and selfish minds. Of course, though all this is awfully important to society, it simply does not matter to *science* a straw. Now my theory, like the theory of Evolution, is fundamentally scientific; at the moment I am rather laying stress on its possible social reactions chiefly because that is the side that will interest you people most." A murmur of assent rippled towards him.

"You can cut out the scientific part, old man," interjected Harry Granville.

"No, I can't," responded Kenneth, eagerly. "The idea is based chiefly on a study of fossils. Now it is essentially a scientific conception, though I am applying it more immediately and more directly to humanity than one can most scientific ideas. That's because it's bigger, more funda-mental than most ideas. Darwin, you know, spotted the fact that the living families of animals and plants have evolved by stages from the older and more primitive groups. Yet in his day, though some of the more important fossils were known, there was nothing like the mass of data from the past that is available to-day, but as he expected, when the inter-esting extinct creatures became better known, many of them turned up in beautiful series in the rocks which seemed to prove Evolution up to the hilt. A bird's-eye view of the whole faunas of the different geolog-ical epochs affords at first an apparently splendid proof of Evolution. You know the chief facts now generally accepted?"

"No!"

"Well, some trifling little time ago," he grinned, "a time ago measured perhaps in hundreds, perhaps in small thousands of millions of years, the earliest animals, simple, backboneless creatures, were swimming about in the waters of the sea and there were no higher animals to eat them. Each individual in each species has had to fight, overcome or adapt itself to its environment or go under: and those best adapted to their environment survived, bred, and handed on their qualities. Away back at the begin-ning of the Palaeozoic Age[52] there were no creatures with backbones at all; then came in the lower backboned families, fishes, reptiles — then later on the queer, half-reptile birds and primitive land animals. It is ever so long before we get Mammals appearing, and the higher Mammals and the Primates — the family to which man belongs — only came in right near the top of the series. Well, that looks like a pretty good proof of Evolution, doesn't it?" he appealed to his audience of three.

"Yes, to us it does; go ahead."

"Now for a few years past Palaeontologists have been looking into the detailed histories of those animals, getting far more specimens of each kind, and working them out far more carefully — and some jolly queer things have come to light! The first thing I'd now ask is, *are* creatures always adapted to their environment? *Does* Evolution depend on adap-tation to environment? I'd hesitate now to answer yes. Take the Ammonites, for instance; rolled shells, like cart-wheels, you know, some of them: some like the nicest little flat snails all over pretty patterns: some of them smooth and very demure; there are heaps and heaps of genera of them. They were a tremendously important family. Now, when their histories are looked into in detail, what do we find? In the days when they first began to appear they were not rolled up tight in the way that is most characteristic of them. They were more or less straight, curved back on themselves but very little coiled. As they evolved they coiled themselves up tighter and got bigger and bigger and covered themselves with knobs and fancy ornamentations. So one may say that a highly-evolved Ammonite is a very fancy article, highly decorative segments tightly coiled up. But then they don't all do that at once, or in one line of descent. That's the queer thing. There are so many different stocks of them which started to do that same kind of thing in slightly different but similar ways, and they took different times about it, so that side by side, in the same rocks, you may find some families of Ammonites which have not gone very far along their evolution, and other families of Ammonites which are just about to die out at the end of it. All the different series seem to follow the same general laws and die out automatically. Evolution is not just the modification of a stock in the direct line of descent, for lots of different stocks of the same family may all be evolving on their own lines — taking their own time over it and — and this is *very important, all following a definite course of procedure more or less regardless of their environment.* That is very important, that is an idea of the first magnitude, and one due entirely to recent Palaeontological work. Most ordinary people have now got it into their heads that creatures have adapted themselves to fit their environments, but the fossils are beginning to throw a good deal of light on a new side to it and it looks very much more likely that on the whole things evolved in harmony with certain laws which *may* have nothing whatever to do with environment in lots of cases. It appears almost as though *any* actual race were bound to follow a certain course, and when the time came, die out — die out of itself and not be crushed out by superior competitors."

"That does not seem to me so very strange," murmured Rose Amber.

"No, I suppose it doesn't, because you have not been trained as a biologist," Kenneth answered. "But it is a recent idea in Palaeontology, at least, it is recent as a scientific conception with any backing, as a thing one can *demonstrate*. We always used to assume, for instance, that the great big reptiles, Ichthyosauruses, for instance, died out by competition with superior land animals — but now we know they didn't; they died out apparently of themselves. Well, there are heaps and heaps of queer cases like that coming to light in the detailed work people are now doing on fossils. A few, very few of the bigger Palaeontologists, like Osborne and Smith Woodward,[53] are beginning to be extremely puzzled and trying to account for it, but it is not easy to go so far from the beaten track. Things don't seem clear, and to my mind that is because we have got our whole

144

human focus wrong. You know yourself, from experience with a spy-glass, for instance, if you focus on a ship near shore you cannot turn the glass right away to sweep the horizon; the focus is blurred. Well, that flashed across me years ago. As a poignant realization I mean. And what I have been trying to work out ever since is the point of view of the new focus we need to enable us to understand these things."

Kenneth leaned forward, his face eager, his immediate perceptions carried away by the intensity of his interest of his subject. He searched the eyes of his hearers, and in them glimpsed real understanding only in Rose Amber's.

"Hitherto we have always looked upon individual animals, individual men, as being in a way ultimate units, as having a direct line of ancestors, also as representing final self-contained units. So that each cat, each horse, each human being we saw as independent, individual units living in an inorganic world. Now *that* is where we are wrong: I don't believe they are! I believe we are only what I might call intermediate units. I believe they and we are all part of a larger unit, which, hitherto, we have been able to ignore, but which, as our scientific knowledge of this world gets more complete, we will *have* to take into scientific consideration. At present, you know, we can only dimly begin to perceive it. And no wonder, because we are actually part of it. Yet we have an analogy of an inferior sort at hand. You know, all of you, everybody knows that our bodies are made of cells, and that each of these cells has its own peculiar individual life. The cells then only originate in the direct lines of descent from other living cells. There are specialized cells in each type of the tissues, the blood, or whichever part we may consider, but ultimately, if we go back to the beginning in individual men or animals, all these cells are in the direct line of descent from a single pair of cells and are modi-fied in adaptation to their special position in the complex we call the body. Life in each individual cell of our complex selves begins in a certain way, adapts itself to its environment, follows its evolution — for we may justly call it that, though it is generally called growth — and is a definite unit. But it is more than a mere unit of its own type; it is a part of a more complex unit of a higher type. You know how much more we are than a mere aggregation of cell units! The cells composing our brains — each lives its life along prescribed lines, and they are, one and all, individual units — and what does our brain mean to *us*? Ah, something greater, more glorious than any brain-cell could ever conceive, a something which is more than the total of all the brain-cells, a super-something — a *consciousness*, which we each call Ourselves. But we, individually, each unit self of us is not in the least conscious of all these myriad smaller unit lives which make up ourselves."

Rose Amber, beginning to grasp the conclusion to which he was approaching, leaned eagerly towards him, her face brilliant with a joyous anticipation. "Yes, yes," she breathed, enthralled.

"But now wait a minute," said Kenneth: "There is a strange and wonderful thing in Nature I want to remind you about; the queer, one might almost say abnormal, development of the unit cells of insects. What happens to them? A caterpillar, with all its cells living their normal little lives, finally eats as many cabbage leaves as stuff it satisfactorily — it then decides, or something within it decides for it, to begin to prepare for its metamorphosis. It spins itself a shroud, it lies dormant. *What becomes of the lives, or the evolution, whichever you like to call it, of the individual cells composing it?* It is suddenly jerked off the rails. You know all insects, not only caterpillars, fundamentally rearrange all their organs during metamorphosis. It is almost as though they liquefied themselves and re-crystallized out in a different way.

"Look at the tadpole's tail. When a little tadpole has grown its legs and is beginning to think about hopping on to the bank, what happens to the private lives of the individual cells in its tail? Those cells, which have hitherto followed their routine, being born from other cells and passing through their life-histories normally, are now disregarded, re-absorbed, their evolution cut athwart. Now, of course, that is only an analogy, and analogies are rotten if you lay any stress on them, but I am just giving you a glimmering of my idea, and what I think the whole process of the big evolution of the genera and species peopling the world may roughly be compared with.

"We could not see it, we could not get an idea of it so long as we dealt only with the present time and the creatures living round us. The whole process is too immensely vast, and our minds were focused on the individuals living around us, which we grouped into species and genera. But now, through Palaeontology, we are getting a longer view, focusing back on stages of the life of the well-nigh interminable ages past, in which individual species and genera melt into each other and fuse. We begin at last to see the queer way in which the evolution of the different genera of animals, following its normal course, is jerked off the rails by some apparently inherent force, something which has apparently nothing to do with the physical environment of the creature it affects. Now in that *I* see a larger growth. I see the units of plants and animals, including human beings of to-day, all as minor units of a greater unit, as much vaster than we are, as you and I are vaster than the single cells which form our bodies. As this greater unit grows, it depends on the normal, ordinary development of the individual lives of the animals in this world, which Darwin called Evolution, but which I call Growth of a Cosmic Unit. When a fresh stage in its growth comes then the evolution of these minor units is cut athwart.

"Evolution, as Darwin saw it, remains a true conception, but it is not an *ultimate* truth, and so when we seek to interpret all the processes of Evolution without taking into account these larger effects of the growth of the greater unit, we fail. Scientists will always find innumerable things inexplicable until they take that into consideration. Of course, we will never comprehend this larger life which is composed of the fusion of the units on our own scale of magnitude all round us. But we may at least have the realization that it does exist. We appear to ourselves to be too isolated to be part of a greater unit-body — but we must not forget that the electrons in an atom are proportionately as far away from each other as planets.

"Our fused consciousnesses must produce a super-consciousness.[54] But of what we might call our Greater Unit's Super-consciousness, we can have only the very faintest glimmerings.

"We know in our own case that the individual activities of our own brain-cells give rise to what we call consciousness. But our own brain-cells — what have they of realization of what we mean by love, or music, or the beauty of a sunset?

"In those strange waves of feeling or passion that quiver through crowds, that surge through nations, I see some of the vibrations of this Super-consciousness of our Greater Unit. And as we evolve, as we link up the thought of the peoples more closely, by telegraph wires and telephones and the daily newspaper, so that our thought synchronizes, so will this become more definite.

"The Greater Unit which composes this world, of which we are but intermediate units, is a great series down to, and perhaps below, the individual electrons which compose the unit atom — this Greater Unit is to us what we are, but something more than we are, to our individual body-cells. The activities of this Greater Unit are so much beyond our comprehension — more, for the whole series is on a higher grade of complexity — as are *our* thoughts and loves to the cells of our bodies — *we* have consciousness, and our united consciousnesses compose a Super-consciousness. Some people have faintly sensed it and called it God — but it is not that, this next great unit in Creation's series. God, I take it, in everyone's mind, is something more infinite, vaguer. This Greater Unit is a material thing, great, complex beyond our comprehension, but still in the series of complexities known to us."

"Glorious! You have made it real!" said Rose Amber. "But — but isn't it — in some of the older religions, isn't the idea foreshadowed?"

"Oh, yes, in a way," Kenneth immediately agreed, "but very vaguely; more vaguely than Darwin's work was foreshadowed by Lucretius. It is only when an idea is put clearly, when there are anything like *scientific* facts with proofs, capable of some sort of demonstration behind it, that

147

the idea becomes vital, and can take hold of modern humanity. The mystic, particularly the Eastern mystic, has always spoken of himself as part of the immense whole of God. My idea is something different from that mysticism, something more precise, something at least partially scientific.

"This larger unit, which we creatures on this particular little planet compose, cannot be compared to the 'infinite godhead' of the religions; it is itself but a minute fragment of the universe. Possibly the idea of a special World-God may be related to it — but that idea was very anthropomorphic and unfounded. To realize how small in one way is my conception, look at the wonderful conceptions of modern Astronomy. We know that our solar system, far from being central, far from being even important, is but a minute speck of dust in the wheeling tail of a super-nebula.[55] There is a fascinating new idea recently developed by astronomers that the Milky Way, with its thickly-scattered solar systems, may be the wheeling tail of some system of systems arranged not unlike a nebula's fragments, and that all this universe of solar systems has a definite limit and is again a very speck in a greater series of universes. You see how small is my conception of the Greater Unit of life on this world, after all, immense as it appears when we look at it from the point of view of our own individual lives, immense as is the change of outlook in the whole scientific and philosophic world which its realization would bring about."

Kenneth sprang up, impelled by the force of his idea to action, but tethered by his hearers, he only walked to and fro across the room.

"Science, with its little spy-glass fixed upon the miracle of our individual bodies, had its focus re-adjusted by Darwin. He opened to us the vista of a whole evolution, with its series of organic form, following organic form, each adjusting itself to its environment, surviving catastrophe only when it had adapted itself wisely, handing on the torch of life to its descendants, which were like it. Before that, man saw in himself the special creation God placed in the centre of the world, the beasts around him subservient. With the spy-glass adjusted by Darwin, and re-adjusted in minute particulars by a myriad other workers since his time, we have scanned a new horizon. But *all* the processes of evolution, with apparently strange gaps and strange inherent behaviours in long series of life-forms, we have not understood. And now it is time to change the focus of the world's gaze on the things around it. I, or my child or my grandchild, or one of my spiritual children, will once more turn the wheel that guides the focus of mankind. Then we will see the facts of all our sordid life, not as a conglomeration of scattered fragments, but as parts of a greater unit whose life we form, who lives and grows, and whose stages of growth and development come cutting athwart the individual life or

evolution of any one of *us*, however much our evolution may have hitherto followed ordinary laws." He stopped, baulked by the immensity of
his conception in relation to his verbal incapacity.

"But I can't explain it all to you in detail. If I were to talk for a year
I could not give you the ramifications of this idea. It obsesses me. It
entrances me. It ultimately satisfies me to be a part of a definite, to some
degree comprehensible, unit, instead of being an isolated speck lost in the
immensity of the Sidereal System.[56] It profoundly satisfies me to know
that my consciousness, definite, comprehensive, though limited, ultimately subserves a greater super-consciousness; my life, fleeting and
trivial, definitely fits into a greater life, as the cells in my body are doing
within me in my own life. These cells are replaced as they individually
die, but through them I retain the very memory of incidents in my life
long past. So may I as a unit vessel, the brain-cell perhaps, of this larger
and more complex super-consciousness hand on remembered beauty.

"Yet this conception is not illimitably vast; it is a comprehensible unit.
Thank God for that — the Infinite crushes me. On paper I can even indicate its commensurability — see." He snatched a paper from his book
and scribbled diagrams.

"Of course, you know that a chemical atom is in itself a planetary
system of still more minute units, but, numerous as they are, they too are
not innumerable; then comes the atom congregating in vast numbers
together, but the numbers are not innumerable; they are only to be
numbered in millions squared to form the single cell. Then come the unit
cells in my own body, in vast numbers but still not innumerable; they,
too, are numbered in terms of millions squared. Then come we and the
animals, still not unlimited, a concrete reality of the same order as the
others in the series. It makes me exult!" He glowed, his mind, leaping
up the ladder of commensurate complexities stood exulting in the
sunlight of truth overpeering mountains.

"Humph, I don't like the idea," said Granville, down on the earth. "I
prefer the old-fashioned idea that I am of some importance as an individual."

"So you are," conceded Kenneth.

"Well, you considerably reduce my self-esteem," Granville professed
chagrin.

"That may be good for you," suggested Rose Amber, mischievously,
laughter bubbling to the surface over the clear deeps she saw revealed in
her heart's yearnings. This, this met the long dreams of her girlhood.

"*I'm* content to be an intermediate unit in something greater, but I
know this is what people will *hate*," said Kenneth.

"Tell me," Mrs. Harvey interposed, "even if the world accepted and
realized this wonderful conception, how would it affect social life?"

"Didn't Darwin's idea of evolution affect social life? Didn't he over-turn the old theological ideas of a specially-created Heaven and Hell, and with it man's intolerance? Didn't he free truth from the shackles of a dogmatic theology?"

"Yes, but this — ."

"Well, this will fight with the present lot of ideas that are hampering the world — hindering, diseasing, for all we know, the life of the Greater Unit. Look at the diseased city dwellers among us, down-trodden, stunted creatures filling the slums in every country in the world. How did they get there? Largely by the supposition that we are separate indi-viduals, and that the 'fittest' must survive, that the weakest must go to the wall, that a strong, successful, rich man is good to carry on the human race, that the rich material success of the few is all that matters. It is *not* all that matters." He spoke fiercely. "Every one of these miserable, dwarfed specimens of humanity are diseased tissues, fleshy sores in the body of the Greater Unit. Do you think if people realized that such things are not isolated strains doomed to individual extinction, but are diseases in the greater, sublimer creature of which we form the tiny parts, they could allow it to go on? No! Consider your own body. If you have an ulcer in your tissues, can you do useful work? Is your consciousness able to deal with noble and beautiful things? Then how should this Greater Unit, with festering sores in its side, be able to do the greater, super-work that is its part in the universe?

"Yet it is *our* responsibility, ours! We make its tissues. Consider the analogy of our own bodies again. If you get a bit of dirt in your finger and it festers, what is happening? One set of the little unit cells that compose your body, the phagocytes,[57] are perturbed; they come along in crowds to cleanse and sweeten and set the tissues right again. Though they have no realization of *us* they act as if they knew that if a part is diseased the whole unit suffers. So they destroy the diseased fragments — eat 'em up and give the sound tissues a chance. Are we, as thoughtful men and women, to be put to shame by the unconscious phagocytes of a man's body and fail to do our part for the life of the Super-conscious-ness? Oh, the effects of this new conception should reach from the geological laboratory to the farthest corner of our social system. I could talk for hours; I could talk for days and not exhaust the side-lights on the subject. Whether I or my son or my son's son will succeed in satisfying the scientific world that the thing is demonstrable, I don't much care. Erasmus Darwin[58] had a grandchild, Charles, who impressed his view upon the world. If I fail myself, my children or my spiritual children will succeed."

"That last bit sounds more like a prophet than a scientist," said Harry, uncomfortably impressed by the fire of the fervid conviction before him.

"What matter? Truth is one. The two methods of reaching it meet at the top."

"Darwin didn't go in for this sort of social application of his discoveries." Harry was impelled by his discomfort to persist.

"Let me be trite — History never repeats herself; she gyrates upwards."

"People won't believe they are only *part* of anything. Where is your dignity; where is your equality of man?" Granville continued.

"Of course they'll hate it. That's the thing my idea will have to fight. The frightfully rooted prejudice Darwin had to fight was dogmatic theology. The frightfully rooted idea I'll have to fight is every man's belief in himself as an *ultimate* unit. Religions, theories have always treated men as separate definite individuals. Man won't give that idea up without a bitter fight."

"Didn't St. James say: 'Ye are members one of another?'"[59] asked Mrs. Harvey.

Her sweet voice brought the group back to the soft echoing shadows of the dim arches of the cathedral, soothing them and easing their eyesight after the piercing glare out in the celestial vastness to which Kenneth Harvey had tempted them flutteringly to attempt to soar.

Kenneth accepted her suggestion eagerly: "Yes, of course, Christ knew this truth, and some of the Apostles dimly perceived it. But that does not put it clearly enough for the modern man. Anyone can accept without uneasiness a vague general statement like that! All through the past people have given lip service to such big ideas in that kind of non-understanding way. It didn't tie them any more than being 'members' of a congregation. But now, if the idea is clearly stated, with at least a partial *demonstration*, with scientific facts behind it, it will *grip*. There'll be ructions once people realize it."

"What will the scientists say?"

"Ah! How many of them have vision? That I have to find out."

"Mighty few of them will be prepared for that kind of vision!"

Granville was sore and uneasy. Though he had never expressed it, he had been hurt and somewhat offended that his munificent gift of the professorship had been put on one side by Kenneth, and he was now wounded and nervous of the possibility of being wounded further where he was most vulnerable — in his belief in a personal immortality. For, although Harvey's scheme offered a personal immortality as a minor unit in something greater than he had ever imagined, he had always man's proud feeling that he was "little lower than the angels"[60] as a finite person and important unit.

Rose Amber, musing, said: "The war has made people think so much of these things — so many homes are desolated — ."

Kenneth eagerly broke in: "Yes, and that is an aspect of it so important, so illuminating. Don't you see that the war, instead of being as so many think, the crash and break-up of our civilization and good old order, is really the re-arrangement of the units of life at the beginning of a higher phase — a new and better order. That fits in with what I said just now of the cell units in a caterpillar that is at the last stage before it becomes a butterfly — all its cells re-arranging, its old order breaking down — apparent destruction re-arranging the myriad cells in its body. Looked at from their point of view, war — calamity — but from the insect's point of view, the greater unit they compose, the beginning of a glorious phase when the cells re-arranged form part not of a crawling ground worm, but a winged, beautiful creature.

"That is how the war is to me; something, with all its agony to individuals, which is not a calamity or breakdown, not destruction and horror, but something which is a metamorphosis for the human race, something in which the loss and anguish of the broken individual lives is made up for a myriad times over by the greater glory of the future to which they are all contributory units."

Granville grudgingly admitted: "The first constructive or cheering word I have heard about the war!"

Kenneth replied: "If there were not something of that sort behind it all life would be a nightmare horror, but there is something like this behind it, and at last man's power to probe all the different universes within and around him is beginning to show a faint glimmering of light — ." Turning to Harry Granville, he said, "You see now, Harry, why I cannot possibly settle down to an ordinary routine professorship. I have something bigger to teach."

CHAPTER
25

A CHANCE REVELATION

ROSE was on a three days' visit to Mrs. Harvey. It was quarter day, and Harry Granville made a point of being personally available for his tenants in the country then if possible, but Rose Amber's bedroom had been repapered and painted, and he wanted to make sure that everything was right before she returned: he could not trust his adored one's comfort to servants and their chance muddles. So for the first time since they were married Rose Amber was separated from her husband.

"It is a great event, this brief return to the narrow white bed of my girlhood." She laughed and sang about the house, pretending there had been no interval, taking up the arrangement of flowers, following Mrs. Harvey from room to room.

"Butlers bother me," she said. "It's so delicious to be in a house without the risk of meeting one. Of course, I just love our own big home, but I would like to have a little one, too. I think I must make Harry buy a cottage that isn't big enough to hold a butler, where we can go away whenever we feel inclined."

Kenneth was out all day, either working at the University or one of the museums, so the two women had long hours to themselves.

Mrs. Harvey had not lost the hope that Kenneth would return to the more normal ways of ambition. "Perhaps if you talked to him?" she said tentatively to Rose Amber, who shook her head.

"I am not sure that I want him to be like other people."

In the evenings, after dinner, they talked about his work, and Kenneth read aloud to them a short paper he was writing. Already it had been re-written many times and the reading aloud suggested further revision.

"The insanity of editors paying by the word," he grumbled. "It's child play to write fifty thousand words on the subject one knows, but to condense it into five thousand is the very devil."

"I don't think editors will pay you anything for it at all," said Rose Amber mischievously.

"They won't," he looked at her whimsically. "Scientific writing never does get paid for — except now and then when a man brings out a successful book. All the real work comes out in the scientific journals, and the writers don't get a red cent from them."

Since the time of Lilian's betrothal a brotherly kiss on the cheek had always passed between Rose Amber and Kenneth, and in the familiar room the old custom was revived when she said, "Good night." She barely noticed the kiss; it merely accentuated the absence of the passionate embraces of her husband. "There are as many kinds of kisses," she thought, "as there are people." She went to sleep trying to invent a name for the tepid, neutral family kiss on the cheek that was little more than a handshake.

The second day of her brief visit was just like the first, but was perhaps more poignant; to-morrow she was leaving them. The suggestion to go to a theatre was negatived. "Oh, no," she said; "we have not nearly done talking."

When she said "Good night" she put her face up placidly for Kenneth's kiss and he stooped and gave her one swift touch right upon the lips. It seemed to him little different from the previous evening, and Rose Amber turned to go out of the door, outwardly as calm, as unstirred as she had ever been by this friendly symbol. But within, her heart was quivering with surprise, with amazement at herself. As his lips had placed their light touch upon hers, she felt as though a sword, swift as lightning, had passed through her whole body, leaving it unharmed but strangely vitalized and joyous. The after-sensation was an actual vibration of the nerves unknown to her before, physically delicious, in spite of the outraged and amazed protest of her mind.

As she lay in bed, sleepless, bewildered, ashamed, she tried to discover some excuse, some explanation for the mysterious and unexpected reaction. It was two days since her husband had embraced and kissed her; but never had his kisses roused such a physiological tumult within her. Could it be that their absence had left her hungering for his kisses unconsciously, hungering so much that the mere touch of a man's lips, himself undisturbed, unconscious, set her quivering with response? Response! How often had Harry been aware of a certain lack of that within her, deep, tender and true though her love had been? Could it be — the thought delighted her — that at last she was growing up? Harry had often told her that young girls did not know the full joy of a kiss, the richness of a husband's embraces. Perhaps his absence had worked like a charm upon her and when she returned to him she would know the complement of that rapture which in him had puzzled her, and left her partly envious. The thought soothed her. Kenneth was forgotten, and his kiss meant nothing. It had been but the little flag fluttering its announcement of the thundering express to follow; but the vane of the weather cock whirled by the rushing of a great wind. To Rose Amber her body had ever been the instrument of her mind, her possession, not herself. Contact with Lilian and Kenneth had instructed her too well in the facts of zoological development for her mind to goad an undeveloped instrument. Yet she longed for the fullness of her powers, had ached like any child "to be grown up." It seemed to her that the time was coming, that those few days in town were epochal, that she had acquired new powers. Did human hearts and human possibilities also ripen slowly and suddenly become potential? They must!

This little placid interval had been a turning point, more solemn than a birthday to a child of seven years old; it seemed to her that she was entering a new phase of her life; she was grown up. She longed for Harry, for the anticipated warm rapture of her home-coming.

CHAPTER
26

FIRE AND ICE

A S the train drew up to the platform Rose Amber looked eagerly from the window, waiting with throbbing heart for the first glimpse of Harry. There he was! The rough home-spuns setting off his fine shoulders and lean strength. He was looking in the wrong carriage, his eyes eager but roving. Rose Amber, standing beside the door, half smiled, watching for the change in his expression when he saw her. There! A light danced in his eyes and he flung open the carriage door, his hand gripped her elbow, and the happy excitement of meeting him again wiped out all memory of the thought that she was curious to note the extent of her own rapture.

They were in the motor together, his arm was round her, his kisses hot upon her cheek, her neck, her lips, her shoulders before she thought of herself at all. Then she came to the conclusion that she had been a goose and that nothing in the whole world could be more delightful than being welcomed home by Harry.

A few moments later she was alone in her bedroom, preparing for tea. She sat down in an armchair to think about her feelings, but a maid came in to take off her shoes and to discuss the new wallpaper in the bedroom, so that the excitement of an arrival was maintained. She ran downstairs eagerly for tea and Harry's delight in her presence worked that wonderful magic, the elimination of everything but the present moment.

The intimate tenderness of the night was upon her, a night penetrated by the mysterious sweetness of the faint echoes of ferine loves which slipped into the room with the moonlight. Since she had been a bride, never had she waited for her lover with such palpitating eagerness. She felt she longed that to-night her marriage should be crowned with the uttermost fullness of mutual joy.

Harry's love, like a warm flame, surrounded her. But in spite of her eager willingness, it did not penetrate nor stir her uncontrollable pulses. She did not know the key which could unlock them, nor the art or nature of their expression. The sweetness which she felt towards Harry was mental, spiritual, maternal. She asked herself — is that not enough? What need to repeat those once experienced throbs of bodily pulse? She had hoped in vain for their intoxicating co-operation; now she reproached herself for that hope.

"I am absurd to expect so much," she thought: "I, of all people, too, who know so well how little most get out of life."

Echoes within her consoled her with the old mis-statements that woman's part in love is and should be passive, that the rapture of the body known to man is not for her. These sophistries silenced the deeper instinct within her, and she consoled herself with them; for like so many modern women, she did not really know that they were mis-statements and threadbare.

She woke in the morning and opened her eyes on the rich beauty of her bedroom, happy to be home again, and turned with warm tenderness to her husband for his morning kiss. How enveloped she seemed in love! Surrounded by waves and depths of it and all the manifold gifts of love that a man, strong and rich, both in worldly and bodily possessions, can give to the adored woman. Her heart sang with gladness for all that was hers, and though she felt that she was not herself giving what seemed its fair counterpart, she joyed that by accepting she could give so much joy. She resolutely wiped out of her memory the thought of that one swift inkling of the something more she might have had.

CHAPTER

27

THE HERO'S PASSION

KENNETH Harvey's short crystallized statement of the great idea which permeated his mind was at last finished. His résumé presented a concrete idea, incomplete but still an idea sufficiently clothed for him to want the opinion of some brother scientist. He intended to present his paper to the Royal Society, but as he was not yet an F.R.S., it would require a sponsor from among the Fellows.

"Whom shall I ask to take this responsibility?" he asked himself. The professor who had presented his recent series of monographs was, of course, the right person, but Kenneth wondered very much whether he would agree to having his name associated with this new and much more vital piece of work. "I know very well that to most academic naturalists I shall appear to be off my head. Will he dare!"

So, without suggesting that he wanted the paper ultimately to be placed before the Royal Society, Kenneth took it round to the one important man whom he thought might be sympathetic, Professor Xaner, F.R.S., and asked him as a personal favour to read it and give him an entirely frank opinion of it.

Professor Xaner was cordial. "Ah!" he said, "I have been reading your recent papers with much interest; you are making a fine name for yourself. I shall look forward to reading this," he tapped the paper which had just been placed in his hands. "Yes, drop round to my club next Friday; I will have read it by then, as it isn't very long, and we can talk it over quietly."

Friday came. Kenneth met the professor in the vestibule of the club. He felt at once a change in his attitude. He was kinder, almost more cordial, but the young man caught him looking over his gold-rimmed glasses curiously, as though he was saying to himself, "Dear! Dear! What am I to make of this new specimen of youthful folly?"

Over their coffee in the smoking-room, after dinner, Professor Xaner obviously postponed coming to grips with his subject, but elaborated unexpected theories about music-hall artistes, and a surprising interest in the pantomime.

Kenneth had to break through a delightful tangle of talk to bring the professor directly to the subject which filled his mind. "What do you think of it?"

Professor Xaner hesitated, at a loss for the right word.

"Humph! Charming, charming," he said at last; "quite oriental, a modernization of Mythology." Kenneth flushed:

"This was the man who had himself elaborated ideas on fundamental subjects, played with them in an adventurous spirit," he thought. "How narrow they all are!"

"Doesn't it seem to you to explain a lot of apparently inexplicable and disconnected facts?" asked Kenneth steadily.

"Humph, yes, perhaps," allowed the professor.

"Well, isn't that the supreme test of a theory, that it suddenly relates apparently disconnected puzzles, and all sorts of scattered, loose ideas slip into their place in ordered whole? Now this theory of mine does this — ."

"If one could overlook the fundamental absurdity it might be a useful theory."

"Why is it any more fundamentally absurd than the structure of our own bodies?" asked Kenneth.

"Perhaps it isn't; nothing could be more absurd than that."

"Then why shouldn't it be true?" The young man was eager, swift in his replies.

"Well, well," temporized Professor Xaner, indulgently, "things are not likely to be worked out like that you know."

"See here, isn't it worth considering as an hypothesis?" insisted Kenneth. "Many and many is the mistaken hypothesis that has served Science by leading men on to discover facts in its support, or to disprove it."

"Well, *your* theory is very different," said Xaner; "there doesn't seem to me any way, any scientific way of proving or disproving it."

"With all the unexpected vistas of Palaeontology? Why, they almost prove is already," claimed the enthusiast.

"Of course, unexpected things *are* turning up, but I don't anticipate anything like a scientific proof will ever result."

"Could Darwin's grandfather ever have anticipated the modern work on evolution, or did Mme. Curie guess only a few years ago that now we would be at work on the age of the earth, using as data some of the results of her discovery of radium? Is there anything more unexpected than the way one set of scientific deductions clears up difficulties apparently remote?"

"Well, well, I like young enthusiasm." Professor Xaner was indulgent.

Kenneth was disappointed but not dismayed by his attitude. "See here," he said suddenly, "would you present that paper to the Royal Society?"

"I should think *not!*" Professor Xaner, F.R.S., sat up in his chair electrified. "You surely have not thought of it?"

"I did, quite seriously." Kenneth's calm was an outrage. The urbane professor suddenly turned acid.

"Well, I advise you not to, young man. That is if you don't want to ruin your reputation as a serious scientist."

"I suppose there were a lot of people who said that sort of thing to young Darwin?" enquired Kenneth. "And I believe even after his theories were fairly well established the chair-throwing was not confined to clergymen. There is a record of a stirring meeting at the British Association of Science."

"Tch, tch, the things are not comparable."

"Aren't they?" asked Kenneth. "To me they jolly well seem to be. Copernicus, Darwin, and whoever it is that impresses this new conception to the world, form a series, a series of great focus-changers."

The young man rose in the fire of his wrath. Professor Xaner sighed, bewildered and sorry, thinking to himself, "I have met chaps before who go mad just on one point and are still able to do brilliant work on sound lines in other directions"; aloud he said, "Lay it aside for a bit and think about it and get on with your solid work, your Palaeontology. Describe your new fossils — *they* are *real.*"

"I have been thinking about it for over five years," retorted Kenneth.

"Pooh, that's nothing," said the elder man: "double that, and come to me again, and if you keep on doing work as brilliant as your recent memoirs, you will be an F.R.S. yourself by the time and you can spring it on the Society without needing to get a previous convert." He chuckled and thawed at the idea.

"If you refuse to back my work I need not expect anyone else who has a position in the scientific world to be more adventurous."

"Perhaps."

"I suppose all pioneers have to break down indifference and opposition?"

"This isn't pioneering, it's dreaming."

"I'm really disappointed."

"Forget it."

"You make me feel up against a stone wall, not knowing which way to turn."

"Let the world wait another five years for your theory."

"Impossible."

"Conscience would not let you rest?"

"Yes."

"A bad case."

"I'll publish it independently as a pamphlet."

"Rot — privately printed and therefore scorned."

"I'll try to get some ordinary publisher to launch it enlarged a little as a book."

"Ruin your reputation."

"Shall I have it translated and brought out in some more adventurous foreign journal?"

"No."

"Try my luck with one of the half-crown magazines?"

"For mercy's sake — no. Chuck it into a bottom drawer and forget it."

"I must talk it over."

"Do."

He thought "With whom?"

"There is no one but Rose Amber who at all understands. Talk I must. I'll go north by the first train next morning."

An hour before tea-time next day, unannounced by previous letter or telegram, Kenneth called on Lady Granville. The butler put him into the drawing-room with an invitation to sit down while he had the garden searched for her ladyship.

Deeply ensconced in the most comfortable chair, wedged by cushions, warming himself in the sunshine from the window, surrounded by a litter of novels, lay the exuberant form of Alastair O'Donnahaw. Seeing Kenneth he heaved clumsily and ineffectively as a polite recognition, and then laughed his great cheerful bellow to indicate and excuse the fact that he had no intention of rising.

Rose Amber, in garden gloves, came flying in.

"Why, Kenneth, how lovely." She welcomed him eagerly. "But is anything wrong? You look so frowny."

"Pulled up," he said. "I want some intelligent advice."

O'Donnahaw interposed: "Introduce me to him!"

The introduction effected, tea and light chatter kept the impatient Kenneth on tenterhooks until he pointedly asked once more for her advice.

Rose made a grimace to him. "Let's go and get it from the sea." She drew on her garden gloves and took him through the avenue to the top of the cliffs, where the fine, short grass, mingled with Rest Harrow, growing on a film of wind-blown sand, crept to the black brows of basalt that overhung the sea.

They sat down in the sunshine within a yard of the edge and Kenneth produced his compromising document. "It will lose me my scientific reputation if I publish it, they say," he announced in high scorn. He dashed his hand into the offending pages.

Rose Amber's look swam through space to his secret wishes. "Then publish it," she said briefly.

"Fine! I like that." He turned a glowing face towards her. "And I would to-morrow, only if the scientific johnnies chose, they could make such a tangled cobweb of disapproval round it that my idea would be mummified for ever and never reach the people whom I want to take joy in its liveness."

A seagull sailed up to the top of the cliff, its bright wings a glint of ivory. It poised a moment like a wind-thrown fleck of foam and sank out of sight. So high were Rose Amber and Kenneth above the sea that the waves beating beneath them sounded like a droning bee.

"Can anything really cut athwart the course of a new truth?" asked Rose Amber, after a long pause.

"No, but they can hinder it for centuries. Look how the priests of the Church hindered Astronomy; and the priests of our day are scientists, medical officers and University professors. In their hands lies immense power when they choose to combine."

"Bother," said Rose Amber, putting the problem aside till inspiration should come. "Feel how warm the grass is. Weren't you jolly glad to have an excuse to get here instead of staying in London?" She twisted the fine grass blades round her fingers. "Let's make the wind decide," she said suddenly; "the wind and the sea. You have got a copy of it, I suppose," she asked, playfully cynical.

"Oh, yes, rather!"

"Well, then, let's throw it up. If the wind carried it out to sea, then you will have to keep it hidden away for another long period. If its pages are left here, on the grass at the top, facing the sun, then it has to be published at once in the light of day."

"Right oh," said Kenneth, and threw the precious packet up into the still air, letting it fall as it would. A sudden mischievous gust of wind came and was about to swirl it away. Kenneth could not bear it. As often happens, through pretending to trust to chance he discovered that solution of the puzzle he really desired.

He made a grab, and his arm shot out behind Rose Amber, capturing the sheets just as they were about to follow the seagull. And at that moment when his arm was almost round her waist, for the papers had blown past her, Harry Granville came within sight of them. From where he stood, a little way behind them, the dark arm was silhouetted across Rose Amber's white back.

That it was shortly withdrawn and that in the hand were a lot of fluttering papers Granville did not observe, nor would it have had any significance for him. He saw only the dark, strong arm across the outline of the slim, white back.

Suddenly the blood sang in his ears, the veins in his forehead knotted like writhing snakes. The incredible seemed to take on reality before his eyes. He came swiftly toward them. Rose Amber, unaware of the volcanic fires behind her, turned happy eyes on him.

"Come and decide for us, darling," she said. "He would not trust the wind and the waves after all."

Harry, clenching his hands, said, "Do you know that it is nearly dinner-time?"

Kenneth had stood up, his right hand outstretched, but Harry only nodded.

"No, is it really?" Rose Amber asked. "Come along, you will be famished, Kenneth."

"Don't your duties keep you in town?" asked Granville, still controlling his voice.

"Usually they do, but I was in a fix and I wanted advice. A leading scientist had not been so appreciative of my work as I had hoped." He spoke stiffly.

"So you seek applause where you know you will find it." Harry Granville spoke with a venomous slowness which was foreign to him. It brought Rose Amber's eyes upon his face. Even she, utterly innocent, could no longer ignore the torrents of unspoken rage that streamed from her husband. She looked at Kenneth and saw by his face that he, too, was engulfed in the storm — but on the defensive, not knowing the quarter whence would come the attack. Suddenly something deep within the heart of Rose Amber leapt centuries back into the past. She was a savage woman rejoicing that two males should fight for her, and, at the same time, the real modern woman was outraged and horrified by her husband's unreasoning suspicion.

The men were silent, and the time seemed to have rushed backwards. She could hear the whirring of its run-down wheels in her ears; then mercifully it stopped. It seemed as though she had been whirled back through the centuries while the men were frozen beside her. She passed through every stage to savagery and was thankful that she was left still in human shape. She felt the whole gamut of primitive passions, of hate and scorn for Harry, of joy that there should be someone there to fight him. Then suddenly the monstrous bubble burst and she came out into the present and found herself once more a sweet virtuous young wife sitting in the sunshine on the cliff she knew so well. She shook herself, thinking it had all been a momentary nightmare, but as she looked at the men she could still see their souls baring their teeth at each other. Now she was safely in the present again, a modern, well-bred woman in whose presence scenes did not happen. She suddenly laughed, a rippling gurgle of laughter, real and most uncontrollable. It was the right note; it dispelled the electric anger in the air and the men fell back a pace and turned to follow her as she sprang up. She took an arm of each, half-running like a little girl.

"Food," she cried. "After all that awful journey up from town poor brother Kenneth needs his food badly."

And Harry cursed himself for a fool, and set the whole of his strength to dispelling all the horror which had yawned before him. Rose Amber prattlingly told him how the precious paper had nearly blown away and how Kenneth at the last second had saved it. Instinctively she spoke of this, though she had no knowledge of the real intensity of its significance to Harry.

Kenneth insisted on taking the night train to town. When he left both Rose Amber and Harry went down the steps to help to pack him into the motor. The two returned slowly to the drawing-room together, and Rose Amber sank into a sofa. Harry shut the door and came swiftly toward her, he fell on his knees beside her and took her in his arms. "My darling, my darling, I adore you, say you love me!"

"There is a teeny, weeny spot in my hard heart that *thinks* — ," her playful voice was soft with love and forgiveness.

Her words were drowned in his kisses.

CHAPTER

28

JUSTICE

THE next morning Harry, once more moody, ashamed of himself, haunted by flecks of unspoken fear, went for a solitary walk to face his obsession and to have it out. He came to the edge of the cliff and found the grass still showing two patches of brighter green where the leaves had been pressed over by the weight of the two who had sat there yesterday. He stood facing them, on the spot where he had stood yesterday, intent on the imagined figures opposite him. Cursing himself for a fool and a low-minded scoundrel, yet he was soothed to notice that the two green patches where they had sat were an irreproachable distance apart. He stood intent, facing the vivid memories, his back to the sea, his feet firmly planted six inches from the edge. His smooth hands, folded over each other, trembled slightly. He relived every gesture, every word of their brief encounter of the previous afternoon, and followed to their burrows every idea which had but popped across the trail of his mind in its heated and speedy journey yesterday.

Behind him the seagulls sailed up, wheeled and sank again into the murmur of the sea. His intent gaze detected now and then a slight movement in the grass blades, which were slowly righting themselves, drawn upward by the sunlight. They held his outward vision, but within his heart he was standing awed in the presence of the judgment seat — himself both the judge and the prisoner at the bar.

Memories of Vera flickered round him like fine thongs of a lash flaying him. In what had he failed her? Now the head of an imp of malicious and cruel suggestion dodged up and flung at him the threat that he might lose Rose Amber in the same way. But what was the way? Could a man more passionately adore than he adored Rose Amber in reality, and in his deluded youth had adored the phantasy, the dream of Vera? He saw in the clear light which penetrated him that an obsession of jealousy distorted his vision. He saw that he himself and not any "painter fellow" had in thought polluted the atmosphere around his adorable and heavenly Rose Amber.

"Confound that fellow, Kenneth Harvey," he thought with irrational fire. "The chap was decent, of course, but confound it that he should be able so to interest my darling."

His thoughts, at first cutting a clear course for themselves through the monster weeds of his imagination, soon lost their sharp edge. The machinery of his mind began to whirr, revolving without making progress. Again his eyes were riveted upon the two patches on the grass. What was he to do to hold utterly his precious monopoly in his darling's every breath? Nothing else would content him. His thoughts sank through the surface of words to the deep intensity of inexpressible feeling.

Suddenly a cheerful sound, a gurgling torrent of happy laughter like a reverberated, strengthened echo of Rose Amber's laugh of yesterday rang out. Alastair O'Donnahaw, R.A., walking to refresh himself after painting a titled neighbour of the Granville's, hailed Harry suddenly.

"Begorrah, is it preaching to all the snakes from Ireland ye are?" Granville, hearing the laugh and not taking in the sense of the words, startled by the sudden shattering of his dream-reconstruction, retreated before the invader, and took a step backwards.

He went over the edge of the cliff.

Silently, more swiftly than the seagulls, he descended toward the sea and crashed upon a boulder above the water level.

A circling islet of foam in a pool by the waving green seaweed was stained crimson by a trickle of blood. The waves splashed on as quietly as they had splashed a moment before. But the air sixty feet above them was shattered and rent by the shouts of the artist, who, leaning on his well-padded stomach, craned his neck over the edge of the cliff, begging for an answer from the man he could see beneath him. Then throwing down his stick, and not noticing that his cap had fallen and been caught by the wind and was also slowly descending to the shore, O'Donnahaw started running. Now he cursed the solitude along the cliffs which five minutes before had delighted him, for no one came to help him. He was sweating, exhausted and incoherent, before he had reached the nearest cottage.

Granville was not dead, the doctor declared, though the men who carried him up to the house spoke of the "corpse," for he lay so rigid on the improvised stretcher.

Alastair O'Donnahaw, stricken like a guilty man, feeling himself unreasonably, monstrously thrust into inadvertent crime by a stupid blunder of fate, did everything he could to help. When his horror allowed him a moment to think, it seemed to be very little. He telegraphed for relations, for friends, for lawyers, for specialists from town. He fought down a horrible fear that someone would suggest that he was actively instead of passively guilty, and when all he could do was done and none had made the monstrous suggestion, he departed and vowed never to set foot in Northumberland again. He shook off the nightmare.

Alastair O'Donnahaw, who feared that Rose Amber might search out the actual spot of the disaster and feed her grief by brooding on its vivid horror, had bribed the cottagers to profess ignorance of the details of the accident. O'Donnahaw himself dexterously avoided telling her exactly where her husband had been found. His kindly heart hoped thus to soften the dreadful realization for the wife and save her the visualization of the nightmare. It was so much the sight of things which stirred his own acutest emotions. Forgetting his own peculiarities as an artist, he fancied others were like himself in this; little did he think that his kindly doing unto others as he would be done by would only result in greater sorrow for the very one he sought to shield.

Granville was brought home unconscious and wholly incapable of movement. His back had been broken low down and the blow on the side of his head had been so severe that the first effects of the concussion lasted for two interminable days, during which he was unconscious.

Rose Amber, melting with impotent tenderness, watched through the long hours while his eyes remained fixed on vacancy. The eyelids, frozen in their descent, but half covered the blank terror of those unseeing eyes. In a few hours skilled nurses were by the bedside, but the wife took from their waiting hands everything which she herself could minister. The bandages, half covering Harry's head, seemed to hide from her the real person of her husband, and the form upon the bed lay like a strange, immobile chrysalis into which the winged strength of his life had retreated. Had he lain before her in the semblance of his old self the pillow which she had so often in warmth and tenderness shared with him would have been soaked with tears. But the well-nigh frozen and encased image congealed her heart. It was too strange, too terrible for reality. To bring back to it warmth and life, to release it from its casings would demand all the strength within her; she dared allow no weakening tears.

For hours she sat or knelt watching, eager to serve were service possible.

At last, on the second day, the eyelids flickered. Rose Amber signalled to the nurse without taking her long, tender gaze from the questioning, fluttering eyes beneath them. Along this slender line of communication she poured out all the strength of her love. The wondrous stream of human vitality reached his heart from hers, and her will transmitted to him a sense of healing. A soft breath trembled from his lips, and his eyelids closed in gentle, natural relaxation.

The nurse was satisfied, did all she had been instructed to do, and sent for the doctor.

The next day, after a little sleep, Rose Amber came once more to the bedside and stroked and kissed the two passive hands. Only one of them responded, and that so feebly that its fluttering, fumbling touch rent her heart. She kissed the hand again and laid her cheek against it. There was recognition, a soft, bewildered tenderness in the eyes gazing out from that bandaged head.

"Kenneth — where's Kenneth?" he whispered: "send — ."

Rose Amber, strangely startled, repeated, "Kenneth?" but obtained no response.

"If it's a friend, M'lady, who can come, better send for him."

"Do you want Kenneth?" Rose Amber asked gently. She could not really tell, but she thought the eyes said "Yes."

Kenneth, in response to an urgent telegram, came at once; but no answering look of recognition appeared in the eyes when the weary eyelids half opened at the disturbance of his entry. Kenneth stayed for two days, visiting the sick-room frequently, but neither his presence nor Rose Amber's words brought any sign of recognition from Harry Granville.

"Why should he have sent for you?" asked Rose Amber.

"Hanged if I know," said Kenneth, but thought to himself, "He couldn't think well enough of my business capacity to want me as a trustee or guardian or anything if he is thinking of his will." Aloud he said, "It must have been a passing idea on his return to consciousness. I will stay if you like."

"No. your work is important. I will telegraph if he asks again."

The doctor endeavoured to maintain the pretence that Granville might recover, and neither he nor any of the relatives and friends who came to the house told Rose Amber the full extent of Harry's injuries. It was not apparent to them whether or not she realized the certainty of her husband's doom. All her energy was devoted to nursing him, to sustaining and comforting him, and for the rest of the world she had a vague, half-smile of thanks for the many kind offers of help which poured in upon her.

When Granville recovered sufficiently to speak a few halting words at a time he made no mention of Kenneth. Indeed, it was doubtful from the little that he said whether his mind concerned itself or not with the life it had so nearly left. Rose Amber and her tenderness alone seemed to touch his mind. Whenever she was in the room his eyes followed her, gazing upon her with that deep and piercing sadness, that embracing penetration seen only in the eyes of those sick unto death. She never left him save for the minimum of necessary sleep.

After this period of quiescence — it lasted for several weeks — once more he suddenly mentioned Kenneth.

"Do you want to see him?" Rose Amber asked softly.

"Yes."

"I will send at once."

"Queer chap," breathed the lips upon the bed.

When Kenneth came, dumb in the awkward way of healthy visitors at a death-bed, Harry looked at him for some time without speaking. He wanted to say so many things, but the superlative effort they required to shape them overcame the impulse. At last he whispered.

"Shake hands."

Kenneth stooped, giving all the warm pressure which his curbed strength dared.

"Say your theories are all rot."

Kenneth, startled, anxious as everyone is to pacify one who suffers, felt he could not immediately disown his precious beliefs. Rose Amber, who was beside them, turned toward him an imploring look.

"I do not grudge them — my life," the sick man went on slowly and then paused. Neither Kenneth nor Rose Amber spoke. Kenneth, thinking that his brain was perhaps a little affected, laid no great stress on his words, but Rose Amber, knowing how rational he had been ever since he had returned to consciousness, was puzzled. *Was* the mystery of the accident connected with Kenneth? Impossible! And yet — she must ask Kenneth about it afterwards, when she went down with him into the hall. The whispering voice on the bed was continuing:

"They can't have — I won't let them have — my immortality."

Kenneth, longing to be kind, said soothingly, "The essential immortality remains, the beauty of life is perpetually handed on."

The eyes upon the bed made protest. "Not true — say you know — your theory's not true."

"Of course, I may be mistaken," conceded Kenneth, generously.

Harry was silent, his eyes pleading for more, but Kenneth could not give it.

"Well, I have shaken hands," murmured Harry, "that's right."

His eyes closed wearily. Neither of his hearers knew of the long fight with himself which made that handclasp possible, and Harry, too weary to explain, was yet relieved by his conquest of himself.

As Harry seemed to have no more to say, after a long, expectant pause, Rose Amber slipped out with Kenneth, but he could not explain to her Harry's puzzling request for his recantation, beyond suggesting that Harry naturally yearned for a very personal immortality — with Rose Amber to share it.

"There's something in his mind I don't understand," said the wife. "I feel sure there is something terrible I have not been told."

The confusion deliberately originated by Alastair O'Donnahaw's desire to prevent Rose Amber ever yielding to a possible suspicion that her husband had attempted to commit suicide had left her very uncertain as to the true story of the accident. Whenever she remembered her transient sense of nightmare that afternoon when the three of them had been on the cliff together the day before it happened, the thought that in some way Kenneth was connected with the accident naturally suggested itself. But his present obvious frankness and the remembrance that he and Harry had parted in friendliness the day before temporarily satisfied her that the idea was grotesque. Harry's fall had been, it must have been, as everyone said, a simple accident while Harry was trying to get a little flower which grew over the edge of the cliff. Had not dear old Alastair O'Donnahaw from the distance seen him fall?

CHAPTER
29

A TUMBLE IN THE SNOW

THREE months later Rose Amber was a widow. She was so worn, her vitality was so sapped that after the funeral she collapsed. Mrs. Harvey for the first time felt that Kenneth's need of mothering was of secondary importance, and took the girl into her arms.

"I shall take you to the mountains, my darling," she said, and proceeded to arrange for a long stay in one of the highest and most comfortable of the many hotels in Switzerland designed for convalescence.

She lay in the sun, snow glittering near. Pictures of the past flashed through her brain, and on her lips once more burned Harry's kisses, bringing tears to her eyes and the ache of sadness to her heart. Incredibly, inaudibly, intangibly, yet inevitably the essential meaning of the word *escape* crept through her.

"Escape from what?" She would not allow herself to think of that, the past was too full of tender memories — she turned to the other side of the picture. There was escape *into* something fresh, into a recovered freedom, into a world in which she could mingle freely with anyone, with everyone who attracted or who needed her. No longer enclosed by the passionate love of one, the wide reaches of the world were once more her dwelling place. She was turned out of Eden, the world was a desert; but the world was wide and men and women went freely to and fro upon it.

"Is Paradise always enclosed by a wall?" she asked Mrs. Harvey one day.

The older woman was puzzled to find an answer. She had been given no clue to the long and formless, unembodied thoughts with which Rose Amber's spirit had hovered. "Paradise?" she asked, vaguely.

"People seem to me either happy and enclosed in their happiness or unhappy, or at least neutral, and out at work or play in the world. Now that I have been turned loose on the world again I must do some work of some sort or another. You see, unhappy people always do unless they are fools."

"Oh, you are never thinking of going back to old Mr. Joshua — ."
Mrs. Harvey had not realized that Rose Amber's larger dreams were of
potential work. "Surely you don't need to work now. You are left quite
well off, dear, aren't you? My home is always open to you — you mustn't
think of working."

"Darling," Rose Amber responded, with a hug. "I'm quite rich now.
The country house and land, of course, go to Harry's brother, but the
town house and all his invested money are mine. I have two or three
thousand a year."

"Then you mustn't think of going and working," protested Mrs.
Harvey.

"All the more need to work." Mrs. Harvey stroked her hand.

"I wonder," Rose went on, as though thinking aloud, "if young
people and inexperienced people see *essential* truths swiftly and clearly
and much better than older people: only they don't know the solid difficulties that confront them when they touch reality. It's *so* hard," she
sighed whimsically, "actually to cope with matter! It's obstinate, it has its
own laws, it has all, to some extent, got the qualities of india-rubber, and
tends to go back however much you pull it about."

"What are you going to do?"

"I don't know, oh, I don't know!" Rose Amber's sudden eagerness
waned. "Get strong first. I'm very tired and very — *sore*."

A tear trickled down her cheek. "I feel almost as though I, too, had
failed Harry, though it wasn't really my fault; it was something in the
nature of things, in the nature of us both. Though he was adorable and
I loved him so — I just missed *something*. I wonder, I wonder if he knew?
If he did it must have made him unhappy."

"No man could have been happier, could have adored you more than
he did," interposed Mrs. Harvey.

"I *wish* I knew whether people who have 'changed their world' know
anything about what we are thinking and feeling here."

"If they do God won't let them be unhappy about it," Mrs. Harvey
reassured her.

"Do you think," asked Rose Amber eagerly, "that if Harry knows
anything about our thoughts now he will know that I gave him every bit
of love that was ripe in my heart? He was older than I — and perhaps
needed more. Does he know that he had all I had then to give?"

With the approach of Christmas, visitors from many parts began to
crowd the great hotel. Mrs. Harvey, so long divided between her two
children, welcomed the opportunity of having them together with her,
and insisted that Kenneth should spend a fortnight with them. Kenneth
arrived with a sledge-load of parcels from the London shops which Mrs.
Harvey had commissioned.

Acquaintances turned up with the crowds from London, and Rose Amber soon found herself entangled with engagements to skate, to learn to ski, to career down long runs of snow face downwards.

Scarlet and blue, orange and crimson, tartan and gold — the patches of colour made by the bright jerseys twinkled in and out of the snow like the fragments of a kaleidoscope. Rose Amber, in white wool, with a black skirt to her knees, wore her colour in her cheeks.

Showing off her new mastery of the treacherous ski, Rose Amber, for once erect, her feet side by side, carrying her with them as they glided downwards, called for Mrs. Harvey's witness to her accomplishment. But, spurred by her triumph, her feet escaped her, and in a moment she had cannonaded with a burly mass of orange wool from out of which two skis stuck at angles like a couple of long pins in a pin-cushion.

She plunged, a helpless white ball, into the heart of the orange obstacle, the long lathes of her feet crossing over the orange man's head enclosed the tangled pair as in a cage.

"Begorrah," said a big voice from the middle of it all, "if any more of ye are coming let me bury me head deep first."

Rose Amber, gasping her breathless apologies, was too shaken by laughter and the inextricable tangle of her position to feel the shock of anguished memory which an ordinary meeting with Alastair O'Donnahaw would have occasioned.

"Faith alive! If it isn't my precious fairy lady," he gasped as he slithered on his back vainly struggling to get a hold which would enable him to heave her gently off his chest.

Kenneth and Mrs. Harvey, weakened as they were by laughter, were both required to effect the rescue. Then Rose Amber and O'Donnahaw sat side by side in the snow with their feet tidily crossed at right angles to their legs and picked pieces of frozen snow out of their hair, and circumvented clotted dabs of half-melted snow on their way down their necks.

"Faith, I'll go directly I can, my precious," said O'Donnahaw, "if it's driving me off you'll be after sitting on me like that."

"Where are you staying?" asked Mrs. Harvey.

"At the Grand, where everybody stays."

"So are we, we have been there for some time."

O'Donnahaw struggled to his feet and, staggering, put an arm on Kenneth's shoulder. The impetus of his weight sent the two men gliding down the bank together.

"Faith, shall I go at once? I wouldn't for the world vex her by reminding her of the evil news I'd had the bad luck to carry her once," he said to Kenneth, when they were beyond range of the ladies.

"I don't think so. Rose Amber is not a coward, and she can't live in

London in the set she does and hope never to run across you by chance. A meeting with you was inevitable."

They all went into the hotel together.

Mrs. Harvey, speaking later to her son, declared that "it couldn't have happened better."

"It's the first meeting that's always so bad, and coming across him in that ridiculous way, laughing and choking with snow, there wasn't time to realize that he was the same man who brought her that terrible news."

When Mrs. Harvey suggested to Rose that O'Donnahaw would go to another hotel she swiftly decided against it.

"He's a darling to think of it, but I'm not going to be silly like that."

In the quietest corner of the drawing-room one evening she allowed O'Donnahaw to sit with her: she wanted to talk to him, and the sunny days in the open were filled with fragmentary chatter and laughter.

"Did you tell me the truth — *then?*" she asked him. Her deep, questioning eyes dated the "then."

"Now it's come," he thought to himself, and fine beads of perspiration sprang out upon his forehead.

"Faith, and I did, my precious. Don't be thinking of it again. 'Tis the Lord's will and it's all past."

Rose Amber, perceiving his discomfort, felt brutal, but persisted.

"Did he say nothing — nothing at all?"

"Nothing, on my solemn oath," answered O'Donnahaw, bravely.

"But I can't see *how* it could have been an accident. He was so sure-footed, he knew the cliffs so well."

Alastair O'Donnahaw, still haunted by the thought that there was no witness of his complete innocence, did not dare to express the discomfort he felt, and, kicking himself for a liar, had to maintain the story he had first told. Rose Amber sighed, not fully satisfied.

"Even still I often cannot sleep at night wondering how it was *possible*. He said such a strange thing, you know," she confided, feeling the inarticulate sympathy in the big heart beside her. "He said he didn't grudge Kenneth his life so much as his immortality, he wouldn't let him take that — his theories take that. You are sure Kenneth didn't meet him on the cliffs? I have had an absurd hysterical feeling sometimes, a nightmare, that Kenneth and he had a duel."

"*My dear!*" He was intensely relieved that he could so truthfully combat this obsession. "Now settle this thing up for ever. That long stretch of cliff covered with short grass was as bare as the back of me hand for miles. I would have seen anyone who had been with him ten minutes before, and I saw poor Granville quite clearly *alone* at the top of the cliff, and while I was too far away to help — God pity me — I saw him fall over."

"Swear," said Rose Amber, looking at him with all her soul.

"By God I swear! Put that wild nightmare out of your head for ever. Poor little heart! Have you been thinking things like that all this time? It was all so terrible, and you were so dreadfully strained, no wonder you had some hallucinations, but now you are getting well again, for God's sake forget it."

They were alone in the small drawing-room, but even if they had not been alone Rose Amber could not have curbed her tears. She pressed her face into the sofa pillow, sobbing. "I am so glad, oh, I am so *glad*."

Alastair O'Donnahaw seemed her deliverer.

CHAPTER
30

THE SUN SHINES OUT

ROSE Amber was giving a tea party in her private sitting-room in her hotel. Clinging to her hand and dancing with excitement at the prospect of at last seeing Lady Granville's mysterious wonderland was a blue-eyed, golden-haired American boy, seven years of age, named Ivon. He won Rose Amber's heart by the heroic way he adapted himself to the mixture of neglect and over-fondling meted out to him by his parents.

The child, now on the threshold, hung back apprehensively, thinking that perhaps the Fairyland he had pictured would not come up to expectation.

"I have dreamed millions of times what your room would be like," he said, and he entered with his eyes shut, to open them wide when he was led into the middle of the room.

With an exclamation: "Oh, I knew it!" he flew towards a great vase of pink carnations standing on a table near the window, clambering up on a chair and burying his head like an intoxicated bee among the sweet-scented flowers.

O'Donnahaw, whose massive presence had been ignored, picked him up by the middle with one hand and held him high in the air.

"Oh!" squealed the boy, "that's what Momma's husband does. Are you Lady Granville's husband?"

"Not yet!" said O'Donnahaw.

"Why not?" said the boy.

"She won't have me."

"Why don't you make her?" asked the boy. "I'd make her if I was as big as you."

"That's an idea," said O'Donnahaw. "I never thought of trying to *make* her. I have tried to persuade her."

"'Suading's no good; they try that on me sometimes, but if I don't want to, I won't be 'suaded. I will only be *made*."

O'Donnahaw spoke with twinkling gravity: "You advise me to *make* her let me be her husband."

"Yes, and I will be her husband until you make her let you be. Let me get down," said Ivon.

He kicked and squirmed until, as he thought, he had conquered the giant, and ran over to Rose Amber's side. Speaking with a protective air, he said: "Let me be your husband, darling, and help you."

Rose Amber, amused, smiled at him.

O'Donnahaw, catching the smile, wondered whether Rose Amber had heard the child's advice, which had chimed so well with his own feeling.

Tea was ready: Mrs. Harvey, looking round, asked, "Where is Kenneth?"

O'Donnahaw grinned: "The last time I saw him he was having a dancing lesson."

"I know," chirped Ivon. "The pink lady was teaching him."

"Oh, ho!" O'Donnahaw chuckled.

"Surely Kenneth can dance," said Rose Amber.

Ivon, sitting opposite her, held her hand with a protective air: "Not very well, darling, you see, it's so soon since he was eman — man — cipated!"

"What do you know about that?"

"I heard him 'splaining it all to the pink lady. He is very young, he said."

"Young?"

"Kenneth said he is only three or four years old. But *I* think he looks big for that. He says he is only just hatched out of his chrysalids. I think it is funny that, although he is younger than me, he should be bigger than me. How does he do it — grow so fast, I mean?"

"He takes a whole bottle of castor oil every night before he goes to bed." O'Donnahaw winked portentously at Rose Amber.

Ivon was impressed. "Momma had to whip me last time to make me take even a teaspoonful."

"You unprincipled monster," said Mrs. Harvey. "Don't listen to him, Ivon, he is telling you nonsense stories."

Rose Amber chimed in: "Mr. Harvey grew so big by learning his lessons very well."

"Who taught him?"

"Life taught him. Life's lessons hurt."

"Lessons can't hurt," said Ivon, "it is being whipped for not doing them that hurts."

"Life's lessons can hurt' when life takes you in hand you will see, young man."

"What is it in life hurts most?" said Ivon.

"Love!"

"Love mixed with women hurts like Hell," said O'Donnahaw.

"Hush!" Mrs. Harvey was thankful to see Kenneth arrive.

"There you are! Escaped the toils!" laughed O'Donnahaw.

"These modern dances are puzzlers," he said, sinking into a chair.

O'Donnahaw chortled: "It is no good; it is no good; I have been engaged to the pink lady meself!"

"Engaged! What nonsense!"

"You wait! She told me yesterday she was only engaged to two men, and three is the proper number for a Swiss season."

"How do you know?"

"Faith, wasn't I the third to be engaged to her meself last year? She told me to do the thing thoroughly, she needs to be engaged to three people at once — one to skate with, one to snow-play with, and the other to dance with."

"Which one will she marry?" said Rose Amber, mischievously.

"Faith alive! The pink girl's engagements have nothing to do with marriage."

"Then, why be engaged?"

"Oh, the air up here makes one so confoundedly romantic."

"Pity I came here then," said Kenneth. "I am not engaged at all, and don't want to be, in that way, at any rate."

Rose Amber's eyes reproached O'Donnahaw. He drew her apart from the others, and she said: "You relieve me; I thought you were serious when you proposed the other day and said that I had broken your heart by not marrying you, and now I am glad to know it was only a jest."

O'Donnahaw changed, and real passion came into his face. He smote his mighty hand upon his knee. "Faith alive, you are not imagining that I was not serious *with you*! I never spoke of *marrying* to anyone else. It is not to be compared with a pink flirtation. Oh, me darling, it has taken every bit of me strength not to take Ivon's advice and *make* you marry me."

Kenneth, though not hearing their words felt the tenour of their talk. He caught the atmosphere of intensity around O'Donnahaw, and thought: "By heaven, O'Donnahaw! Was it possible? But why not? With his artist's eye and passion for beauty, she must be distracting to him. But what was Rose Amber herself feeling?" Kenneth strained to catch the reflection of her heart's atmosphere, enclosed so well by the outwardly demure, unruffled sweetness of her bodily presence, and saw there some trembling, nascent feeling he had not yet detected. "Impossible! Surely she would demolish O'Donnahaw in the twinkling of an eyelash. And yet — these big, masterful, vital men sometimes have a way with women."

Suddenly he realized that if O'Donnahaw became Rose Amber's husband he would hate him, and the mere contingent potential hatred filled him with rage. He had never hated before; it was a new sensation, a poison juice — a vertigo — a hell.

Rose Amber could not surely — Rose Amber must not be *allowed* to marry a second too dominant male. His mind seemed suddenly to whirl into flame.

Time passed; he did not know how long. The next thing he heard was the prattling of a child. Little Ivon had taken out a handful of carnations from the vase.

"Oh, Ivon!" said Mrs. Harvey. "That is naughty; put them back!"

"No; I want them," said the boy.

"That is no reason why you should take them; they are Rose Amber's."

"But why should she have them all and Momma and me have none? That is not fair."

Mrs. Harvey, with memories of her old-fashioned nursery, said: "Little boys do not argue."

"I do. Yes, it's not fair!" the modern child replied.

Mrs. Harvey's experience had not included a real American democrat. "If you are very good, and ask properly, perhaps Lady Granville will give you one," she said.

"But why should I have to ask? You have no right to have them all when we have not any. If you have got more than you should have, I can take half without asking."

"Socialism already, begorra!" chuckled O'Donnahaw.

Rose Amber sat down near the child. "Put them back for just a moment while I talk to you about them, Ivon."

"Yes, darling; of course, now that I am your husband, I must obey you."

He put the flowers back in the vase.

"Now why should you have them all and Momma and me have none?"

"Can you count up to a hundred?" said Rose Amber.

"I guess so; I can count up to a million."

"Have you ever counted how many people there are in this hotel?"

"No."

"Guess how many there are."

"A million."

"Surely not as many as that!"

"It is difficult to find out."

"First, let us see how many rooms there are. What is the number of your bedroom?"

"Our bedroom is No. 127 on the Third Floor."

"And you and your Mamma sleep in the same bedroom, and Mr. and Mrs. Smith sleep in the same bedroom next to yours. So you will see there are more than 127 people in the bedrooms we know about. Now count the carnations in that vase."

The first time he counted twenty-six, and the next time twenty-three.

"So there are only twenty-three flowers, you see! Can you give even *one* each to 127 people?"

His little brows puckered up. "Well, buy more carnations, or make them."

"Could you make them?"

"Guess I could if I was a fairy!"

"But you see we have no fairy just at the moment and only twenty-three carnations. Who is to decide who is to have them?"

"I will."

"But why should it be more fair for you to decide than for me? You see if every little boy in the hotel were always taking carnations because they had not got any, the poor carnations would spend all their time being snatched from one person by another, and carnations do not like that; they like to stay still in water. Now if you like you may take them all away and give them to as many people in the hotel as you can."

"That would not be really fair, either," he said. "Why does not God make more carnations? That is what I would do if I were God. Then I would give *you* an extra big bunch, because you are a peach and I love you."

"Ah!" said Kenneth, "that is what God did do, picked on Lady Granville to give that big bunch of carnations to."

"You may have half of them," said Rose Amber, rising and taking them out of the water, "and now you must go back to your mother."

After Ivon had gone, Rose Amber said, with comical, shamefaced apologies: "What frightful ethics have I been teaching?"

"Jolly little beggar," said Kenneth.

The silhouette of Rose Amber stooping to talk so seriously to the eager child at her knee glowed in his memory. His mind brooded on it. "That is how Rose Amber should be throned — with a child at her knee — a child at her knee. A child. Whose? Ah! What lucky man? . . . "

She glowed in his mind, a maternal radiance.

A few months later Kenneth Harvey and Rose Amber sat together under the pine trees of an Alpine slope, opposite them the jagged crests of the Dents-du-Midi pierced a wreath of translucent clouds. Their bodies burned with the exultant fire of the air from the snow fields. Together they had come up through the open vistas, knee-deep in flowers. Now, at their feet were drifts of snow still nestling in the hollows, crystalline and pure, save where the wind-blown pine seeds and light-brown scales had been dropped by air currents upon their rippled, glittering surfaces.

"You are mine, you know," he spoke masterfully yet quietly, with a serene certainty.

She knew it, but played with reluctance, as with a fan, to hide lips ready to be kissed.

"I'm not sure," she wavered.

"You are sure. Don't play with me, beloved, after all these years of separation, of service in bondage to fates we had to work out — the time has come — now — *now*. . . . "

"But why to-day rather than yesterday or to-morrow?"

"Because the time and the place and the loved one *are* at last all together — and we know it."

"But — your lips look so stern."

"And yours so kissable."

"Your eyes are so deep."

"And yours so luminous."

"Can you think of so small a thing as a single home with — a — *wife* in it?"

"However far a man's thoughts may roam, isn't that the biggest thing he can *experience*? Come home, at last, my love!" He opened his arms and drew her up to him in silence.

Rose Amber stood in Kenneth's arms. Between her lips and his had just passed the swift vitalizing passion of the kiss of betrothal.

Beauty, softer and stranger, but not less vivid than that of her fresh, young girlhood, shone through her, and Kenneth felt as the captain of a ship, long storm-tossed, entering the brilliantly-lit and welcoming harbour. In a short space of moments they experienced an aeon of peace.

At last their lunch was remembered, and extracting its paper-wrapped fragments from their pockets, they fluttered down to mundane life.

"What lots of things we have to do! Where shall be begin?" Rose Amber's voice was a song.

"Begin by living," Kenneth answered.

"Ourselves?"

"Yes! Fancy you and I really living for the first time, having crept up through the chrysalis stages — through little tadpoles in a pond — all that sort of thing, until we are now fully fledged, winged — ourselves."

After an interval of rapture, Rose Amber, woman-like, eager to provide a material body for the dreams her lover shared with her, asked: "And what shall we do precisely?"

"Have children!" Kenneth spoke reverently.

Rose Amber, palpitating, flushed at the joyful thought: "Oh, I hope so, but, you know, twice I have been disappointed."

"Ah," said Kenneth, deeply remorseful on her behalf, "it is not much apparently, the father's share in parenthood — but his strength and self-control have a part to play to balance the mother's — I won't fail you, my beloved."

Kenneth, steady-eyed, was a pilot she could trust to steer in the swift, clear, central current leading to health and joy and power unfathomable, safe from the unbridled whirlpools on the one side and asceticism on the other.

She whispered, "I'm afraid of the storms and stresses of passion — I'm . . ."

He thought of Sir Harry Granville and his exotic love, and as she quivered so flower-like he melted with protective tenderness.

"I know. You need never fear that we shall not go *together* — even into the innermost experiences. You know, darling, I fear the mud-flats of asceticism."

"Your eyes are steady as a pilot's, Kenneth. Harry's used to flicker and melt and burn — but yours are clear and calm, like the stars you have gazed at so long. Oh, darling — do you really love me? Do you?"

She was swept into his arms; his eyes, gazing so near her into hers, melted in the burning fusion of love.

"My love, my life," he murmured, and put an end to all words with kisses.

With soft finger-tips she stroked his forehead and his eyelids and slipped gently from his arms at last.

"Enough," she laughed. "I'm answered. I'll never *ask* again. But you must tell me — often."

"Often. Every day a thousand times. In all my words and deeds there will be an expression of the one and only important thing — I love you!"

"There will also be the outward, everyday aspect of our lives," said Rose Amber. "What shall we do with that part of us?"

"Work."

"Your big theories! You'll publish them?"

"I don't know." He hesitated, thinking of the rebuff dealt out by the Fellow of the Royal Society.

"But you must, you must! Defy the scientific quibblers and scoffers! Beat them down by your triumphant certainty."

"My lovely generous one," he said. "It may be that the time is not yet ripe for my theories. I may be only the *next* Focus-Changer's

Grandfather. How would you tolerate me as a mere ancestor and not the great man himself?"

"Ah, but *you are* the great one for *me*. Your work widens science and enriches life."

"And your work?"

Rose Amber was eager. "Don't you see how your work is the key of all I was striving after for humanity. I was seeking for a cure for every one's loneliness and sorrow. You're giving us that. Together we must prove that humanity is not only divided up into pairs of lovers; it is knit up into one great wonderful thing — and the signing of a paean of joy to God in two lives may mean something sublime in the life of the Greater Unit."

Time stood still for their long kisses to penetrate and enrich Eternity.

"Ah, my sweet!" His lips parted from hers laughing.

"But I fear, I fear I'm only the epoch-maker's *grandfather*! How long can you love a man whose only claim to greatness is that he will be a grandfather?" He tossed back his head, the sunlight caught the firm pillar of his throat. Rose Amber kissed it.

"So long as he is also the father of my child — *always*."

NOTES TO THE NOVEL

1 (PAGE 2) *Lewis Carroll* was the pseudonym of Charles Dodgson (1832–1898). Dodgson was also Professor of Mathematics at the University of Oxford and author of eleven mathematical books which he published under his own name.

2 (PAGE 3) *Formalin*. An aqueous solution of the chemical compound formaldehyde, with a pungent odour commonly used as a preserving medium or for fixing microscopic slides. Highly toxic.

3 (PAGE 4) *Microtome sections*. A microtome is an instrument that uses a blade made of diamond, steel or glass for slicing sections in preparation or examination under a microscope.

4 (PAGE 5) *A six-plate quarto in the Transactions*. The *Philosophical Transactions of the Royal Society*. A journal produced by The Royal Society (see note 9), established in 1665. Famous contributors included Newton, Faraday and Darwin. In 1887 the journal split into two sections, one for physics, maths and engineering (A) and one for biological sciences (B). The journal still exists.

5 (PAGE 5) *Xylol*. A chemical compound consisting of xylene and ethal alcohol, used for cleaning bones.

6 (PAGE 9) *Dame Nature in the Water Babies*. Charles Kingsley (1819–1875). *The Water Babies* first appeared in book form in 1863. Kingsley's endorsement of Darwin was included in the second edition of *On the Origin of Species* (1859).

7 (page 10) *Zoology*. Branch of biology that pertains to the study of animal life.

8 (PAGE 10) *Morphology of a family of animals and its bearing on evolution*. Morphology is a branch of biological sciences that focuses on the structure and form of organisms.

9 (PAGE 10) *The Royal Society*. Originating officially in 1660, the oldest academy of scientists in Britain.

10 (PAGE 12) *"My eyes shall see new truths."* Almost certainly a reference to *Psalm* 119: 18: "Open thou my eyes that I might behold wondrous things out of thy law."

11 (PAGE 19) *Board schools*. Schools established by the Church of England to promote a religious education.

12 (PAGE 20) *The Village Blacksmith*. A poem by Henry Wadsworth Longfellow, first published in 1841.

13 (PAGE 27) *Lady Hamilton* (1765–1815). Mistress of Lord Nelson.

14 (PAGE 28) *Shoolbreds*. Well-known furniture and interior design store on Tottenham Court Road. Closed down in 1931.

15 (PAGE 33) *Darwin*. Charles Darwin (1809–1882). Author of *On the Origin of Species* (1859), *The Descent of Man and Selection in Relation to Sex* (1871) and *The Expression of the Emotions in Man and Animals* (1872). His expedition on 'The Beagle', which lasted over five years, from 1831, is perhaps echoed in the novel by Kenneth's own five years travelling around the world.

16 (PAGE 34) *Divorce reform*. Between 1909 and 1910, a Royal Commission began examining the need to reform Victorian divorce law which had made it difficult, particularly for women, to end marriages. The Commission's recommendations for cheaper and simplified proceedings did not result in any immediate change. Increasing numbers of divorces during and after the First World War heralded further pressure for change, especially from groups representing women of property over thirty, who had in 1918 been enfranchised. A Private Member's Bill introduced in 1923 — which passed as the Matrimonial Causes Act — made adultery by either husband or wife the sole ground for divorce. A wife no longer had to prove additional faults against the husband. Campaigning in the early 1920s also led to the Summary Jurisdiction (Separation and Maintenance) Act in 1925 which extended the grounds on which either partner could obtain a separation.

17 (PAGE 41) *Linnaeus*. Carl Linnaeus (1707–1778). A Swedish doctor, botanist and zoologist, he was known as the father of modern taxonomy, and also had a huge influence on the development of ecology.

18 (PAGE 42) *Discontinuity*. It seems likely that Kenneth is thinking here of the writings of the French philosopher Henri Bergson (1859–1941), whose theory of duration arose from his engagements with the writings of Herbert Spencer (who had coined the phrase 'survival of the fittest') and whose writings on time, memory and evolution were central to modernist aesthetics, and, notably here, of importance to Virginia Woolf. In *Time and Free Will* (1889) Bergson argued that you could not measure a moment, that time was subjective, mobile and incomplete. Bergson's *Creative Evolution* (1907) seems also to be making a central contribution to Kenneth's developing worldview, although later in the novel he rejects Bergson as 'Not radical enough. Too blurred' (*LC*, p. 118).

19 (PAGE 47) *Tennyson*. Alfred Lord Tennyson (1809–1892). Succeeded

William Wordsworth as poet Laureate in 1850, a post he held until his death.

20 (PAGE 47) *Georgians*. Poets whose work appeared in a series of five anthologies edited by Edward Marsh. The first was published in 1912. Poets most keenly associated with the movement are Lascelles Abercrombie (1881–1938), Edmund Blunden (1896–1974), Rupert Brooke (1887–1915), Wilfrid Gibson (1878–1962), Edward Thomas (1878–1917). Later in the century the term became derogative.

21 (PAGE 51) *Chloral*. A widely-used sedative in the nineteenth century. Also used to prepare microscope slides.

22 (PAGE 53) *"Physican, heal thyself"*. Luke, 4: 23.

23 (PAGE 57) *Palaeontologists*. Palaeontology: the scientific study of prehistoric or ancient life which lies on the boundaries between biology and geology, and uses fossils as one of its main sources of evidence.

24 (PAGE 57) *Dr Walcott*. Charles Doolittle Walcott (1850–1927). An eminent American palaeontologist.

25 (PAGE 57) *Silurian*. Geologic period that extends from 443.7–416 million years ago.

26 (PAGE 59) *Fenians*. A movement founded in America by the Irishman John O'Mahony in 1858 and known in Ireland as the Irish Republican Brotherhood, later to become the IRA. Fenians believed in Irish independence which they thought could be won only by an armed revolution. The term Fenianism was sometimes used in Britain by the political establishment during the 1860s for any form of mobilization among the working classes or those who expressed any Irish nationalist sentiments.

27 (PAGE 59) *Triceratops*. A dinosaur that lived in the Late Cretaceous period, between 68 and 65 million years ago.

28 (PAGE 59) *Ichthyosaurus and Plesiosaurus*. *Ichthyosaurus*: a dolphin-like reptile that existed in the early Jurassic period between 199.6 and 189 million years ago. *Plesiosaurus*: a large marine reptile which existed between 199.6 and 175.6 million years ago.

29 (PAGE 61) *Megatheriums*. A genus of elephant-sized ground sloths endemic to Central America and South America.

30 (PAGE 68) *Lavoisier*. Antoine-Laurent Lavoisier (1743–1794), the so-called father of modern chemistry who found and named oxygen and hydrogen, and also established that sulphur was an element.

31 (PAGE 71) *Galton*. Francis Galton (1822–1911), a half-cousin of Charles Darwin; geographer, explorer, meteorologist. Galton invented the term eugenics, the aim of which he claimed was "to bring as many influences as can be reasonably employed, to cause the useful classes in the community to contribute *more* than their propor-

tion to the next generation" (*American Journal of Sociology*, Volume X; July, 1904; Number 1) see http://galton.org/essays/1900–1911/galton-1904-am-journ-soc-eugenics-scope-aims.htm. Galton coined the phrase "nature versus nurture". The application of eugenicist ideas and their numerous and horrific consequences have meant that his reputation is controversial. His unpublished novel *The Eugenic College of Kantsaywhere* (*c.* 1910) can be found at: http://www.ucl.ac.uk/library/special-coll/ksw.shtml.

32 (page 73) *Frail barque.* A small ship. Perhaps a reference to Shelley's poem 'To Wordsworth' (1816), "Thou wert as a lone star, whose light did shine / On some frail bark in winter's midnight roar!"

33 (PAGE 74) *Epithelia.* One of the four primary tissues of the body, classified according to their shape, and whether or not they appear in layers.

34 (PAGE 85) *F.R.S.* Fellow of the Royal Society.

35 (PAGE 93) *Niggers.* By the 1900s this term was recognised as pejorative and became increasingly offensive as the century progressed.

36 (PAGE 94) *Coolies.* Indian or Chinese migrant manual labourers. Derogative. Early in the twentieth century many were Indians, employed under a system of indenture; later they were paid the lowest possible wage. Penang was a British colony from 1786–1957. Britain was highly dependent on Malayan rubber exports, particularly in the run up to World War II.

37 (PAGE 106) *Epiphyte.* A plant that grows, above ground, using other plants for support, often parasitically.

38 (PAGE 111) *John Milton.* English poet (1608–1674). Milton wrote four divorce tracts between 1643–1645: *The Doctrine and Discipline of Divorce, The Judgment of Martin Bucer, Tetrachordon*, and *Colasterion*. These argue for divorce on the grounds of incompatibility.

39 (PAGE 113) *Chatelaine.* A woman who owns or controls a large house.

40 (PAGE 115) "*Gather your roses* . . . " from Robert Herrick's poem 'To the Virgins to Make Much of Time' included in his volume *Hesperides* (1648).

41 (PAGE 116) *Newton.* Isaac Newton (1642–1727). English mathematician, physicist and astronomer. His *Philosophiae Naturalis Principia Mathematica* (1687) laid down the principles of modern mechanics.

42 (PAGE 117) *Copernicus.* Nicolaus Copernicus (1473–1543), Renaissance astronomer. His *On the Revolutions of the Celestial Spheres* (1543) is seen as the starting point of modern astronomy.

43 (PAGE 118) *Mrs Eddyism.* Mary Baker Eddy (1821–1910) was the founder of Christian Science. In 1875 she published *Science and Health*

which proposed a philosophy of healing not through medicine but faith.

44 (PAGE 118) *Bergson*. See note 18.

45 (PAGE 118) *De Vries*. Hugo Marie de Vries (1848–1935) was a Dutch botanist and one of the first geneticists. He is known for suggesting the concept of genes, for introducing the term mutation and for developing a mutation theory of evolution.

46 (PAGE 118) *Coral atolls*. A circular coral reef surrounding a lagoon.

47 (PAGE 127) *Michael Angelo* (1475–1674). Italian renaissance painter, sculptor, poet, architect.

48 (PAGE 128) *Harry Lauder*. Scottish entertainer and singer (1870–1950).

49 (PAGE 133) *Carnegies*. Andrew Carnegie (1835–1919): Scottish industrialist and philanthropist who earned his immense wealth in the steel industry.

50 (PAGE 135) *Chwang Tsze*. Chwang Tsze Zhuangzi or Chuang-tzu (born *c.* 369, Meng, China — died 286 BCE). Most significant early Chinese interpreter of Daoism. Daoism taught that enlightenment comes from the realization that everything is one, the dao, but that the dao has no limitations or demarcations and whatever can be known or said of the dao is not the dao. He held that things should be allowed to follow their own course and that no situation should be valued over any other.

51 (PAGE 138) *Yale with Wieland, New York with Osborne*. George Reber Wieland (1865–1953). Paleontologist and fossil collector. Wrote two important volumes *American Fossil Cycads* (1906 and 1916). Henry Fairfield Osborn (1857–1935). American palaeontologist. Discovered and named, among many other dinosaurs, *Tyrannosaurus Rex* (1915) and developed a theory of evolution counter to Darwin, known as the "Dawn Man" theory based on the Piltdown Man discovery, in which fossilised bones of an orangutan were falsely placed and claimed to be the bones of early man. The hoax was not exposed until 1953.

52 (PAGE 143) *Paleozoic Age*. This period extends from 542–251 million years ago.

53 (PAGE 144) *Smith Woodward*. Arthur Smith Woodward (1864–1944). An expert on fossil fish who worked in the Department of Geology at The Natural History Museum. Perhaps most famous outside scientific circles for his involvement in the Piltdown man case.

54 (PAGE 147) *Super-consciousness*. Owes perhaps to Jung's idea of the collective unconscious which argues that alongside an individual consciousness is a universal psychic system which does not develop but is inherited and which is common to all.

55 (PAGE 148) *Super-nebula.* Gas and dust shells secreted by stars near the end of their lives.

56 (PAGE 149) *Sidereal System.* As opposed to solar time, the sidereal system is oriented to the position of the stars in the night sky, rather than the sun.

57 (PAGE 150) *Phagocytes.* White blood cells that work to remove bacteria, or other harmful or dying cells from the body.

58 (PAGE 150) *Erasmus Darwin* (1731–1802). The grandfather of Charles Darwin. Doctor, poet, chemist, biologist and precursor to evolutionary thinking. His *Zoonomia* (1794) which was twenty-five years in the writing, was an attempt to create a comprehensive survey of diseases and treatments.

59 (PAGE 151) *'Ye are members one of another.'* In fact this is St Paul, *Ephesians*, 4: 25.

60 (PAGE 151) *"Little lower than the angels."* *Hebrews*, 2: 7, or *Psalm*, 8: 5.